EDINBUR(

THE EUROPEAN UNION SERIES
General Editors: Neill Nugent, William E. Paterson

The European Union series provides an authoritative library on the European Union, ranging from general introductory texts to definitive assessments of key institutions and actors, issues, policies and policy processes, and the role of member states.

Books in the series are written by leading scholars in their fields and reflect the most up-to-date research and debate. Particular attention is paid to accessibility and clear presentation for a wide audience of students, practitioners and interested general readers.

The series editors are **Neill Nugent**, Visiting Professor, College of Europe, Bruges and Honorary Professor, University of Salford, UK, and **William E. Paterson,** Honorary Professor of German and European Studies, University of Aston. Their co-editor until his death in 1999, **Vincent Wright,** was a Fellow of Nuffield College, Oxford University.

Feedback on the series and book proposals are always welcome and should be sent to Steven Kennedy, Palgrave Macmillan, Houndmills, Basingstoke, Hampshire, RG21 6XS, UK or by e-mail to **s.kennedy@palgrave.com**

General textbooks

Published

Laurie Buonanno and Neill Nugent **Policies and Policy Processes of the European Union**
Desmond Dinan **Encyclopedia of the European Union** [Rights: Europe only]
Desmond Dinan **Europe Recast: A History of the European Union** [Rights: Europe only]
Desmond Dinan **Ever Closer Union: An Introduction to European Integration (4th edn)** [Rights: Europe only]
Mette Eilstrup-Sangiovanni (ed.) **Debates on European Integration: A Reader**
Simon Hix and Bjørn Høyland **The Political System of the European Union (3rd edn)**
Dirk Leuffen, Berthold Rittberger and Frank Schimmelfennig **Differentiated Integration**
Paul Magnette **What is the European Union? Nature and Prospects**
John McCormick **Understanding the European Union: A Concise Introduction (5th edn)**
Brent F. Nelsen and Alexander Stubb **The European Union: Readings on the Theory and Practice of European Integration (3rd edn)** [Rights: Europe only]

Neill Nugent (ed.) **European Union Enlargement**
Neill Nugent **The Government and Politics of the European Union (7th edn)**
John Peterson and Elizabeth Bomberg **Decision-Making in the European Union**
Ben Rosamond **Theories of European Integration**
Esther Versluis, Mendeltje van Keulen and Paul Stephenson **Analyzing the European Union Policy Process**
Hubert Zimmermann and Andreas Dür (eds) **Key Controversies in European Integration**

Forthcoming

Magnus Ryner and Alan Cafruny **A Critical Introduction to the European Union**
Sabine Saurugger **Theoretical Approaches to European Integration**

Also planned

The Political Economy of European Integration

Series Standing Order (outside North America only)
ISBN 978–0–333–71695–3 hardback
ISBN 978–0–333–69352–0 paperback
Full details from www.palgrave.com

Visit Palgrave Macmillan's
EU Resource area at
www.palgrave.com/politics/eu/

Britain and the European Union

Andrew Geddes

First published 2013 by
PALGRAVE MACMILLAN

This book is designed as a replacement volume for the author's earlier work *The European Union and British Politics*.

Palgrave Macmillan in the UK is an imprint of Macmillan Publishers Limited, registered in England, company number 785998, of Houndmills, Basingstoke, Hampshire RG21 6XS.

Palgrave Macmillan in the US is a division of St Martin's Press LLC, 175 Fifth Avenue, New York, NY 10010.

Palgrave Macmillan is the global academic imprint of the above companies and has companies and representatives throughout the world.

Palgrave® and Macmillan® are registered trademarks in the United States, the United Kingdom, Europe and other countries

ISBN 978-0-230-29194-2 hardback
ISBN 978-0-230-29195-9 paperback

This book is printed on paper suitable for recycling and made from fully managed and sustained forest sources. Logging, pulping and manufacturing processes are expected to conform to the environmental regulations of the country of origin.

A catalogue record for this book is available from the British Library.

A catalog record for this book is available from the Library of Congress.

10 9 8 7 6 5 4 3 2 1
22 21 20 19 18 17 16 15 14 13

Printed in China

For my mother and father, Norma and Peter Geddes

Contents

List of Illustrative Material

Tables

Figures

Boxes

Acknowledgements

I am grateful to Professor Ian Bache and Professor Simon Bulmer, my colleagues at the University of Sheffield, and to Professor Hussein Kassim of the University of East Anglia for help with and suggestions regarding parts of this book. Any errors of fact or omission are, of course, my responsibility.

Heartfelt thanks, as ever, to Federica, Jacopo and Beatrice for bearing me with me while I worked on this.

ANDREW GEDDES

List of Abbreviations

AFSJ	Area of Freedom, Security and Justice
BCEM	British Council of the European Movement
BIE	Britain in Europe
BIS	Department for Business, Innovation and Skills
BNP	British National Party
BSE	Bovine Spongiform Encephalopathy
CAP	Common Agricultural Policy
CFSP	Common Foreign and Security Policy
CIE	Committee of Independent Experts
CJEU	Court of Justice of the European Union
CMSC	Common Market Safeguards Campaign
COES	Cabinet Office European Secretariat
CoR	Committee of the Regions
CRE	Commission for Racial Equality
DCLG	Department for Communities and Local Government
DECC	Department for Energy and Climate Change
DEFRA	Department for the Environment, Food and Rural Affairs
DoE	Department for the Environment
DWP	Department for Work and Pensions
EAEA	European Atomic Energy Authority
EAS	External Action Service
EAW	European Arrest Warrant
EC	European Community
ECHR	European Convention on Human Rights
ECRG	European Conservatives and Reformists Group
ECSC	European Coal and Steel Community
EDC	European Defence Community
EEA	European Economic Area
EEC	European Economic Community
EFTA	European Free Trade Area
EMS	European Monetary System
EMU	Economic and Monetary Union
EP	European Parliament
EPC	European Political Cooperation

EPP	European People's Party
EQ	Economic Association Committee
ERDF	European Regional Development Fund
ERM	Exchange Rate Mechanism
ESC	Economic and Social Committee
ESDP	European Security and Defence Policy
ESF	European Social Fund
EU	European Union
EUMF	European Union Migration Forum
FCO	Foreign and Commonwealth Office
FDI	Foreign Direct Investment
FRG	Federal Republic of Germany
FSG	Fresh Start Group
GDP	Gross Domestic Product
GDR	German Democratic Republic
GLA	Greater London Authority
GNI	Gross National Income
HI	Historical Institutionalism
IGC	Intergovernmental Conference
IMF	International Monetary Fund
JHA	Justice and Home Affairs
JMC(E)	Joint Ministerial Committee (Europe)
KBO	Keep Britain Out
MAFF	Ministry of Agriculture, Fisheries and Food
MLG	Multi-Level Governance
NATO	North Atlantic Treaty Organization
NFU	National Farmers Union
NRC	National Referendum Campaign
ODP (E)	Overseas and Defence Policy Committee (Europe)
OEEC	Organisation for European Economic Co-operation
OLP	Ordinary Legislative Procedure
QMV	Qualified Majority Voting
RDA	Regional Development Agencies
REGLEG	Region with Legislative Powers
SEA	Single European Act
SGOEU	Scottish Government Office in the European Union
SLG	Starting Line Group
SNP	Scottish National Party
STV	Single Transferable Vote
TEC	Treaty establishing the European Community
TFEU	Treaty on the Functioning of the European Union

TUC	Trade Unions Congress
VAT	Value Added Tax
UKIP	United Kingdom Independence Party
UKRep	UK Permanent Representation to the EU
WAG	Welsh Assembly Government
WEU	West European Union

Introduction

The debate about Britain and the European Union (EU) is about the past, present and future of British politics, about Britain's place in the world and about national self-understandings. This book specifies the profound effects of membership on British politics and addresses the fundamental debate about Britain's place and future in the EU. The book is not intended as a technical manual detailing the mechanics of British relations with the EU; rather, it focuses on why, how and with what effects the EU has become one of the most contentious issues in contemporary British politics. It shows that the 'choice for Europe' made by British political leaders in the 1960s and 1970s was essentially defensive and that Britain has moved into an outer tier, or what could be called the EU's 'slow lane'. Britain is outside both the eurozone and the Schengen passport-free travel arrangements. There are also strong calls from Conservatives within the coalition government that came to power in 2010 for further repatriation of powers from the EU, or even exit. Few British political leaders have embraced 'the European project', while opposition to European integration has remained a powerful political undertow in British politics. Since the 1990s, public opposition to European integration has grown, while political leaders have lacked the intention, or capability, or vision or opportunity to develop alternative visions of Britain's place in the world that could challenge euroscepticism.

The book also documents the major changes in the scope of the 'European project'. Although it has sometimes been represented as such in Britain, the intention of European leaders was never to create some kind of glorified free trade area. There was always a core political purpose informing the development of European integration. This political purpose has underpinned polity-building efforts at EU level since the 1990s and, in particular, the move to create an economic and monetary union with a single currency. Britain has opted out of this key development, but cannot opt out of its effects and consequences. The EU has moved to a high level of economic

1

and political integration, while the eurozone crisis that was unleashed by the effects of the post-2008 credit crunch has pushed the EU towards stronger forms of economic governance, including fiscal policies. This means that the EU now impinges directly on the EU and its citizens, and cannot be passed off as a largely technical exercise concerned with regulating the single market.

While the EU's future is uncertain and the effects of the financial crisis will take years – if not decades – to play out, member states have made huge investments in the European project and its disorderly collapse would probably be catastrophic. However, European leaders have not articulated a clear vision of the EU's future that chimes with EU citizens. In the postwar period, the EU could be hailed as a guarantor of peace and security after the horrors of war. This justification does not work so well nearly 70 years after the end of World War II. The ideologies of federalism and European unity seem not to resonate, while populist politicians on both right and left target a supposedly out-of-touch Euro-elite. British governments have long preferred a looser, more intergovernmental structure with a strong focus on market liberalization, but this vision does not command widespread support. The Conservative–Liberal Democrat coalition government elected in 2010 has made it clear that it prefers to stand aside from the travails of eurozone governance, although Prime Minister Cameron knows full well that Britain cannot stand aside from the effects of the crisis. Britain is now located within an outer tier, or slower lane, of the EU. This is not a new development. Britain first secured use of 'opt-out' provisions in the Maastricht Treaty, agreed in 1992, although the debate then often focused on when Britain would 'catch-up' by, for example, joining the euro. This debate has now changed and appears to involve acceptance of a re-defined relationship with the EU that is neither fully 'in' nor fully 'out'. In July 2012, in response to questions in the House of Commons, David Cameron contended that:

> I think we should not be frightened of a variable Europe, with variable countries involved in variable projects. Our national interest is the single market, trade and co-operation over foreign affairs, where we have a huge amount to bring to the table. Our interest is not in being in the Schengen agreement; our interest is not being in the single currency. We have to be a bit more relaxed about a Europe of different types of membership. (*Hansard*, 2012)

Whether this is a sustainable position is a key question that is central to analysis of the future of Britain, within or outside the EU. The extent of this 'variability' is one key question. It is highly unlikely that many – if any – member states would voluntarily choose to be located in the slow lane with the UK, which does then raise questions about Britain's influence on EU decision-making, particularly as the EU moves towards a higher level of economic integration encompassing fiscal policy and the regulation of banks. If Britain's national interest is in the single market, as Cameron claimed, then exclusion from eurozone economic governance could be a major problem as rules are made and developed over which the British government has little influence, but the effects of which on the British economy are likely to be strong. Opting for the slow lane is a hugely important strategic choice that raises major questions about Britain's future in or out of the EU. Britain is slowly moving towards an outer tier or slower lane of the EU. The coalition government could also be seen as preparing the ground for this redefined relationship. In July 2012, Foreign Secretary William Hague announced a comprehensive audit of British relations with the EU to report in 2014, i.e. one year before the planned 2015 general election. He denied that this was a move towards withdrawal or disengagement. However, such an audit is very likely to be used to sustain Conservative arguments for a re-cast relationship with the EU, and the repatriation of powers in areas such as social and employment policy. The audit is entirely consistent with the movement towards a slow lane, or outer tier, of the EU. It could also help to buy time with Conservative eurosceptics that have pushed hard within the coalition government since it came to power, in 2010, for a redefinition of Britain's relations with the EU.

The constraints of dissensus

While this book looks at Britain and the EU, it also specifies the major shifts that have occurred in the European project since its inception in the 1950s. European politics have been transformed during the last 60 years by economic and political integration within the EU but Britain has been marginal to key developments. British governments have not resolved domestic political tensions that have long characterized relations, while levels of public support for European integration in Britain lag behind those in many other member states. More to the point, attitudes in Britain towards the

EU since the 1990s have hardened into a strong streak of opposition to the EU known as 'euroscepticism'. Such 'permissive consensus' as there was in Britain, whereby citizens in EU member states would allow their national governments some space to pursue their EU objectives, has long since been eroded (Lindberg and Scheingold, 1970; Hooghe and Marks, 2007). Hooghe and Marks (2008) argue that there has been a shift across Europe from permissive consensus to 'constraining dissensus', with political leaders facing euroscepticism. This is particularly evident in Britain, where the consensus was fragile in the first instance. One reason for this is that 'signals' on the EU issue sent by political leaders have been lukewarm, at best. Britain stood aside from the first steps towards European integration during the 1950s and has spent a good part of the time since it joined in 1973 agonizing about the EU's shape, form, scope and direction. The result is that British vacillation has occurred from the sidelines, rather than from 'the heart of Europe'. Some see this as a shortcoming or failing that strikes at the heart of British politics. Others see the continued development of the EU as a threat to national sovereignty and self-government. The following is a checklist of British 'awkwardness':

- Britain did not join the first supranational European organization, the European Coal and Steel Community (ECSC), when it was founded in 1951 and did not take seriously the Messina negotiations in 1955 that led to the Treaty of Rome.
- Prime Ministers Macmillan and Wilson made unsuccessful applications in 1961–63 and 1967, respectively, which on both occasions were vetoed by French president de Gaulle.
- There have been, and still are, divisions within and between the main parties on membership (in the 1960s and 1970s) and on the effects of membership (since accession).
- Britain sought a renegotiation of the terms of accession soon after joining in 1973, with a divisive referendum in 1975 on the renegotiated terms.
- In 1979, the Conservative government led by Margaret Thatcher disputed its level of contributions to the EEC budget. The issue was not resolved until 1984.
- Strife broke out within the Labour Party over Britain's EC membership, which became a core bone of contention that led to the creation of the breakaway Social Democratic Party in 1981,

comprising figures of a more pro-European persuasion such as Roy Jenkins and Shirley Williams.

• Margaret Thatcher's Bruges speech in 1988 gave rise to what we now know as 'euroscepticism', asserting a vision of a Europe of nation states that opposed key aspects of plans for future European integration.

• During Thatcher's time in office between 1979 and 1990, six cabinet ministers resigned on European issues (Leon Brittan, Michael Heseltine, Nigel Lawson, Nicholas Ridley, Sir Geoffrey Howe and, finally, Thatcher herself).

• The Maastricht Treaty of 1992 and sterling's ejection in September 1992 from the Exchange Rate Mechanism (ERM) led to great disruption within the Conservative Party. John Major issued a 'put up or shut up' challenge in June 1995 to Conservative eurosceptics.

• The post 9/11'war on terror' and conflict in Iraq once again exposed tensions between UK Atlanticism and competing calls for closer relations with key EU states, particularly France and Germany.

• The Labour government led by Tony Blair did not resolve its attitude towards the creation of an Economic and Monetary Union (EMU) and the establishment of the single currency, the euro.

• Albeit in 'second order' European Parliament (EP) elections, there was a strong performance from the United Kingdom Independence Party (UKIP) advocating withdrawal from the EU.

• David Cameron made an unsuccessful attempt in December 2011 to oppose the 'fiscal compact' (the Treaty on Stability, Coordination and Governance in the Economic and Monetary Union, to give it its proper title). Little more than two months later he made a swift *volte-face* to accept a Treaty-based instrument to enforce strict budget controls on member states, albeit with an opt-out for Britain.

This is a long list, at the contents of which are explored more closely in the chapters that follow. It would be unfair to label Britain as uniquely Europe's 'awkward partner' (George, 1998). Other member states can be 'awkward' or 'reluctant', too. Norway and Switzerland have even chosen not to join. Britain has actually engaged relatively enthusiastically with some forms of cooperation and integration,

particularly as an enthusiastic advocate of single market liberalization, and played a leading role with the French government in cooperation on defence and security policy. Britain also has a good track
record when it comes to implementation of EU laws. But, crucially,
Britain has been on the sidelines for key steps in economic and political integration, both when the organization was founded in the 1950s
and, more recently, with the creation of the euro and the response to
the post-2008 economic crisis. Public opinion data show that British
people declare less knowledge of, interest in and confidence in the EU
than citizens in many other EU member states, while they are also
more likely to construe the EU as a threat to national identity.

Since the credit crunch and subsequent economic crisis, there have
been declining levels of public confidence in the EU and in EU institutions across the EU. This corresponds with a more general lack of
confidence and trust in political institutions and politicians that has
become an important and wider dynamic in contemporary European
politics. Even in the context of declining trust and confidence, people
in the UK have remained amongst the least supportive of European
integration. Eurobarometer surveys of EU-wide public opinion
provide insight into attitudes to the EU in the UK. The May 2011
survey found 63 per cent of British respondents tended to distrust the
EU, compared with 24 per cent who said that they tended to trust it
(which was actually a 4 per cent improvement in trust since the same
question had been asked in the autumn 2010 Eurobarometer survey).
The EU-wide average figures are 41 per cent trust and 47 per cent
distrust. Interestingly, respondents in Britain to the May 2011 survey
almost equally distrusted the EU, the national parliament and the
British government (63 per cent, 64 per cent and 65 per cent, respectively). When assessing the most effective level for responding to the
economic crisis, respondents in Britain seemed to show relatively
more confidence in national government, with 35 per cent seeing the
national government as best able to take effective action against the
crisis (the EU average being 20 per cent). British respondents had less
confidence in the EU, with just 10 per cent seeing it as best able to
take action compared with an EU average of 22 per cent.

The paradox of ever-closer union

Given this doubt, vacillation and scepticism, why has Britain
become so integrated? Why has the EU worked its way into the
nooks and crannies of the British political system? Despite evidence

of a lack of support in Britain for European integration and some doubt that it is the best way in which to respond to key challenges such as the financial and economic crisis, the EU is a fact of life in contemporary British politics. Britain has become deeply integrated with other EU member states, in both economic and political terms. Britain's trade is strongly focused on the EU, while access to the single market helps attract foreign direct investment (FDI) to the UK (HM Treasury, 2011). Much of this integration has occurred 'under the radar' and can be labelled as 'quiet Europeanisation' (Bache and Nugent, 2007). As will be seen, many key policy areas are extensively 'Europeanized', in the sense that they are largely governed within an EU framework. Europeanization has changed the 'standard operating practices' within the British political system and worked its way into institutional roles, party debate, policy-making, devolution and interest representation.

The precise amount of legislation that arises from EU decisions is a matter of debate. Some have claimed that up to 80 per cent of British law is made at EU level, but this is an exaggeration. In June 2006, responding to a written question in the House of Lords, the trade minister, Lord Triesman, stated that: 'We estimate that around half of all UK legislation with an impact on business, charities and the voluntary sector stems from legislation agreed by Ministers in Brussels. Parliamentary analysis of UK statutory instruments implemented annually under the European Communities Act suggests that on average around 9 per cent of all statutory instruments originate in Brussels' (House of Commons Library, 2010: 14).

The EU's remit is wide-reaching. A quick glance at the Lisbon treaty (agreed in 2007 and ratified in 2009) reveals that the EU's remit extends to: external action, foreign, security and defence policy, citizenship, the single market, agriculture, fisheries, free movement, border checks, asylum and immigration, civil and criminal and police matters, justice and home affairs (JHA), transport, competition, tax, economic and monetary policy, employment and social policy, public health, consumer protection, industry, the environment, energy, commercial policy and financial provisions. Given that British political elites have often been divided and public opinion has been sceptical, why has Britain become quite so engaged with European integration across such a wide range of issues? The next section explains the conceptual approach that this book will develop in order to address the issue of British engagement with European integration across its many levels and dimensions.

The conceptual approach of the book

The puzzle that this book addresses is that of why, given reluctance, doubt, scepticism and awkwardness, Britain has become quite so integrated with the EU. It cannot have happened by chance; neither can we put it down to some conspiracy. The reason must lie within the actions and preferences of political actors within the British political systems and the effects of these actions, whether intended or not. Thus, rather than claiming that Britain has some kind of psychological problem with European integration rooted in some sense of its 'national identity', this book focuses squarely on the interactions between the British system and European integration over a period of more than 50 years. To do so, it is important to gather some conceptual tools that can help us organize and make sense of these complex interactions and their effects.

A wide range of theories have developed that seek to account for engagement with the EU, decision-making at EU level, and also for the effects that European integration can then have on domestic politics. These theories are introduced and discussed throughout the book. This section pays close attention to the analysis of the effects of developments over time and the insights offered by historical institutionalism (HI). Thinking about events over time points to the value of historical perspectives that allow the assessment of continuity and change in British relations with the EU, while also exploring the ways in which European integration has become absorbed within the organizational and conceptual logics of British politics; or, put another way, the extent to which British politics has been 'Europeanized'. HI is very focused as an approach to understanding the effects of previous decisions on current choices. It could be seen, simplistically, as implying that 'history matters' and that, to understand current debates about Britain in Europe, we need to pay attention to past decisions and their effects. HI is more than a mere statement of the obvious importance of history for politics. HI is also interested in what can be called the 'politics of time' and the ways in which decisions made at particular points in time and for particular reasons can become locked-in and difficult to change. It also looks at the conditions under which change is possible (Pierson, 2004).

HI does appear to create a useful conceptual vocabulary for understanding British relations with the EU, as well as the more general tendency to institutional persistence in British politics. HI tends to focus on the longer-term impact of decisions made about Europe in the 1950s and 1960s, and also how the effects of European integration on the British political system are mediated by established practices and ways of doing things. The term most commonly associated with HI is 'path dependence', meaning that previous decisions shape future options. It could be argued that a 'path' of awkwardness for British relations with European integration was established in the 1950s from which it has since been difficult to deviate. The argument would be as follows: decisions made in the postwar period about Britain's relations with other European states – which themselves drew, of course, from deeper-rooted national self-understandings and ideas about Britain and its place in the world – have since continued to affect attitudes towards European integration.

If the proposition that cause and effect are not necessarily contemporaneous is accepted, then current political events can have longer-term causes whose origins lie in institutional arrangements that have become entrenched and which limit possibilities for future policy development. Attention is drawn to issues of timing and sequence so that formative moments or conjunctures can be distinguished. Thus 'it is not only a question of what happens but also of when it happens. Issues of temporality are at the heart of analysis' (Pierson, 2000: 251). Levi (1997: 28) likens the effects of this institutional entrenchment on policy choices to the branches of a tree: 'From the same trunk, there are many different branches and smaller branches. Although it is possible to turn around and clamber from one branch to the other – and essential if the chosen branch dies – the branch on which a climber begins is the one she tends to follow.' Institutional processes can become reinforcing, with the result that the further one goes down the path, then the harder it becomes to change course. It also implies potential path inefficiency: the longer-term outcomes may be less desirable than those that would have arisen if an alternative path had been chosen. The classic issue here is Britain's decision not to join the ECSC and EEC in the 1950s, although policy-makers at that time would not have been be able to anticipate path-dependent inefficiencies at the time decisions were made and act in advance to remedy long-term disadvantages.

Historical institutional analysis thus focuses on the ways in which institutions 'constrain and refract' politics and 'shape both the strategies and goals of political actors' (Fairbrass and Jordan,

2001: 7). Furthermore, as Pierson (1998: 30) argues, member states can play a key role in the decisions that shape the EU, but can also agree to policies that then fundamentally alter their own positions in ways that could not have been anticipated at the time the original decisions were made. As European integration proceeds, then a range of additional actors (sub-national government, EU institutions, other member states, EU pressure groups) impinge to greater or lesser extents on supranational decision-making processes and can limit the ability of the British government to influence outcomes. Moreover, these outcomes can differ from those that were initially foreseen at the time when the original decision to cede sovereign authority was made; meaning that European integration's 'path' can have unanticipated consequences.

This historical dimension has important social effects on the capacity for European integration to become fully embedded over time as a central component of the interests and identities of British political actors. The extent to which political actors learn (or not) to become European is central to assessment of the EU's impacts on British politics. The next section of this chapter develops a more systematic exploration of some of the factors that might help explain Britain's conditional and differential engagement.

To adopt an HI perspective appears an appealing choice, but three sets of issues can be raised that help to qualify this approach. First, it will be clear throughout this book that previous decisions have had effects on later choices; but so, too, have ideas about Britain's place in the world. We can account for institutional processes, but must also be attuned to the ideas – about state, nation, sovereignty, the market and the welfare state – that animate these processes and the ways in which they are articulated in political debate. Second, the implications of HI seem quite clear. Britain has, over time, located itself in the EU's 'slow lane'. It is not in the Schengen free movement zone, it has opted out of the euro and also opted out of the development of eurozone governance within the so-called fiscal compact. It is difficult to foresee circumstances under which Britain would deviate from this 'path' towards a slower lane or outer tier of the EU. It is also hard to see which other member states would want to join the UK in this location. Finally, we can ask whether the past is a reliable guide. If the 'weight of history' is the key driver of Britain's relations to the EU, then what happens when the world changes? The Danish physicist Niels Bohr observed that 'prediction is very difficult, especially about the future'. The world is now radically different from the one that Britain faced in the 1950s and 1960s, when choices about European integration were first made. The Cold War had ended. The so-called BRICs (Brazil, Russia, India and China) are fast-rising powers. European countries have been gripped by economic crisis, have ageing populations and creaking welfare systems. They seem far less dynamic than many of their more nimble international competitors. The USA, too, appeared to be shifting its focus. In his 2010 announcement on US military strategy, President Obama made it clear the USA would increasingly look east towards Asia and the Pacific in its foreign and defence policy. The US government also expressed its frustration with the inadequacies of the response from eurozone countries to the economic crisis. The past may no longer be a reliable guide to the future and the 'weight of history' might not provide the most reliable account of the future of Britain in the EU. Perhaps the EU is the solution to the basic problem of how to respond to this changed world (of economic reform, responding to climate change, sustaining welfare provision), or perhaps the EU is part of the problem and needs to be radically reformed – or even abandoned – if adequate responses are to develop in the face of these challenges. British governments will seek to play a role in these debates, but will do so from the EU's slower lane or outer tier.

Conditional and differential engagement

This book shows that Britain has chosen to move into the EU's slow lane and also that other member states have been happy to accommodate this choice as a way of pursuing their objectives without having to keep the British onside. This move to the slow lane is emblematic of Britain's *conditional* and *differential* engagement with the EU. Engagement is conditional, in the sense that identification with the EU seems not to be deep-seated and appears based on pragmatic calculations about costs and benefits, rather than any attachment to European ideals. It is differential, in the sense that Britain has opted out of key aspects of European integration (most notably the Schengen system of border free travel, and the euro), while some areas of British political life have clearly been more affected than others. The 'path' of ambivalence or scepticism, from which it has subsequently been hard to deviate, was established in the 1950s, with the attendant consequence that 'Europe' has not become deeply embedded within the preferences, identities and interests of either Britain's political elite or its population. At the same time, the European context has changed, with other actors (EU institutions, other member states, pressure groups, sub-national governments) becoming more deeply involved in the decision-making process, with the effect that central government has become one of many centres in the EU's political system. Thus, Britain's conditional and essentially defensive 'choice for Europe' has also been exposed to the dynamics of new forms of supranational political integration that challenge some of the core underlying premises of British politics. The solution has been the move to an outer tier from which Britain has chosen to observe the debates that will shape the EU's future, but will find it more difficult to make its voice heard. The reasons for this will become clear. British governments have either not been able to make the case in Britain for Europe, as happened under New Labour between 1997 and 2010, or have not had the intention to make the case, as has happened under the Conservative–Liberal Democratic coalition since 2010.

Britain in Europe and Europe in Britain

This section specifies two ways of thinking about conditional and differential engagement. The first of these can be labelled 'Britain in Europe', and centres on the analysis of British relations with the EU and the role of British governments in attempting to shape Europe's institutional architecture. The other is 'Europe in Britain', which focuses on the impacts of European integration on British politics.

The kinds of question raised by the Britain in Europe theme include:

- What factors have motivated British policy towards the EU?
- Have British governments possessed the capacity to turn preferences into EU priorities?
- Have British governments been particularly effective players of the EU game?
- How have British policies towards the EU changed over time, and what factors have contributed to these changes?

The focus from the 'Britain in Europe' perspective tends to be on inter-state relations, analysis of the UK's role within the EU and the attitudes of various UK governments to the development of European integration over the last 60 years. This shows the ways in which Britain has engaged (or not) with European integration since the 1950s and how Britain has sought to use its influence in the councils of Europe across the wide range of policy issues with which the EU is concerned. Britain's European policy has contained three central elements based on perceptions of the UK, its interests and its place in the world:

- The UK has a preference for intergovernmental structures that enshrine the central role and legitimate authority of national governments. This combines with a dislike for 'federal' solutions to European problems, and a self-consciously pragmatic and sceptical attitude to discussions of grand projects and the EU's *finalité* (or final destination).
- The UK places strong emphasis on the Atlantic alliance as the core element of British foreign policy. This was an approach affirmed by Tony Blair in 2003 in a speech to UK ambassadors when he spoke of the UK as a bridge between Europe and the USA. The war in Iraq gave a practical demonstration of this central tenet of British foreign policy.
- The UK has a preference in the realm of the international political economy for arrangements that promote global free trade which, over 20 years or so, has become support for measures that promote market liberalization and protect the vast concentration of financial service providers in the City of London within the European economy.

In addition to these points, there has been an important change in the underlying political dynamics. European integration used to be an issue of low salience because it was largely a technical issue associated with market-making. It was far easier to build a permissive consensus if few people actually cared about the issue. Since the 1990s, the EU has become a more ambitious project of polity-building. In the era of low salience and largely technical debate about market-making, political leaders could rely on the permissive consensus to give them some space to reach agreements at EU level; however, even in the 1970s, this consensus was fragile and contested. This has become even more pronounced with the movement to a 'constraining dissensus' marked in the UK and other member states by eurosceptic opposition to the EU. It is relevant to think about the factors that drive this scepticism. Influential work on

European integration has pointed to the importance of economic cost–benefit analysis as driving public attitudes. Since Maastricht was seen as 'uncorking' popular opposition to European integration, this has been joined by two other powerful and important factors (Franklin *et al.*, 1994). The first of these is national identity and the ways in which European integration can, or cannot, be reconciled with national identity. The second is a wider public loss of confidence by citizens in the political system and politicians. These factors have stoked euroscepticism. Voters are far less likely to take their cues from political parties and follow their lead. The permissive consensus has been eroded. The EU's move from 'market-making' to 'polity-building' has created more space for euroscepticism in British politics that draws from the representation of the European project as a threat to national identity, as well as a wider disaffection from the political system.

This politicization of European integration also challenges established theoretical perspectives on European integration such as neo-functionalism (supranational actors such as the European Commission in the driving seat) or intergovernmentalism (member states in charge) that, although offering very different perspectives on European integration, effectively saw it as an elite-driven device for resolving socio-economic problems (Börzel and Risse, 2009). There is little room for the citizens and voters in these theories.

The 'Europe in Britain' theme involves analysis of the extent to which European integration has been absorbed into the logics of British domestic politics. The kinds of question that are explored include:

- What impact has European integration had on the organization of the British political system?
- To what extent do British policy priorities, and the organization of the British economy and welfare state, 'fit' with those in other member states and with an emerging EU model?
- To what extent has the EU facilitated the devolution of power to sub-national levels within the UK?
- What impact has European integration had on debates within and between the main political parties?
- In what directions have public attitudes towards the EU developed and what part has the mass media played in shaping these views?

The first point requires the inclusion of decision-making in Whitehall, the organization of the British polity, but necessarily looks 'out' from Whitehall to think about the role of sub-national government. Indeed, the term 'sub-national government' hardly conveys the major changes that have taken place within the British political system. When the issue of 'multi-level politics' within the EU is considered, then it might seem logical to look at the growth of the supranational layer at EU level. However, this misses a crucially important part of the picture because it only looks 'up' to Europe. Power and authority in the UK political system has also moved 'downwards' and 'outwards': 'downwards' to sub-national government, and 'outwards' to the market and forms of delegated governance, as a result of privatization and agency governance. In such terms, the UK is an increasingly disunited kingdom.

A key advantage of combining the 'Britain in Europe' theme with the 'Europe in Britain' theme is that it prevents the simplistic assumption that European integration simply 'happens' to the UK, as though the EU were a supernatural phenomenon with its own mysterious powers, rather than a supranational organization of which Britain is a leading member. 'Europe' does not just happen when government ministers fly to Brussels, Luxembourg or Strasbourg to meet ministerial and official colleagues from other member states, or deal with EU institutions located in those cities. If this were so, then this would imply that decisions made at EU level would follow a simple and inexorable logic of integration driven by higher forces that render it both inevitable and detached from national politics. This is conspiracy theory, not serious analysis. It is more useful to identify the ways in which British governments have consciously chosen European integration, the reasons for and effects of these choices, and the ways in which economic and political integration have become integrated as central concerns in British politics.

This perspective has a further implication. European integration is not simply a foreign policy issue detached from domestic politics. It works its way into domestic decision-making structures. It does not mean a simple amendment of these domestic structures to 'fit' with a standardized EU approach. Instead, we will see that the British political system refracts, rather than simply absorbs, the effects of European integration. Adaptation occurs with 'national colours' (Green Cowles *et al.*, 2000). Analysis of the ways in which the British political system shapes, or is shaped (and perhaps transformed) by, European integration provides a key perspective on British relations with the EU (and on other key changes in British politics), while also facilitating understanding of the 'Europeanization' of British politics without assuming that the nature of British political change is unidirectional and linked exclusively to the impact of European integration. Europe is but one potential source of British political change.

This can be better understood if the UK political system is seen as nested within a series of interlocking relationships that extends 'down' to the sub-national and 'up' to the supranational. The key remains the 'national' circle, although devolved power to sub-state governments in Scotland, Wales and Northern Ireland, as well as integration within the EU, have fundamentally changed this 'national' circle. Furthermore, the ways in which sub-national, national and supranational government are enmeshed indicates the extent to which British politics and policy have become Europeanized.

Organization of the book

This book assesses Britain's role in the EU and the EU's impacts on British politics. This introductory chapter has sketched some fundamental themes. As an organizational point, it is useful for the reader to bear in mind that the issues that are to be assessed cannot be easily compartmentalized. For example, the economic crisis and eurozone debate affects policy and institutional choices, but also has effects on party politics. This means that it is analysed from a variety of perspectives throughout the book. To help the reader navigate their way through the analysis, there is cross-referencing to indicate these areas of overlap. There now follows a brief outline of the key purposes of the book's chapters.

Chapter 1 extends the analysis to explore explanations for British 'awkwardness' and contends that the ways in which domestic institutional structures refract the impacts of European integration need to be central to analysis of the EU and British politics.

Chapter 2 surveys Britain's relations with emerging structures of European economic and political integration from the end of World War II until 1973. Central to this are the positions of British governments at the time of the Treaty of Paris (1951), the Treaty of Rome (1957) and the failed membership applications of 1961–63 and 1967.

Chapter 3 assesses Britain's role within the EU between accession in 1973 and the fall of the Major government in 1997. This chapter also begins to develop the Britain in Europe theme through evaluation of the stances of successive British governments on the Single European Act (SEA) (1986), the Maastricht Treaty (1992) and the Amsterdam Treaty (1997). The pace of European integration quickened considerably after the mid-1980s. As the pace has quickened, so has the capacity of European integration to strike at the heart of British politics.

Chapter 4 analyses the EU polices of New Labour between 1997 and 2010, and the coalition government since 2010. It avoids unrealistic assessments of whether these governments moved Britain 'to the heart of Europe' and, instead, focuses on the balancing of inter-state relations at EU level with the complexities of domestic politics.

Chapter 5 analyses the EU's main institutions (the Council of Ministers, the European Council, the European Commission, the EP, and the Court of Justice (CJEU)) and explores the attitudes of British governments to these institutions, the ways in which the development of law-making capacity at supranational level affects some of the fundamental precepts of British politics. This chapter also assesses forms of representative politics at EU level.

Chapter 6 analyses key EU policies: the budget, Common Agricultural Policy (CAP), single market, regional development, social policy, regional policy and environmental policy. The focus is on policies that have often been core to the EU's ambitions and/or are in areas of low politics. In all these areas, attention is paid to British government preferences and their attainment.

Chapter 7 assesses the EU's move into areas of high politics since the 1990s, including the creation of an EMU with a single currency, the development of common migration and asylum policies, and stronger cooperation on foreign, defence and security policy. The chapter assesses the stances of British governments on these highly significant policy developments.

Chapter 8 shifts focus to explore the Britain in Europe theme more fully in order to assess the 'fit' between the organization of the British polity and EU structures. This chapter explores the ways in which the organization of the British state has affected its ability to deal with the EU. The chapter also explores the effects of devolved power to Scotland, Wales and Northern Ireland.

Chapter 9 examines the impact of European integration on British party politics. The stances of the main political parties on

European integration are outlined, and the debates within and between the parties on European integration are evaluated. The most vigorous and divisive debates have often occurred *within* rather than *between* the parties as the fractious behaviour of the Labour Party (in the 1980s) and the Conservative Party (since the 1990s) demonstrates.

The book concludes with an assessment in Chapter 10 of the influence of these factors and some reflections on Britain's place in the EU. The overall aim is to assess conditional and differential engagement with the EU. As has already been noted, it is usual to encounter analyses of Britain's role within the EU that highlight the UK's inability to come to terms with key aspects of European integration. This is an important question and one that this book addresses. But it is equally pertinent to ask why – given evident scepticism at both elite and popular level about 'the European project' – Britain has become quite so engaged with the EU. Where are these points of engagement, and how can the differential nature of this engagement be explained? Finally, to return to the point made at the beginning of this chapter, we can also assess the extent to which Britain is 'in' the EU and how this relationship might evolve in the future.

Chapter 1

Britain on the Edge of Europe

This chapter analyses a variety of factors that could help to explain British relations with the EU and the impacts of European integration on British domestic politics. These include Britain's geographical position, and its distinct history and institutions that could contribute to positive or negative attitudes at governmental and public levels. It is, however, argued that geography, history and identity do have effects, but that these effects cannot be understood unless they are located in the context of the British political system; by which is meant not only institutions and processes, but also the ideas that inform and animate this system. Thus, we can hypothesize that, if the organization of the British political system is a key factor, then, in those areas that tally with domestic political preferences and institutional logics, there may well be British support for European integration because it can make the attainment of domestic political objectives more likely. Similarly, if EU objectives do not accord with British preferences, then reluctance or awkwardness could be anticipated.

This chapter begins by addressing some basic definitional and terminological issues. It discusses terms such as 'integration', 'supranationalism' and 'sovereignty', and provides a short overview of the EU's development. It then examines the extent to which factors such as geography, interdependence with other EU member states, and history and identity help to explain British relations with the EU. It goes on to explain how and why these factors need to be located in the context of the key features of the British political system.

What are we talking about?

A potentially puzzling aspect of analysing European integration is the plethora of terms used to describe it: the EU, the European Economic Community (EEC), the European Community (EC), the Common Market, the Union and the Community, to name six. It may be even more puzzling that, basically, all refer to the same organization. The key point is that the Maastricht Treaty (1992) created the EU and, since the Treaty was finally ratified in November 1993, it has become usual to see references to the EU. This is the term most frequently employed throughout this book. At various points, however, readers are likely to encounter other terms or acronyms such as the Common Market, the EEC or EC. All these terms have historical, legal or political importance. To highlight their significance and explain the development of European integration, terms other than the 'EU' will be used when appropriate. These situations will be clearly explained, and the relation between these terms and acronyms, and what we now know as the EU, will become evident. When analysing events before the Maastricht Treaty that created the EU, it is accurate to refer to the EEC, EC or Community, as will often be done in the book's earlier chapters. Also, it should be noted that when terms such as 'Britain' and 'the British government' are used, they are shorthand terms that refer to the far more complex workings of the British political and administrative systems. Even at times when the great ship of state has appeared to be proceeding serenely, there has been furious activity in the engine rooms below.

The EU is both an economic and a political entity, and seeks integration at both levels. The precise link between these two processes is, however, a matter of great contention. Some argue that economic integration should be separated from the political, while others maintain that no such separation is possible. Underlying this debate is an undeniable drive towards economic integration in Europe, accompanied by the development of a political-institutional framework to back up economic objectives. All statistics show that the EU is increasingly becoming a single economic area. More than 50 per cent of British trade is with other EU member states. The EU has also assumed an increased role in social and regional policies. Since 1993, all citizens of member states have become citizens of the Union. On 1 January 2002, a single European currency – the euro – entered circulation and the national currencies of the 12 states participating at that time were phased out. Since the 1990s, the EU has also tentatively entered the domain of 'high politics' that impinge far more directly on state sovereignty with increased responsibilities for foreign policy, defence cooperation, policing and border controls. As the EU becomes more concerned with such issues, questions of national authority and national identity come to the fore because foreign, defence, immigration, asylum and monetary policies impinge squarely on collective identities that have tended to be focused on nation-states, rather than international organizations.

Integration

This book is about European integration, but the very meaning of both the word 'Europe' and the term 'integration' need to be explored. The EC emerged during the Cold War, which ended in 1989 and had been composed of capitalist economies in western Europe. In the 1990s, following the collapse of the Soviet bloc, the EC faced the challenge of responding to the 'new Europe'. This immediately makes the point that the EU and Europe are not one and the same thing. The two terms cannot be transposed. Within the wider Europe, beyond the EU, a complex web of interdependent states and markets cooperate in an array of organizations such as the Council of Europe (with 47 member states) and the North Atlantic Treaty Organization (NATO), which includes the USA and Canada. What is significant about the EU, and distinguishes it from other organizations, is that it is supranational. This term will itself be analysed later in this chapter.

Integration has been defined as 'a process for the creation of political communities' within which 'states cease to be wholly sovereign' (Haas, 1971). As such, integration leads to the creation and maintenance of patterns of interaction among participating states with both political and economic dimensions that can also have effects on non-participating, bordering states. Integration has a formal dimension based on outcomes that result directly from political decisions, such as new laws, institutions and policies. It also has an informal dimension where processes such as trade and other cross-border transfers that have effective consequences develop, but are not necessarily dependent on formal, authoritative intervention (W. Wallace, 1990; see also Rosamond, 2000: 13). To facilitate analysis, Table 1.1 presents the five levels of economic integration and the four dimensions of political integration that can be identified (Laffan, 1992).

It is worth reflecting on these distinctions between levels of economic and political integration. In the wake of the eurozone crisis, there were proposals to move to a much deeper level of economic integration that held implications for fiscal policies. This would suggest location at least at point 4 and maybe moving towards point 5 on the scale of economic integration. On the political scale,

TABLE 1.1   *Distinctions between levels of economic and political integration*

Economic integration	Political integration
1 A free trade area within which tariffs and quotas are eliminated between member countries	1 Institutional integration, comprising the growth of collective decision-making structures with common institutions and formal rules
2 A customs union within which tariffs and quotas are removed, and an external tariff is imposed on goods and services entering the Union	2 Policy integration, whereby responsibility for particular policies is transferred to the supranational level
3 A common market within which people, goods, services and capital can move freely	3 Attitudinal integration, which involves growth of support amongst the peoples of the participating countries
4 An Economic Monetary Union involving a single currency and harmonization of some national economic policies	4 Security integration founded on security communities within which the expectation of war between participating states is minimized
5 Total economic integration whereby the same economic policies are pursued in all the member states	

Source: Adapted from Laffan (1992).

there is clear evidence of points 1 and 2, but less evidence of attitudinal integration. Theoretical approaches to European integration labelled as 'neo-functionalism' assumes that the public will catch up and that, as integration develops, loyalties will be refocused. In a time of plenty and economic growth, this may be the case but, in a time of crisis, it is not clear why there should be a growth of support amongst EU citizens for institutions and processes that deliver austerity and cuts, rather than growth.

It is important also to note that, while the EU does influence many of the main issues in contemporary British politics, some key political concerns that have been central to recent general elections – such as health care, education, and law and order – remain essentially national concerns. Even so, Britain's economy, even outside the eurozone, is closely tied to that of other EU member states. In the 1990s, bitter disputes over European integration during the 1990s and the divisions they caused were central to the landslide electoral defeat of the Conservative Party at the 1997 general election.

Supranationalism

A key feature of the EU analysis is that it is supranational: this means that, in certain policy areas – such as trade, competition policy and agriculture – the member states have ceded power (or sovereignty) to Union-level institutions to make decisions that are legally binding on them. This supranationalism is both a central and a controversial aspect of the EU. Its implications for Britain are a key aspect of this book.

The EU Union is a Treaty-bound organization. As this book shows, the EU is based on a series of Treaties negotiated between the member states that then, through legislative, executive and judicial processes at European level, are turned into a set of laws and rules which bind the member states. This law-making capacity and the binding nature of these laws is a distinct and unique feature of the EU as a supranational organization. Supranationalism involves the capacity of EU political and legal processes to turn treaties agreed in international law between participating states into laws that bind those states, as represented in Figure 1.1 and explained in Box 1.1.

FIGURE 1.1　*Basic features of the European Union supranational system*

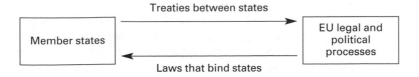

Box 1.1   What is supranationalism?

Supranationalism involves the establishment of formal structures of government above the nation state. It possesses three
key features:

- the institutions of the supranational government are independent from those of member states
- the organization can make rules that bind members and
  has the power to enforce those rules
- the institutions of the supranational government are part
  of a new legal system to which member states and individuals are subject (see Capotori, 1983).

EU law overrides national law, and institutions exist at the
supranational (EU) level that are independent of member
states. Supranational government has clear implications for
national sovereignty. In formal terms, national sovereignty
means that a country has supreme authority within its territory. Any country that is bound by the rules of a supranational
organization no longer has supreme authority and is therefore
no longer fully sovereign.

Britain has long preferred intergovernmental cooperation
to supranational government. Intergovernmentalism implies
unanimity as the basis of decision-making, and allows a veto
to be exercised to protect national interests. However, the
founders of the EC – France, Germany, Italy and the Benelux
countries – were suspicious of political systems based on the
notion of a national veto, and sought to move away from
intergovernmentalism.

Sovereignty

Supranational governance has important implications for sovereignty. The former Labour MP and cabinet minister Tony Benn
once said in the House of Commons: 'I don't know what sovereignty is ... We are talking about democracy.' This pithy observation highlights two points. Sovereignty can be a slippery concept
that means different things to different people, or can even evade

ready comprehension. Second, ultimately, the basic issues that people are most likely to grasp are 'Who decides?' and 'Who decides who decides?'

The 'sovereignty of parliament' is a key constitutional principle in Britain and was defined by Dicey in *The Law of the Constitution* (1885: 39–40) as meaning 'neither more nor less than this, namely that Parliament ... has, under the English constitution, the right to make or unmake any law whatever; and, further, that no person or body is recognized by the law of England as having a right to override or set aside the legislation of Parliament'. The UK is the only EU member state with this principle of legislative supremacy. In effect, this doctrine of legislative supremacy is qualified, rather than absolute. It is qualified, for example, by EU membership; human rights law; and devolution of power to Scotland, Wales and Northern Ireland.

The term 'sovereignty' can be confusing, which is why legislative supremacy is probably a better way of understanding the role of Parliament within the UK political system. This is because sovereignty tends more to be understood as a basic foundational principle of public international law governing relations between states. A *sovereign state* can be said to be one that holds and exercises supreme authority within its territorial jurisdiction, and is recognized as such by other states. It says nothing about the form or type of government, such as whether it is democratic or not. This is often referred to as the Westphalian model (after the Peace of Westphalia, 1648) of territorially exclusive sovereign states with an internal monopoly of violence (the ability to make and enforce law and order), control over external security, a central administration with tax-raising powers and central institutions with policy-making powers (Caporaso, 1996).

European integration does challenge the sovereign authority of its member states. All member states sign up to a supranational body of law that compromises national sovereignty. By ratifying the accession Treaty that took Britain into the EC then, it is possible to say that the British Parliament self-limited its sovereign authority because, in some areas, supranational institutions such as the Council (of Ministers), EP and Commission make laws, while Britain is subject to the remit of the CJEU. Human rights law and devolution complicate the picture and provide a more complex situation of re-ordered patterns of multi-level governance (MLG) in Britain. The EU contributes to this multi-level dynamic, but is not the only factor.

Eurosceptics tend to see the EU as diminishing, if not destroying, the very foundations of British political life through its attack on both state sovereignty and legislative supremacy. The counter-argument made by pro-Europeans is that sovereignty can be more effectively exercised if it is pooled, i.e. states work together and thus recognize the supremacy of supranational laws in areas where they have agreed to cooperate. In a speech in 1966, Edward Heath (1998: 357) provided a poolers' manifesto:

> Member countries of the Community have deliberately undertaken this to achieve their objectives, and, because they believe that the objectives are worth that degree of surrender of sovereignty, they have done it quite deliberately ... When we surrender some sovereignty, we shall have a share in the sovereignty of the Community as a whole, and of other members of it. It is not just, as is sometimes thought, an abandonment of sovereignty to other countries; it is a sharing of other people's sovereignty as well as a pooling of our own.

Britain in the European Union

EU membership has had an extensive impact on British politics, economy and society. Responsibility for important policy sectors has been transferred to common decision-making structures in collaboration with other member states and EU institutions. Good examples of this are agriculture and fisheries, where national policies have almost ceased to exist; measures are, instead, decided collectively within common policy frameworks. The decisions within these EU institutions override national law. Government ministers meet frequently with colleagues from other member states in EU decision-making forums. British government officials frequently board Brussels-bound trains or planes. Interest groups will look to both Whitehall and Brussels because they follow the basic law of pressure group politics: follow the power and seek to exert influence on it. For instance, in the 1980s the British trade unions that had, at one time, been staunch opponents of European integration became more favourably disposed to the EC, as it offered them a route to influence denied to them by the Conservative governments. Political parties from across the EU have also come together in Europe-wide confederations, although the foundations of party politics still remain largely national (Geddes, 2006).

These kinds of development indicate that it is important to understand the workings of EU institutions, and the role of UK governments and other actors within them, rather than to regard the EU as a 'foreign policy' issue detached from domestic issues. European integration is not a foreign policy issue. The EU's remit stretches to a wide range of domestic activities that have now expanded to include issues such as migration and asylum policy. We can consider the ways in which the UK has sought to 'upload' its policy priorities and preferences (and also think about what these are, and how they have developed and changed), as well as the impacts of EU rules and laws being 'downloaded' on the British political system. Yet, at the same time, it is important not to exaggerate the EU's effects and leap to the assumption that the EU alone has driven key changes in British politics. Many aspects of policy – such as health, education and taxation – remain largely beyond the EU's remit, while the organization of the British economy, labour market and welfare state remain quite distinct.

There are also strong elements of continuity in the British approach to European integration. UK governments have long displayed a preference for a vision of Europe and an associated institutional architecture that enshrines the centrality of member states and national governments. Moreover, Britain's European relations have been set against a continued preference for maintenance of strong transatlantic ties with the USA. These preferences can actually connect British governments in the 1970s with those of governments in the first decade of the twenty-first century. They remove some of the lustre of 'newness' from the mantle of 'New Labour' and also help place in context the EU policies of the Conservative–Liberal Democrat coalition government elected in 2010.

For these and other reasons, Britain has often been peripheral to the economic and political integration that has characterized EU history. Having been the leading European nation at the end of World War II, Britain chose not to participate in the development of supranational European integration and has often been marginal since. Hence was born the 'awkwardness' thesis, although there are some risks of hindsight here because, as Wolfram Kaiser (1996: xvi) remarks, it is much easier for contemporary observers to condemn the decisions made by politicians and officials in the 1950s when Britain stood aside from the first steps towards European integration, but this 'is based on the normative assumption that the path taken by the six [EC founder member states] was not only successful but natural, and also morally preferable to the British preference for trade liberalization within intergovernmental structures'. There was scepticism among British ministers and officials in the 1950s about 'the European project'. Britain's interests were seen to lie elsewhere. With hindsight, we could argue that they were mistaken (and there were those who argued at the time that they were), but this could not have been known with any degree of certainty.

The facts are that Britain stood aside from negotiations in the 1950s that led to the EC being created, endured failed applications for membership in 1961–63 and 1967, and finally joined the club on 1 January 1973. Since then, there have been periodic outbursts of opposition to European integration, most notably in 1974–76 while Labour were in power, and also in 1979–84, 1988–90 and – most intensely – 1992–97 under the Conservatives. Discontent has simmered in the Conservative Party since the 1990s and threatens to boil over as a result of the compromises of coalition government with the Liberal Democrats after 2010.

It was after 1992 when the label 'euroscepticism' was applied to opposition to Europe. According to the *Oxford English Dictionary*, the first use of the term 'eurosceptic' occurred in 1992 in *The Economist* newspaper in relation to opposition in Germany to EU-wide standards affecting German beer production. Right-wing euroscepticism surged to the forefront of British politics in the 1990s with devastating effects on the electoral fortunes of the Conservative party. This sentiment has not gone way. In October 2011, 81 Conservative backbenchers MPs defied David Cameron to call for an 'in' or 'out' referendum.

Analysing awkwardness

We now analyse the historical, political and institutional dimensions of Britain's engagement with the EU. The argument that is developed stresses the centrality of domestic politics as the point from which the effects of European integration need to be viewed. It is important to understand the ways in which the key features and characteristics of the British political system refract the influence of European integration and help to create the particular features of debate about European integration in Britain.

Does geography make a difference?

As an island on the north-west edge of Europe, Britain shares a land border with only one other EU member state, the Republic of Ireland. British people speak of 'going to Europe' or travelling to 'the continent', which implies that Britain is physically detached from the rest of Europe. Because of this peripheral location, Britain can also choose to opt in or out of engagement with European countries, or so the argument goes. There are three problems with this contention. Geographers would point out that Britain is part of Europe, understood to be the western extension of Eurasia. Moreover, if geographical peripherality shapes attitudes to Europe, then why have Ireland and Greece tended to be more enthusiastic member states than Britain? And why have attitudes to European integration *within* the UK and *over time* varied? Geographical location alone does not appear a particularly promising explanation.

Functional interdependence

Perhaps, then, the point is that Britain is not exclusively European. The argument here is that Britain is, as Winston Churchill put it, 'with' but not 'of' Europe, in the sense that Britain's European vocation remains contested by competing callings from the Commonwealth, from the 'special relationship' with the USA, and with political relations and trading patterns that are more global than strictly European. In a speech to the House of Commons in May 1951, Churchill asked:

> Where do we stand? We are not members of the European Defence Community, nor do we intend to be merged in a Federal European system. We feel we have a special relation to both, expressed by prepositions: by the preposition 'with' but not 'of' – we are with them, but not of them. We have our own Commonwealth and Empire.

The question still remains a perplexing one. Britain is a permanent member of the UN Security Council, has the world's seventh largest economy, has sought to be the closest ally of the USA in Europe (as the 'war on terrorism' and, very starkly, the wars in Iraq demonstrated), and is a leading member of the Commonwealth. But the UK has become much more closely linked to the EU and its member states (Aspinwall, 2003). Indeed, despite talk of globalization, the UK economy has actually become more *regionally* focused on the EU (Hay and Rosamond, 2002). While in the 1950s and 1960s Britain traded extensively with non-EU member states, since accession British trade has become ever more closely linked to the EU. This is a point also made by Andrew Gamble (1998), who discusses the relation between Europe and the global economy, and argues that European integration is often seen as resulting from underlying shifts in the European and global economies that generate increased interdependence and drive closer economic and political integration in Europe. 'On this view', Gamble (1998: 25) goes on to argue, 'it is the trends towards regionalization of the European economic space through trade and investment flows which is the central reality of the past fifty years'. Hirst and Thompson (1996) identified the emergence of three powerful trading blocs (USA/Americas, Europe and the Pacific Basin) and showed the British economy to be dominated by British domestic capital, with the international operations of British companies strongly focused on the European region.

This raises the issue of the relation between national economies, regional trading blocs and the global economy/globalization. Globalization has been seen as centred on 'a world no longer based on geographic expanse but on a temporal distance constantly being decreased by our transportation, transmission and tele-action possibilities' (Virilio, 2001: 71). Yet, a regionally focused EU economy based on the single market and EMU co-exists with the global economy partly as a reaction to it and partly as a defence against it. Anti-globalization activists identify the huge iniquities associated with global capital and neo-liberalism as a dominant global ideology propagated by the EU and other powerful international organizations such as the International Monetary Fund (IMF) and the World Bank. Also, some EU member states see unconstrained 'globalization' as a threat to their economic and social models. This idea of globalization as a threat has, since the 1980s, been less evident in the discourse and actions of UK governments, which have sought a 'pro-business' EU, the rolling back of the frontiers of the state through liberalization and deregulation of the British (and EU economy), and protection of the financial services industry in the City of London. This ties in with a longer-standing UK preference for global free trade and is another example of the ways in which historically embedded choices (this time in the realm of international political economy) have important effects on contemporary political dilemmas regarding Britain and Europe. In such circumstances, 'globalization' is a movable feast that can be construed by some as an inexorable force that requires certain fundamental realignments of the relationships between states and markets in both a European and global context to which 'there is no alternative', as Margaret Thatcher put it. Yet, this is not the only understanding that is available; for instance, Bauman (2002: 13) argues that globalization also presents an ethical challenge that draws into view the links between the richer and poorer parts of the world, and the ways in which global capital could and should be harnessed.

What effects, then, does regionalization have on economic and political integration? There is a school of thought known as 'transactionalism' that sees the increased intensity of interaction as a driving force for integration and as bringing with it greater identification with other European countries and their peoples. The effects of Europe can hit different groups within society in different ways so that, for instance, big business may be more in favour than smaller businesses, or younger people more supportive of European integration than older people. The general argument, however, is that as goods, capital, services and people move more freely within Europe, as people meet other Europeans, and as the symbols of images of a united Europe (the flag, the anthem, the currency) become more commonplace, then people will become more accepting of European unification and the demand for 'more Europe', with deeper integration, could also grow (Aspinwall, 2003).

However, while it is true that Britain is closely linked to the EU in trade and, of course, through economic and political integration, closer ties over the last 30 years have done little to inculcate deep-seated enthusiasm and demand for more Europe. In fact, trends seem to be in the opposite direction. At best, Britain appears to retain a Churchillian sense of being 'with' but not 'of' Europe. This also suggests that political and social identities are not quite so malleable and so easily refocused on the EU as rather straightforward transactional imperatives might suggest. A holiday in Italy or Spain, or an appreciation of French wines, does not necessarily translate into full-hearted enthusiasm for the euro. In turn, this suggests a continued role for domestic political processes that refract, rather than simply absorb, European influences.

Identities and attitudes

There is strong evidence from the Eurobarometer surveys of EU-wide public opinion that people in the UK are less enthusiastic about the European project. Figure 1.2 draws from data collected in autumn 2011 to compare perceptions of the meaning of the EU in Britain to the EU average. The right-hand side of Figure 1.2 shows more positive views of the EU while on the left are more negative views. There is a stronger association in the minds of people in Britain compared with the EU average. People in Britain are more likely to see the EU as a threat to cultural identity and border controls, as overly bureaucratic and as a waste of money.

Timothy Garton Ash has argued that the answer to the question 'Is Britain European?' is 'Yes, but not only' (Garton Ash, 2001). This raises the question of the complex politics of identity within the multi-national and multi-cultural United Kingdom. There is growing interest in the ways that the EU's move from market-making to polity-building has fuelled euroscepticism, and part of the reason for this scepticism is the threat some see European integration as posing to national identity.

Thomas Risse (2001) compared British, French and German national identities and argued that, since the 1950s, 'Englishness' as

FIGURE 1.2   *What does the EU mean? Britain and the EU compared*

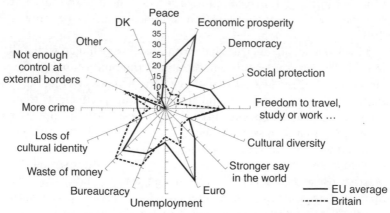

Question: What does the EU mean to you personally (% respondents)?

Source: Eurobarometer (2011a): 50–1.

a variant of British national identity has been constructed as distinct from Europe and as incompatible with federalism or supranationalism. This perspective encourages us to think about the part played by collective social identities of which Risse (2001: 201) identifies four components:

- ideas held by individuals about their membership in particular groups – these attachments are often based on emotional ties
- membership of a particular group can lead to distinctions from other groups, and to differences between in-groups and out-groups – it is a well-known aspect of national identity formation that these are formed in relation to 'the other'
- national identities within the 'imagined community' (*pace* Anderson, 1991) are closely linked to ideas about sovereignty and the state
- individuals hold multiple identities that are context-bound, which means that the real question is 'how much space is there for "Europe" in collective nation state identities' (Risse, 2001: 198).

Risse argues that there is not much space for Europe in 'Englishness'. 'Englishness' could be contrasted with identities within Scotland, Wales and (more problematically) Northern Ireland. Scottish and Welsh identities, in particular, have been strongly influenced by Englishness, in that they have been largely defined in both relation and opposition to it, and could have more space for Europe.

There also exist competing interpretations of British historical relations with Europe such that 'England against Europe' is too sweeping. The 'Anglo-Saxons' may have all the best tunes, as William Wallace (1991) put it, but that does not mean that there are not pro-Europeans in Britain who have a different understanding of Britain's history, identity and place in the world. Moreover, if British history is portrayed as in some way exceptional, then it must be acknowledged that so, too, are those of other European countries. Historical exceptionalism is the European norm, not a peculiarly British trait. Moreover, many 'ancient traditions' that are invoked when historical claims are made are actually quite recent creations. The 'invention of tradition' was a key element of the forging of the British nation-state during the nineteenth century (Hobsbawm and Ranger, 1983; Colley, 1992). Many traditions, such as the grandeur of the state opening of Parliament, embody an attempt to bestow splendour on the constitutional monarch, and thus a particular notion of British history, society and politics.

The practical consequence of interactions between national interests and national identities was late accession in 1973 to the EC which, as Helen Wallace (1997: 68) notes, had profound consequences, in the sense that it was an 'equivocal and pragmatic' shift without 'a conversion to the symbolism of integration' and with the political parties failing 'to embed the discourse of integration as a positive virtue'. Churchill famously saw Britain as at the centre of three circles of influence: the empire, the special relationship with the USA, and Europe (with Europe third on the list of priorities). While the original six countries of the EC concentrated during the 1950s on commercial economic policies, Britain sought to re-establish sterling as an international currency via sterling–dollar convertibility. As Alan Milward (1992: 390) wrote, 'the pound, once good as gold, would now be as good as dollars'. The forced devaluation of sterling in 1967 was a sign that this policy had failed and that Britain's global powers had faded. Rather than being a symbol of national regeneration, joining the EC was an indication of relative decline to regional power status and a diminished role in world affairs. The cognitive readjustment to this role as a European regional power was a painful process as the UK lost an empire and tried to find a role for itself in world affairs.

We now consider the effects of these issues of identity on developments on attitudes to European integration. Easton (1965) has argued that individual attitudes to politics have two components. An *affective* dimension based on ideological or non-material identification and a *utilitarian* dimension based on cost–benefit calculations. This affective dimension can be linked to the work of Ronald Inglehart on the rise of post-materialism in advanced industrial democracies, particularly amongst younger generations (Inglehart, 1971). This meant that material prosperity would stimulate increased interest in non-material issues, such as quality of life concerns. This was seen as also leading to increased support for European integration. Gabel (1998) identified, since the 1990s, the increased importance of utilitarian measures influencing public support for European integration. Since the 1990s, there has been increased interest in the ways in which national identity and the impact of wider public dissatisfaction with politics have fuelled euroscepticism (Hooghe and Marks, 2008). Table 1.1 presents

TABLE 1.2 *Affective and cost–benefit assessments of the UK's membership of the EU*

EU image	Economic balance of UK membership			
	Costs exceed benefits	*Benefits exceed costs*	*They are in balance*	*DK/NA*
Rather negative	25	8	4	3
Rather positive	10	21	7	4
Neither positive nor negative	3	3	4	3
DK/NA	2	1	1	2

Questions:

Q1. In general, do you have a more positive or negative image of the European Union?

Q7. In your opinion, do the economic costs of being in the EU exceed the benefits or do the benefits exceed the costs?

Note: %, base (all respondents).

Source: Eurobarometer (2011b): 14.

cross-tabulated data from the Eurobarometer survey of public opinion in Britain to explore the relationship between affective and cost-benefit assessments of the EU. This allows us to look at how many people gave consistent answers, which means that, if they had a favourable view of the EU, then they also saw benefits of membership as exceeding costs while, if they held an unfavourable view, they saw costs as exceeding benefits. Table 1.2 shows that 25 per cent of respondents were consistently unfavourable, while 21 per cent were consistently favourable. The remaining 54 per cent had more mixed views.

It is absurd to imagine that there is some kind of predisposition in Britain to euroscepticism, as though it were some kind of national trait or characteristic. Euroscepticism is a choice, not some component of 'national character'; it derives from political beliefs, not from primordial instinct. Essentialist beliefs about sceptics as some national character trait neglect the variation in attitudes on Europe within Britain and that these are shaped by historical, social and political context.

These attitudes must come from somewhere and be shaped by something. Some argue that media coverage can have powerful effects. Since the 1990s, large circulation daily newspapers at the high and lower end of the quality spectrum, such as *The Sun*, *Daily Telegraph*, *Daily Mail*, *The Times* and *Daily Express*, have been consistently and vocally eurosceptic. Politicians have also seemed fearful of press influence and eager to court the approval of newspaper barons. Philip Stephens (2001: 67) argued that the national press, 'weaned on the confrontations of the Thatcher/Major years, is undoubtedly hostile to an approach which sees Europe as a partner rather than an enemy', while Peter Riddell (1998: 112) claimed that 'the shift in the press during the 1990s probably had a cumulative impact on influencing public attitudes, particularly during the absence of a clear lead from politicians'. Most British citizens also have little direct exposure to the EU and will use the context of domestic politics to acquire information. The EU is an issue from which, as Gavin (2000: 356) puts it, people are 'one stage removed' as most have little direct experience of the EU (see also Franklin, 1994; Anderson and Weymouth, 1998). Various media outlets newspapers, radio, television, blogs and the like play a key role in providing information about European integration. The Eurobarometer survey has also asked people in Britain about their perceptions of various media sources. As Figure 1.3 shows, radio and TV broadcasting is seen as the most objective, while press reporting is seen as more prone to negativity. The perception of negative press coverage was stronger in Britain than in any other EU member state. Eurobarometer polling also shows that people who feel themselves to be well-informed about the EU were more likely to criticize the positive or negative bias of media coverage (Eurobarometer, 2011: 11).

Interest in the role and impact of the press also arises from a sociological interest in the role that newspapers can play in national identity formation. The 'we-feeling' that newspaper reading can invoke was memorably put by Benedict Anderson (1991: 35):

> The significance of the mass ceremony is paradoxical. It is performed in silent privacy in the lair of the skull. Yet each communicant is well aware that the ceremony is being replicated simultaneously by thousands (or millions) of others of whose existence he is confident, yet of whose identity he has not the slightest notion.

FIGURE 1.3   *Perceptions of the British media*

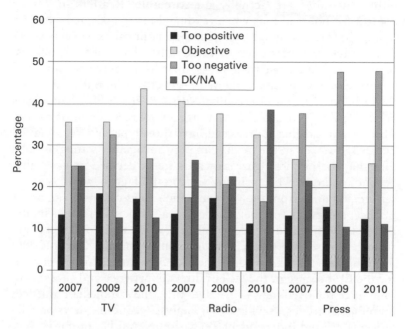

Source: Eurobarometer (2011b).

Billig (1995) argues that everyday representations of 'we', 'us' and 'them' communicated on a daily basis by newspapers contribute to what he calls 'banal nationalism'. National newspapers can help develop and sustain national communities. Brookes (1999: 248) argues that one of the key attributes of a national press is the representation of 'the nation as the natural political and cultural unit'. To support this observation, Brookes analyses the Bovine Spongiform Encephalopathy (BSE) and foot and mouth crises of the mid-1990s to show how it had an 'us' (Britain) versus 'them' (Europe) element, in the sense that specific incidents such as the March 1996 EU ban on British beef were turned into general arguments about whether EU membership was in Britain's interests. Anderson and Weymouth (1998) surveyed both pro- and anti-European newspapers to argue that the British press has become more hostile to the EU and that proprietorial influence has been very influential. They also argue that the EU has contributed to the problem through its own 'great public relations disasters'.

Research evidence suggests that the effects of newspapers on public attitudes are actually questionable. Readers may well control for political bias when reading a newspaper, may select a newspaper because it accords with their political views, may select a newspaper for entertainment value rather than political analysis, or may well not trust their newspaper as a source of impartial advice. Evidence points to limited press effects on public attitudes towards politics and politicians (Norris *et al.*, 1999). Individuals are more likely to use a wide range of sources for information. These various media sources can have three types of effect (Gavin, 2000: 356–7). First, the media can play an 'agenda-setting' role by directing the publics' 'gaze' towards items deemed newsworthy. Second, there can be 'priming' effects that go beyond agenda-setting and arise from the ways in which news coverage can affect public perceptions of the salience of a particular issue. Finally, there can be 'media dependency' effects, when a lack of direct experience increases the public's reliance on the media. Gavin (2000: 357) suggests that this media dependency is particularly important for the EU because of the lack of direct experience and subsequent 'one stage removed' news coverage. In a study of media influences on public attitudes, Gavin (2000) analyses economic news on television (BBC and Independent Television News) because it is well-established that economic news has important effects on political attitudes, while television is a preferred and relatively well-trusted medium. This research suggests that television coverage of economic news 'is an unlikely platform for the development in the UK of European solidarity or identity'. This conclusion is reached by demonstrating that EU stories on British television news often centre on intra-EU squabbles and conflicts, rather than 'Europe versus the world' stories that could inculcate the 'we-feeling' among Europeans. Few stories were found that emphasized the civic entitlements that European integration could bring. In such terms, television news was found to reinforce zero-sum ideas of national sovereignty with EU member states arguing across a range of issues in line with their well-established national preferences. The result is that, in terms of 'agenda-setting' and 'priming', the public's gaze is not directed towards material benefits of membership and, in terms of 'media dependency' effects, there is little scope for the development of an awareness of rights and entitlements as part of an integrated Europe. The EU is typically represented as clashes and disputes.

This section has illustrated the importance of identities within the multi-national British state and the influences upon them that can, in turn, shape views of the EU. It also focused on the ways in which the EU is represented in public debate in the UK. However, it was also argued that attitudes cannot be understood in essentialist terms, as though they are some never-changing component of 'British identity'. Instead, they need to be located in the context of the interactions between historical, socio-economic and political processes that shape and are shaped by them. These can be grouped under the heading of 'domestic politics'.

The importance of domestic politics

As noted in this book's Introduction, the ways in which decisions made at earlier points in time have lasting effects that are still felt in contemporary politics is a key insight provided by historical institutional analysis. The next step is to identify where, how and why historical influences have shaped British attitudes to European integration, without either assuming that Britain is exceptional, or taking national myths for granted. Rather, if decision-making processes remain strongly grounded in national contexts, then this suggests that we need to explore some key conceptual and organizational features of the British polity.

It has been argued that Parliament and the attitudes of the main political parties need to be central to this approach. For example, Aspinwall (2000) argued that when the impact of EU policy on national authority is high, then there is a greater need for balancing by party leaders between pro-EU and anti-EU wings of their parties. He also argued that when the size of the governing majority is small, then there is more need for balancing. The government of John Major (1990–97) is a good example of this search for balance. By his own account, Major (1999) veered during his time in office from unbending man of principle to consensus-seeking party manager. At the time of the Maastricht Treaty, Major argues that his pursuit of British interests during the negotiations was based on principle: 'I genuinely stood apart from both sides', he wrote, 'and decided upon the policy I believed to be right; it was coincidental that it fell smack between the two' (Major, 1999: 273). Later in his memoirs, survival instincts and party management took precedence as EU tensions intensified. In the mid-1990s, he wrote that: 'To have one wing of the Party up in arms was sufficient. Two would have been cataclysmic if I was to keep the Party in one piece. For me, the strain and frustration of trying to maintain a balance between the two sides was immense' (Major, 1999: 616). A relatively small band of hard-line eurosceptics was also able to wield disproportionate influence in the mid-1990s because of the Conservative's small majority. Aspinwall's (2000) analysis focused on the majoritarian aspects of British electoral and party politics. The coalition between the Conservatives and Liberal Democrats after the 2010 election questions majoritarianism. While the Conservative party is more eurosceptic than at any point since Britain joined the EC in 1973, it is also the case that the coalition agreement and moderating influence of the pro-EU Liberal Democrats constrains eurosceptic influence on the government. Cameron, as Prime Minister, has to balance within his party and within the coalition. The tensions within the coalition became apparent in the aftermath of the setbacks of the 2012 local elections when the Conservatives lost 405 seats, the Liberal Democrats lost 336, while Labour gained 823. There were calls from some backbench MPs and the right-wing media for the Conservatives to move to the right on issues such as tax, Europe and immigration, although such a move would be incompatible with the coalition agreement that emerged in the aftermath of the indecisive 2010 general election (see Chapter 4). Deputy Prime Minister Clegg argued that he would try to hold the centre ground while Cameron, too, had pursued an electoral strategy that sought to occupy more 'centrist' positions on issues such as health, education and the economy.

Analysis of the party system underlines the importance of considering domestic political factors that mediate the relationship between Britain and the EU. The parliamentary arena was the key location for the euro-turmoil that affected British politics in the 1990s. Forster (2002a) argues that, since the Maastricht Treaty ratification saga of 1992–93, there has been a broadening of the debate beyond the parliamentary arena to include also a wider public debate. One effect is some reduction in the ability of party leaders to control the terms of the debate and use party management techniques. Usherwood (2002: 228) points out that the development of extra-parliamentary groups can lead to a radicalization of anti-EU politics and can potentially instigate a pressure cooker effect as the distance increases between the (marginal) pro- and (much more vociferous) anti-EU wings of British politics.

Focusing solely on Parliament and the main political parties gives important insight into the origins, development and effects of pro- and anti-EU sentiment in Britain, but can also mean that the analysis fires on just one cylinder. Other factors also mediate the relationship between Britain and the EU, such as the organization of the state (including the role of central, sub-national and local government), socio-economic priorities and their relation to EU priorities. Wilks (1996) observed that it is useful to consider the extent to which the UK is an 'awkward state' in terms of, for instance, the balance between centralized and decentralized political authority.

Conclusion

This chapter has examined basic characteristics of the EU and some explanations for Britain's relations with the EU. It has been argued that the ways in which a series of choices has become embedded within the domestic political context is central to analysis of Britain's relations with the EU. Geographical location, functional interdependencies and identities were not seen as compelling explanations in themselves. Instead, it was argued that they need to be located in the context of the key features of the British political system and the ways in which this gives meaning and resonance to ideas about the impact of geography, interdependencies and identities. Moreover, it is also important to bear in mind that other member states face precisely the same issues. They, too, will be influenced by their location, history, interdependencies and identities; but the effects of each of these will be evident in the context of domestic politics and may well be different. As in Britain, we can also expect these effects to change over time. In analytical terms, this points to the importance of history, but also to the social context of politics and the importance of ideas about issues such as identities within the British multinational state.

In this book's Introduction, reference was made to the 'weight of history' argument. To this can be added the ways in which Europe is constructed as a domestic political issue (for example, as a threat or opportunity; as a component of national identity, or as a menace to it). Broadening this discussion out can also help to locate this debate in terms of key reference points within what is known as 'new institutional' analysis. For example, this book analyses inter-state relations and negotiations centred on the pursuit of British interests and policy preferences. However, it is shown that interests and preferences will both shape and be shaped by the historical and social 'construction' of the European issue in British politics. Moreover, the meaning of Europe, as a social and political construct in British politics, will change over time. To illustrate this point, the next chapter analyses the origins of the debate about Britain and European integration that occurred in the 1950s and 1960s.

Chapter 2

Looking In from the Outside

Britain's relations with the EU until membership in 1973 can be related to the character of that organization (supranational and with lurking federal ideas) and to key developments in British domestic and foreign policy. The two went hand-in-hand as Britain stood aside from the first steps taken towards European integration in the 1950s, then re-evaluated its role and sought membership of the EC in the 1960s and 1970s. The chapter develops the 'Britain in Europe' theme by providing an overview of Britain's relationships with the EC from the postwar leader of a landslide Labour government, Clement Attlee, until accession under Prime Minister Edward Heath in 1973. The chapter is particularly concerned with the factors that shaped British government attitudes towards supranational integration, the capacity to attain UK European policy objectives, and the ways in which these preferences and objectives changed over time between the late 1940s and the early 1970s. In the 1950s, the development of European integration is assessed alongside Britain's long-standing preferences for free trade and the maintenance of economic relations with the Commonwealth and USA, an aversion to supranationalism, and a desire to recover great power status. In the face of competing influences, British governments in the 1950s chose not to participate in the early moves towards European integration. This stance was re-evaluated in the early 1960s and led to membership applications in 1961–63 and 1967, both of which were rebuffed by President de Gaulle of France. A key underlying point is to demonstrate the ways in which national history and national self-understanding played (and still play) a key role in British relations with the EU, and were powerful contextual factors that facilitate understanding of the 'construction' of European issue in British politics.

From the contemporary vantage point, it is easy to judge the choices that were made by Britain's political elite when the first steps towards European economic and political integration were taken – and the lack of 'European vision' implicit within them. Yet, whilst 20–20 hindsight is a great asset for the contemporary historian, in the 1950s it could not have been known that the ECSC would develop into what we now know as the EU. As is also shown, it would have been a remarkable about-turn for the British government in the early 1950s to abandon its foreign and trade policy priorities, and throw in its lot with the supranational ECSC and its progeny, the EEC.

East versus West

After World War II, Europe was divided, and faced severe economic and political challenges. To the east, the Soviet Union consolidated its strength. To the west, states looked to their principal ally, the USA, for help. As Story (1993: 11) puts it, 'Europe had become an object of world politics with the shots being called by the great powers.' American assistance to Europe came in the form of Marshall Aid, named after Secretary of State George C. Marshall, who developed the plan to rebuild west European economies. Around $13 billion worth of aid was distributed among west European countries between 1948 and 1952. West Germany was the main beneficiary of Marshall Aid, receiving $4.5 billion. This served to draw it firmly into the Western bloc. By establishing the Organisation for European Economic Co-operation (OEEC) in May 1948, the Americans sought to involve recipient countries in the Marshall Aid distribution process. Significantly, the British, then the strongest power in Europe, resolutely advocated intergovernmental cooperation in the OEEC, rather than the institution of supranational structures with powers over member states.

The USA was keen to see the establishment in western Europe of open capitalist economies with liberal-democratic political systems. It made sound economic and financial sense for the USA to seek to restore the economies of the west because it could then trade with them. Hence, the USA was a sponsor of European integration and sought the inclusion of its closest European ally, the UK, in this organization. It was not only the external threat from the east that perturbed the Americans; there were also strong Communist parties in France and Italy. The restoration and consolidation of economic prosperity within a liberal, capitalist order was seen as a defence against Communism in these countries.

On Soviet insistence, Marshall Aid was not accepted in eastern Europe. Both Czechoslovakia and Poland rejected it. This, and the

Czech Communists' seizure of sole power in February 1948, led Britain, the Benelux countries (Belgium, the Netherlands and Luxembourg) and France to form the Brussels Treaty organization in March 1948, whereby they pledged mutual military aid and economic cooperation. Also in March 1948, the three Western occupying powers in Germany – France, Britain and the USA – unified their occupation zones and convened a constitutional assembly, which introduced currency reforms that created the Deutschmark. This caused similar steps to be taken in the east of Germany by the fourth occupying power, the Soviet Union. A Soviet attempt to blockade Berlin in the winter of 1948 (which, although occupied by the four powers, was surrounded by the Soviet zone of occupation) was breached by Allied airlifts.

In April 1949, the Treaty of Washington established NATO. This firmly committed the USA to defend western Europe. In September 1949, the Federal Republic of Germany (FRG) was created. In October 1949, the German Democratic Republic (GDR) was established in the east. The division of Germany provided firm evidence of the Iron Curtain that had fallen across the continent of Europe.

Intergovernmentalism versus supranationalism

It has been argued that British political elites made three fundamental miscalculations about the first steps taken in the 1950s towards European economic and political integration (Beloff, 1970):

- British governments held the view that supranational integration was idealistic, rather than practical, and that it would inevitably fail. The EC's federalizing tendencies would soon founder on the rocks of member states' national concerns. The evidence for this is that the British refused to join the ECSC and the European Defence Community (EDC), and only sent a senior civil servant to the negotiations that led to the Rome Treaties of 1957.
- Britain believed that the problems of the postwar era could be met by establishing a free trade area (EFTA), and that supranational integration was unnecessary.
- The British under-estimated the obstacles to accession once that course of action had been decided upon. French President de Gaulle blocked the applications made by Macmillan (1961–63) and Wilson (1967).

Box 2.1   What is federalism?

There are many strands of federalist thought and different types of federal system in operation around the world. In *federal systems*, such as the USA and Germany, neither the central nor the regional level of government is supposed to be subordinate to the other. Federalism is seen as generating effective central power for handling common problems, while preserving regional autonomy. Five main features of a federal system of government can be highlighted (Wheare, 1963):

- two levels of government – one general, the other regional
- formal distribution of legislative and executive authority, and sources of revenue between the two levels
- a written constitution
- a supreme or constitutional court to adjudicate in disputes between the two levels
- central institutions, including a bicameral legislature within which the upper chamber will usually embody territorial representation, as is the case with the US Senate and the German *Bundesrat*.

In the EU, there are some signs of federation. There is a multi-level system linking the sub-national, national and supranational. In addition, an established body of European law overrides national law. The CJEU acts as umpire in disputes between supranational and national levels of government. However, in terms of its budget, the EU is far from being a fully-fledged federation as the term would normally be understood, and neither should it be assumed that it is necessarily locked in some trajectory that will lead inevitably towards federation. Bulmer and Wessels suggest that what is emerging is a system of 'co-operative federalism': the EU and national governments share responsibility for problem-solving in some areas because neither of them has the legal authority or policy competence to tackle the challenges that they face on their own (Bulmer and Wessels, 1987).

The restoration of nation states after World War II had dashed the hopes of constitutional federalists who had sought a United States of Europe. In their opinion, only such a dramatic step could transcend the bitterness and divisions that had plagued the continent and generated two world wars in the space of 30 years. For them, ways forward in a Europe of nation states were unclear. In the meantime, nation states were re-established and became closely linked to the performance of welfare state functions that further served to consolidate the national state as the recipient of citizens' loyalty.

It was clear that a basic divide was emerging between Britain, on the one hand, and the six countries that were to found the ECSC in 1951, on the other. The Attlee government was prepared to sponsor cooperation with other European countries, but primarily as a way of ensuring that Britain remained top dog. The Foreign Office view was that 'Great Britain must be viewed as a world power of the second rank and not merely as a unit in a federated Europe' (cited in Ellison, 2000: 16). The British had no intention of participating in a supranational organization, but supranational plans that fundamentally changed relations between European states were being hatched. The Benelux countries had already in 1948 taken steps towards pooling their sovereignty when they set up a customs union.

It has been argued that the European policies of the Labour government (1945–51) and Conservative governments of the 1950s directly contributed to the outcome that was supposed to be avoided: the fear that Britain would become, as Labour's postwar Foreign Secretary Ernest Bevin put it, 'just another European country'. Early tensions between supranationalists and intergovernmentalists became apparent at the May 1948 Congress of Europe in The Hague, where over 700 prominent Europeans met to discuss the future of the continent. The outcome of the meeting was creation of the Council of Europe in May 1949. It was located in Strasbourg, on the Franco–German border, in order to symbolize reconciliation between these two countries. Britain's preference for intergovernmentalism prevailed in the Council of Europe: decisions in its Council of Ministers are taken on the basis of unanimity. It has come to be identified with the European Convention on Human Rights (ECHR), signed in November 1950. This, after the atrocities of World War II, signified a commitment to human rights as binding on sovereign states. By 2012, the Council of Europe had 47 members and was the largest pan-European grouping.

Schuman's Plan

A core group of west European countries felt frustrated by Britain's opposition to supranationalism and, as the Benelux countries had already achieved in their customs union, sought economic integration. France and West Germany formed the key axis within the supranational project as it emerged in the 1950s. Plans developed by the French foreign minister, Robert Schuman, were for a common market in coal and steel. The ECSC was an attempt to resolve the question of how to restore West German economic prosperity, from which the French would benefit, whilst binding West Germany to a peaceful west European order. The Netherlands, Belgium and Luxembourg had already taken steps to pool their sovereignty, while for the Italians supranational integration could offer an external guarantee of economic and political stability.

Schuman's plan, proposed on 9 May 1950, led to the creation of the ECSC by the Treaty of Paris in April 1951. It created a common market for coal and steel, and supranational structures of government to run the community. Schuman's ambitions were not limited simply to coal and steel. As he put it, 'Europe will not be made all at once or according to a single general plan. It will be built through concrete achievements which first create a de facto solidarity' (cited in Weigall and Stirk, 1992). A leading ally of Schuman was the Frenchman, Jean Monnet, who became the first President of the High Authority of the ECSC (the forerunner of the Commission).

The ECSC broke new ground in two ways: it laid the foundations for a common market in the basic raw materials needed by an industrial society; and it was the first European inter-state organization to show supranational tendencies.

Schuman advocated step-by-step integration. A united Europe was the goal, but it would be achieved through 'spillover' effects. The idea of spillover derives from *neo-functional* theories of European integration. Neo-functional theory centres on the core claim that integration in one area draws in other associated areas (known as 'functional spillover') which can then lead to a re-location of political action because of this shift in decision-making (known as 'political spillover'). The European Commission was attributed a particularly important role in driving spillover, although decisions of the CJEU have also been seen as playing a role in pushing the boundaries of European integration. The weakness of neo-functional theory was that it had difficulty accounting for the pace and tempo of European integration, and also for the occasional bouts of spillback and blockage, rather than spillover. A key weakness is that it downplays the role of member states and national interests.

Britain was not opposed to the creation of the ECSC, but was opposed to British membership of it. As Hugo Young (1999: ch. 2) shows, there was strong opposition from Labour politicians and senior Whitehall mandarins to British participation in the 'institutional adventures' of Monnet and Schuman. Coal and steel had only recently been brought under state control, so ceding competencies in this area was an unattractive proposition. But, more than this, integration also risked offending key trade unions; or, as Herbert Morrison put it: 'It's no damn good – the Durham miners won't wear it' (cited in Forster, 2002b: 299). That said, if supranational integration were to pacify Franco–German relations, then it would be advantageous (it could hardly be argued otherwise). Also, the fact that the US government supported the ECSC affected the British government's stance.

A divide in interpretations of British responses to European integration in the early and mid-1950s has been identified between diplomatic and economic historians (Ellison, 2000: 5). Diplomatic historians focus on foreign policy and see UK policy as motivated by opposition to supranationalism, a strong preference for an Atlantic basis for European security, and a need to balance relations with Europe with those with the Commonwealth and USA (J. Young, 1993). Economic historians focus on financial policy and see that while the EC6 sought to develop a common market, Britain sought to maintain sterling's convertibility with the US dollar as a route to the re-establishment of former glories (Milward, 1992). Whatever the focus, a point that unites the two camps is the general view that Britain was not particularly successful in achieving either its diplomatic or commercial policy objectives.

The European Coal and Steel Community's Institutions

The ECSC was a major innovation in international politics because participating states agreed to relinquish aspects of their sovereign authority to common institutions. This was an ambitious plan and there were those in Britain that saw it as doomed to fail because high-minded ambitions would founder on the rocks of hard-headed *realpolitik*. What these harbingers of failure did not grasp was that the ECSC was not solely motivated by high minded idealism but also by calculations of national interest, particularly French ideas about how to develop peaceful relations with West Germany.

Within the ECSC was the 'High Authority' (the basis for what we now know as the European Commission), but the six member states were keen to have the final say in decisions that were taken. They ensured that this happened by making a Council of Ministers the decision-making body of the ECSC.

Two steps forward, one step back

Stanley Hoffmann (1966) has argued that European integration has tended to falter when it has had to deal with matters of 'high politics', such as foreign affairs and defence, and to prosper when confronted with matters of 'low politics', chiefly trade. In the early 1950s, the morale of federalists was raised by the success of the ECSC, and they looked to build on this success by creating a European Defence Community (EDC). This represented a move into the domain of 'high politics' of defence, security and foreign policy.

In 1950, the leader of the opposition, Winston Churchill, had called for a unified European army acting in cooperation with the USA and West Germany. In office, though, Churchill's Conservative government of 1951–55 was as hostile to supranationalism as had been its Labour predecessor, and it refused to join the EDC. The French Left was also opposed to rearmament of Germany within the EDC. The plan was killed off in August 1954 when it was rejected by the French National Assembly. Instead, in the same month, the six ECSC members plus Britain, as the west European, intergovernmental pillar of NATO, established the West European Union (WEU). The WEU incorporated the vanquished axis powers of Germany and Italy into the collective defence structures of western Europe.

All roads lead to Rome

The creation of the WEU could be portrayed as a triumph for intergovernmentalists and a setback for integrationists, although Milward (1992: 386) argues that the setback provided momentum for the negotiations that led to the Treaty of Rome and creation of the Common Market. By the mid-1950s, integrationists sought a common market, such as that set up by the Benelux countries in

1948. In June 1955, a conference of foreign ministers was convened in the Sicilian coastal town of Messina and a committee led by the Belgian foreign minister, Paul-Henri Spaak, was asked to look at options for further integration.

The British representative on the Spaak committee was a Board of Trade official, Russell Bretherton – 'the sacrificial agent', as Hugo Young called him – rather than a senior minister. This indicated the British government's lack of serious intent. The discussions centred on the creation of a common market and an atomic energy authority. When, in November 1955, Spaak drew up his final report, Bretherton asked that no reference to Britain's position be made. This was seen as tantamount to British withdrawal from the process, an impression that the British government was not concerned to dispel (J. Young, 1993: 47).

The outcome of the Spaak committee was two treaties of Rome signed by the six founder members (Belgium, France, Italy, the Netherlands, Luxembourg and West Germany) in March 1957: one established the European Economic Community (EEC) and the other set up the European Atomic Energy Authority (EAEA or Euratom). Thus, there are three founding treaties of the European Communities: the Treaty of Paris (1951) that created the ECSC and the two Treaties of Rome (1957) that established the EEC and Euratom. Subsequent treaties – such as the SEA (1986), the Maastricht Treaty (1992), the Amsterdam Treaty (1997), the Nice Treaty (2000) and the Lisbon Treaty (2007) – amend these founding Treaties.

The EEC became the predominant organization. Its founding treaty was premised on 'an ever closer union of the peoples of Europe'. It sought the abolition of trade barriers and customs duties, and the creation of a common external tariff, thereby making the EEC a customs union. The EEC was also designed to promote the free movement of workers, goods, services and capital within a common market. The member states transferred to the EEC powers to conclude trading agreements with international organizations on their behalf.

Four main institutions, modelled on those set up to run the ECSC, were created to manage the EC:

- the Commission, a supranational institution responsible for both policy proposals and implementation
- the Council (of Ministers), the legislative authority

- the Common Assembly (now known as the EP), with a consultative role and no legislative authority
- the Court of Justice, to rule on matters of dispute relating to EC law.

The EEC Treaty also made provision for a Common Agricultural Policy (CAP). Agriculture was an obvious candidate for a common policy for three main reasons. First, it would have been illogical to leave this important area of economic activity with member states. Second, the EEC and the ECSC addressed a range of industrial issues, such that an agricultural policy was seen as a balance to these concerns. Third, France, with its large agricultural sector, sought protection for its farmers, as well as access to markets in other member states. Through the CAP, France has been highly effective in translating a national interest to European level and thus protecting one of its key economic sectors.

Much of the Treaty framework was vague and depended heavily on the impetus given to integration by member states. The speed and direction of European integration have always depended heavily on their collective endeavour.

Many have argued that the 1950s were a decade of lost opportunities for the British. John Young detects national arrogance in the views of those such as the former Conservative politician, Anthony Nutting, who argued that 'Britain could have had the leadership of Europe on any terms she cared to name' (cited in J. Young, 1993: 52). The historian, Mirian Camps, also claimed that the 1950s was a decade of 'missed opportunities' in which the leadership of Europe was Britain's 'for the asking' (Camps, 1964: 506). John Young (1993: 52, emphasis in original) goes on to make a contrasting point very clearly:

> Britain could not have had the leadership of Europe *on its own terms* because Britain saw no need to abandon its sovereignty to common institutions, whereas the Six saw this as vital. Britain could only have played a key role in European integration, paradoxically, *if* it had accepted the continentals' terms and embraced supranationalism, but very few people advocated this before 1957.

The British response

By November 1955, the British were developing a plan that they hoped would lure the EC 'six' away from supranational integration and towards the British preference for a free trade association without supranational pretensions. The result of Britain's alternative plan was the creation of EFTA, set up by the Stockholm Convention of July 1959. EFTA was in accord with the British preference for intergovernmentalism. The seven signatories – Denmark, Norway, Sweden, Portugal, Austria, Switzerland and Britain – established a free trade area which brought down barriers to trade between members and sought to keep in touch with EC tariff reductions. Europe was now at sixes and sevens.

By the early 1960s, it had become apparent to the British that EFTA was peripheral to the fast-growing economies of the EC. A powerful trading bloc was emerging on Britain's doorstep from which it was excluded. In the 1960s, the EC appeared to be going from success to success as the Common External Tariff was put in place and the CAP established. Britain was forced into a re-evaluation of previous policy and sought membership of the EC. However, as will be seen, de Gaulle was distinctly underwhelmed by the prospect of British membership and vetoed the first two British accession bids.

The origins of the European Community

A rapid process of European integration was instigated in the 1950s by the institution of the ECSC, the EEC and Euratom. An anti-Europeanism evident in British politics during the 1950s hardened into an anti-Common Market stance motivated by a dislike of supranational integration's implications for the British political elite's view of their country's place in the world (Forster, 2002b).

During the 1950s, supranational integration remained largely confined to the area of low politics and failed to break into the domain of high politics following rejection of the EDC in 1954.

Britain remained aloof from supranational organizations. However, this was not just the product of its distrust of supranationalism; as the former US Secretary of State, Dean Acheson, put it in 1960, the British had lost an Empire and were trying to find a role. Despite decolonization, the Empire/Commonwealth retained a powerful influence over many Conservative MPs and remained 'the main religion of the Tory Party' in the 1950s, as R.A. Butler put it (cited in Forster, 2002b: 299). These historical ties and economic entanglements created some real tensions within the British elite when trade policies and relations with the USA, the Commonwealth and the European Community were discussed.

By the end of the 1950s, a basic divide had emerged in Europe between the EC6 and the EFTA7. The EU proved to be the magnet to which EFTA countries have been attracted. By 2011, most EFTA states had joined the EU (Austria, Britain, Denmark, Portugal and Sweden). Norway rejected membership in referendums in 1972 and 1994, but is associated with the EU through the European Economic Area (EEA).

1960s: Britain says 'Yes', de Gaulle says 'No'

In the 1960s, French President de Gaulle unilaterally vetoed British accession and strongly opposed the development of qualified majority voting (QMV) in the Council of Ministers. Kaiser (1996) argues that the UK had actually come to terms with majority voting as early as 1961. British policy towards the EC was re-evaluated in the 1960s. Both Macmillan (between 1961 and 1963) and Wilson (in 1967) pursued membership of the Community, only to be rebuffed by de Gaulle's veto. The other member states supported UK accession, but the General's '*non*' was enough to block British membership. It was left to Heath to lead Britain into the EC in January 1973.

De Gaulle's vision was of Europe as a third force between the USSR and USA, ideally with France as its leader. He thought Britain would seek to dominate the EC and place it firmly in the US bloc. Britain and the United States shared a 'globalist' perspective, of which central features were commitment to an open world trading order and rejection of protectionism.

Four broad characteristics of British policy towards the EC in the 1950s can be highlighted:

- Aloofness was shown towards Europe based on a perception, as Churchill put it, that Britain was 'with them' against the greater foe of Communism, but not 'of them' in participating in integration.
- There was opposition to the sovereignty-eroding implications of supranational integration. British national identity had, if anything, been strengthened by the experience of World War II. The national sovereignty that had been so keenly defended then was not about to be ceded to supranational institutions in Europe.

- Accession would be a sign of failure and of Britain's diminished status in the world.
- There was development of an alternative policy focused on the Empire and the 'special relationship' with the USA.

By the early 1960s, the British government was questioning its aloofness towards the EC. The 'special relationship' with the USA had been dented by the Suez crisis of 1956, when the USA had declined to support Britain's military intervention in Egypt. The relationship was beginning to seem more special in British eyes than in American, and postwar hopes of partnership had been replaced by an economic and military dependence, by means of which Britain was consigned to a role of 'increasingly impotent avuncularity' (Edwards, 1993: 209).

Britain was also worried that its close ties with America could be supplanted by links between the USA and the EC. The USA feared that de Gaulle's 'third force' aspirations for Europe would weaken the Western alliance, and hoped Britain would steer the EC in a direction sympathetic to American interests. In July 1962, President Kennedy called for an Atlantic partnership between the USA and the EC, including Britain. He wanted to see an outward-looking and open EC, and wanted Britain to be part of it.

In the 1960s, the Commonwealth ideal that nations of the former Empire could cooperate on an equal footing took several dents. Divisions emerged between the 'black' and 'white' Commonwealth over, for example, Britain's less than wholehearted denunciation of the racist South African regime after the Sharpeville massacre of 1961. Conflict also arose between India and Pakistan over the disputed territory of Kashmir, and over the unilateral declaration of independence made by Ian Smith's racist regime in Rhodesia in 1965.

By the time Harold Wilson became Prime Minister in 1964, economic concerns impelled the membership bid. EFTA was not proving a success when compared with the dynamic economies of the EC, and Commonwealth trading patterns were changing as Australia and New Zealand looked to markets in the USA and Japan. Wilson had come to office espousing 'the white heat of the scientific revolution' that would modernize the British economy. Larger markets were needed for high technology industries – such as aircraft and computers – but exclusion from the EC meant separation from the supranational institutions that united fast-growing neighbouring economies.

On all usual economic indicators, Britain was lagging behind the EC. For example, between 1958 and 1968 real earnings in Britain rose by 38 per cent, compared with 75 per cent in the EC. Fear of isolation is apparent in a memorandum sent by Macmillan to his Foreign Secretary, Selwyn Lloyd, in 1959: 'For the first time since the Napoleonic era the major continental powers are united in a positive economic grouping, with considerable political aspects, which, although not specifically directed against the United Kingdom, may have the effect of excluding us both from European markets and from consultation in European policy.'

1973: membership

In 1969, the political complexion of the two countries at the heart of European integration – France and West Germany – changed in a way advantageous to Britain's membership hopes. In France, President de Gaulle resigned and was replaced by Georges Pompidou, who favoured British accession. In West Germany, the new Social Democratic government, led by Willy Brandt, was also keen to see EC enlargement.

Prior to the accession of new member states the founder members laid down a budgetary framework for the Community at a heads of government meeting in The Hague in 1969. This was formalized by treaty in 1970, and provided a classic example of rules that were not to Britain's advantage being determined in the absence of input from the British government. Britain would be obliged to accept more or less the entire *acquis communautaire* – European law, including the budgetary arrangements. When Britain joined, it contributed 8.64 per cent of the budget, rising to 18.72 per cent in 1977. Construction of the EC's 'own resources' was not to Britain's advantage, as it effectively penalized countries with extensive trading links outside the EC and that had efficient agricultural sectors. Goods entering the EC from non-member states encountered the EC's Common External Tariff, which then became part of the Community's 'own resources'. Having substantial trading links with non-EC countries, notably those in the Commonwealth, Britain was disadvantaged from the start by this measure. Britain's relatively efficient agricultural sector meant that much benefit was not secured from the main financial activity of the EC, the CAP and its support system for farmers.

Negotiations on British accession began in June 1970 under the Conservative Prime Minister, Edward Heath. In July 1971, a White Paper was published. It noted some of the disadvantages of membership as follows:

- It was estimated that food prices would go up by 15 per cent over a six-year period because the CAP contained a system of Community preference, which would mean that Britain could no longer shop around on cheaper world food markets.
- Increased food prices would contribute to a 3 per cent increase in the cost of living over a six-year period.
- British contributions to the EC budget would amount to £300 million a year, making Britain the second largest contributor behind West Germany. British contributions would be high because it had extensive external trading links.

Although Heath was pursuing a policy developed by his Conservative and Labour predecessors who had come to the conclusion that EC membership was necessary, if Britain were not to risk economic and political isolation, he was more than merely a pragmatic European. Indeed, Heath was a wholehearted advocate of British membership and remained a convinced euro-enthusiast throughout his political career. In this, he stood apart from many of his eurosceptic opponents in the 1980s and 1990s that started out as supporters of British membership of the EC before becoming vociferous critics.

Edward Heath's political outlook was shaped by formative experiences in his youth, when he travelled extensively in Europe and saw the rise of Nazism at first hand, even being present at the Nuremberg rally in 1938 (Heath, 1998). Heath's maiden speech as an MP in 1951 had extolled the merits of the ECSC and advocated British membership. Heath remained a stalwart defender of the EU and a vigorous opponent of the eurosceptics even after the tide within the Conservative Party had turned strongly against him in the 1990s. On pragmatic grounds, too, Heath was convinced of the merits of British accession. Even though there were some points of contention and some areas where EC and British priorities did not fit, he thought that Britain had little option but to enter the EC and try to shape it from within.

Geoffrey Rippon led the British negotiating team. The application was coordinated through the Cabinet Office in an attempt to prevent Whitehall rivalries and tensions scuppering the application. Since the first accession application in 1961, the pace of European integration had quickened considerably. By the early 1970s, there were 13,000 typewritten pages of Community legislation covering key areas of EC activity such as the CAP and the common market (by the time of the 'big bang' enlargement to 10 new member states in 2004, there were some 80,000 pages). The leading official negotiator, Sir Con O'Neill, summed up some of the frustrations of the negotiating team when he wrote in a 1972 Foreign Office report that: 'None of its policies were essential to us. Many of them were objectionable.' But they had to be accepted if accession were to occur or, as O'Neill also put it, 'swallow the lot, and swallow it now' (cited in H. Young, 1999: 227). That said, the UK did secure some adjustments to EC rules that favoured Commonwealth trading partners for a five-year transition period.

Aside from the negotiation details, there was another crucial element to British accession: the support of the French President, Georges Pompidou. Heath (1998: 367–70) had already established a good relationship with Pompidou. The British–French summit meeting, 19–20 May 1971, was central to UK accession. Pompidou supported UK accession for a variety of reasons. It would allow him to distinguish himself from de Gaulle (Pompidou did not share de Gaulle's distrust of the 'Anglo-Saxons'). Another French rejection of British membership could have irreparably damaged UK–French relations. Finally, when compared with the Labour leader, Harold Wilson, there was little doubt that Heath 'meant it' when he sought full membership and that he would not be distracted by the Commonwealth or USA. In the Salon des Fêtes of the Elysée Palace where de Gaulle had vetoed UK accession in 1963, Pompidou (standing alongside Heath) declared that:

> Many people believed that Great Britain was not and did not wish to become European, and that Britain wanted to enter the Community only so as to destroy it or divert it from its objectives ... Well ladies and gentlemen, you see before you tonight two men who are convinced of the contrary. (Cited in Heath, 1998: 372)

This gave firm impetus to the negotiations, which then required Parliamentary approval. The 1972 European Communities Act gave effect to the accession agreement. Article 2.1 was particularly significant as it noted that:

All such rights, powers, liabilities, obligations and restrictions from time to time created or arising by or under the Treaties, and all such remedies and procedures from time to time provided for by or under the Treaties, as in accordance with the Treaties are without further enactment to be given legal effect or used in the United Kingdom shall be recognised and available in law, and be enforced, allowed and followed accordingly; and the expression 'enforceable EU right' and similar expressions shall be read as referring to one to which this sub-section applies.

This established the principle of 'direct effect' of EC law, which means that EC directives and regulations would become part of national law when agreed at EU level. If a member state does not meet its commitments, then it can be referred to the CJEU. In 1979, the Master of the Rolls, Lord Denning, explained what this meant for British law: 'If the time should come when our Parliament deliberately passes an Act with the intention of repudiating the Treaty or any provision in it or intentionally of acting inconsistently with it and says so in express terms then I should have thought that it would be the duty of our courts to follow the statute of our Parliament. ... Unless there is such an intentional and express repudiation of the Treaty, it is our duty to give priority to the Treaty'.

Parliamentary agreement to membership was secured on 28 October 1971, when MPs voted by 356 to 244 in favour of accession to the Community, but the Conservative government relied on support from 69 Labour MPs who defied a three line whip to support accession. The House of Lords endorsed membership overwhelmingly by 451 votes to 58. The Treaty of Accession was signed in Brussels on 22 January 1972.

British accession occurred just as the economies of western Europe were ending their long postwar period of economic growth. Britain could hardly have chosen a less propitious moment to dip a tentative toe into the waters of supranational economic and political integration. Oil price increases soon helped to plunge the British and European economies into recession.

Conclusion

This chapter has explored the attitudes of British governments towards European economic and political integration in the period from the end of World War II, the commencement of the Cold War, and the onset of supranational economic and political integration, initially through the ECSC and then in the form of the EEC. Across the political spectrum and at the highest official level, there was scepticism about the European project initiated by the French and Germans. The chapter also sought to identify the policy preferences that underlay these attitudes, the capacity to attain these objectives, and the ways in which preferences and objectives changed over time. It was shown that, during the 1950s, in neither commercial nor diplomatic terms, was there a deeply-held view at the highest political level that European economic and political integration was in the UK's interests. The UK was prepared to sponsor integration, but was not itself prepared to participate in the common structures of a supranational community. This was founded on a view that Britain's commercial interests did not lie exclusively with this European grouping, and that a route to recovery of great power status could be found through the Commonwealth and the special relationship with the USA. By the 1960s, it had become clear that the context within which these preferences were exercised was changing: the Commonwealth ideal and the special relationship had both been dented, the UK economy was growing at a slower rate than the EC countries, and European integration was proving to be a success. Taken together, these indicators of relative decline instigated some form of national identity crisis. Britain had won the war, but seemed to be losing the peace. But, rather than being seen as a route to reclaimed influence, European integration was seen by many as amounting to recognition of Britain's diminished place in the world. Any conversion to Europe was unlikely to be heartfelt.

These indicators of relative British decline cannot be ignored. The re-evaluation of British relations with the EU prompted a decision in the early 1960s to abandon the experiment in intergovernmental free trade centred on EFTA, and for Britain to throw in its lot with the EC. The capacity to attain this objective was seriously undermined by the opposition of de Gaulle because, in his view, Britain did not 'mean it' and would steer the EC in the direction of US interests. The change of government in France opened the door to UK membership, as, too, did Edward Heath's genuine and wholehearted desire for British membership.

These developments also have a broader long-term significance. First, as historical institutionalists point out, initial policy choices can have long-term effects because they establish a path for policy developments from which it can become more difficult to deviate over time. UK governments faced problems with European integration during the 1950s and 1960s because, when push came to shove, they did not *believe* in the European project to the extent that the member states did. This also suggests the importance of ideas about Britain and its place in the world. When it did arrive, UK engagement was based on a pragmatic and instrumental view of European integration that remained strongly influenced by preferences for Atlanticism, intergovernmentalism and global free trade. The British political elite were also economical with the truth when it came to divulging to the British people the nature of the organization that Britain was joining. The EC was often portrayed as a common market devoted to trade objectives. The political implications had been clear since the 1950s, but were played down in the UK. This was unlikely to provide fertile ground for acceptance of more ambitious integration plans in the future.

A second point that builds on the historical legacy of these choices made during the 1950s and 1960s is that strong elements of continuity can be detected in Britain's relations with the EU. The maintenance of close ties with the USA, support for a vision of Europe that focuses on the central role of member states, and a preference for free trade and open markets, all provide a link between British attitudes in the 1950s and aspects of New Labour's approach in the first decade of the twenty-first century. Chapter 3 develops these themes by analysing events between 1973 and 1997, and analysing the patterns of continuity and change that have been evident.

Chapter 3

Full-Hearted Consent? Britain in Europe from Heath to Major

This chapter analyses British relations with the EU between 1973 and 1997. Chapter 2 showed how the powerful legacy of postwar events combined with economic and political factors to explain the construction of Europe as a social and political issue in Britain. This chapter takes these analytical strands forward by exploring British relations with the EC/EU from the premiership of Edward Heath (1970–74) until 1997 and the election of Tony Blair's first Labour government. The chapter continues the 'Britain in Europe' theme by exploring the institutional and policy preferences of British governments, and the motivations underlying these preferences; the capacity in negotiation to attain UK objectives; and the ways in which preferences, motivation and bargaining capacity have changed over time. It will be shown that Britain has engaged with important developments in European integration such as the SEA and the Maastricht Treaty, but in ways that were consistent with views about the reach and scope of European integration. British governments have defined their relationship to the EU in relation to a particular normative vision of appropriate political, social and economic arrangements, and of Britain's place in the world.

The chapter will also link with the 'Europe in Britain' theme by indicating the ways in which, during the same period, political and economic changes in the UK (such as economic deregulation and the development of Conservative euroscepticism) had effects on Britain's relations with the EU, and led to serious questions being asked about Britain's continued membership of the organization. Essentially, this centres on the incompatibility or misfit between British 'ways of doing things' and the EU approach. Students of europeanization would identify quite high adaptational pressure on such cases as a result of 'misfit', although the UK's awkwardness has been accommodated through 'variable geometry'; for example,

Maastricht's 'pillars' for the Common Foreign and Security Policy (CFSP) and JHA, and through opt-outs (from Maastricht's Social Chapter, the Schengen framework, and the creation of the euro). The effects for Europe in Britain have thus been limited to some extent, although this does not mean that Britain can isolate itself from the effects of these arrangements, as is clear with the post-2008 eurozone crisis.

1974–75: renegotiation and referendum

EC membership in 1973 was, for Edward Heath, his defining political accomplishment and the one of which he remained most proud. This counted for little when continued British economic decline and major industrial disputes led to the fall of his government in February 1974 and his replacement as Prime Minister by Harold Wilson. As leader of the opposition Britain's membership of the EC posed something of a dilemma for Wilson. As Prime Minister, he had sought EC membership in 1967, but in Britain's adversarial political system he could use EC membership as a device to criticize the Heath government. Moreover, there was deep opposition to the EC within the Labour Party and labour movement. Wilson's strategy was to oppose the terms of accession as negotiated by Heath and pledge a future Labour government to renegotiation and a referendum. This caused tensions within the Labour Party at the highest level (most notably, for the Deputy Leader and convinced pro-European, Roy Jenkins). Wilson's reasoning was that a shift to a broader public debate could avoid deep Labour Party divisions being exposed to the public with the result being, as James Callaghan put it, that the referendum was 'a life raft into which one day the whole Party [might] have to climb' (cited in Forster, 2002b: 303). Labour was involved in some opportunistic U-turns when one considers their 1967 attempt to secure membership, but the depth of opposition within the Party made a referendum an attractive proposition. Harold Wilson gave responsibility for coordinating Labour's opposition to the accession treaty in the House of Commons to the confirmed anti-EC duo of Michael Foot and Peter Shore. The contrast here with Conservative Party management is interesting. Heath had marginalized opponents of the EC and excluded them from the membership negotiations. Labour at this time had anti-marketeers in senior positions within the government and involved in discussions at the highest level about Britain's future in Europe.

After Labour returned to power in February 1974, renegotiation talks were led by the Foreign Secretary, James Callaghan. Callaghan has been described by his biographer as emphasizing from the start 'his coolness about the European project and his intention of dissecting it in its fundamentals'. When officials suggested that there might be some leeway on the budget and the CAP, Callaghan rebuked them, asking if they had read the Labour Party manifesto, and stated that, if they had, then they would discover that the Labour government's aim was a fundamental renegotiation of the Treaty of Accession (cited in Morgan, 1997: 412–13). This was hardly likely to go down well with the other member states. Peter Shore, from the anti-Common Market wing of the party, and, from the pro-wing, Roy Hattersley, then carried out the detailed discussions. This strange arrangement may have appeased Labour's pro- and anti-Common Market brigades, but it baffled other member states.

Why should other member states accede to British demands? There were many good reasons why they might find them irritating. After all, unravelling the complex EU *acquis* to favour the British might prompt other member states to seek some compensation, too. For instance, if the British were to get some help with their budget contributions, then why not the West Germans who were also big contributors?

Britain gained little through the renegotiation that it could not have gained through normal Community channels. The degree of acrimony engendered by the bargaining soured Britain's relations with other members for many years. For what they were worth, the House of Commons endorsed the renegotiated terms by 396 votes to 170 in April 1975. Ominously for the Labour government, and despite pro-Community speeches from both Wilson and Callaghan, a special Labour conference on 26 April 1975 voted by 3.7 million to 1.9 million to leave the EC.

The pledge to hold a referendum helped Wilson overcome divisions within the Labour Party. Indeed, it seems likely that this was the referendum's major purpose. During the referendum campaign of 1975, Wilson suspended the convention of collective Cabinet responsibility so that Cabinet ministers could speak according to their consciences. The 'Yes' campaign commanded powerful political assets despite opinion polls at the outset pointing to a 'No' vote. It had strong support from Fleet Street and from influential business interests, which provided a large part of the £1.5 million spent in the quest for an affirmative vote. It also gathered a powerful coalition of centrist politicians, including Heath, Labour's Roy Jenkins and the Liberal leader, Jeremy Thorpe. By comparison, the 'No' campaign raised just £133,000. It found itself outgunned and was weakened by its disparate character: Tony Benn, from the left of the Labour Party, formed a decidedly uneasy temporary alliance with right-wingers such as Enoch Powell. The outcome, on 5 June 1975, was a two-to-one vote in favour of continued membership on a 64 per cent turnout (Butler and Kitzinger, 1976; King, 1977). The anti-EC National Referendum Campaign soon fizzled out with the rapid disappearance of its 12 regional offices and 250 local branches (Forster, 2002b: 304).

1976–79: Callaghan's difficulties

In April 1976, James Callaghan succeeded Harold Wilson as Prime Minister and inherited a Labour Party divided over EC membership. Labour's rank and file distrusted the EC, even though some prominent Labour politicians, such as Roy Jenkins and Shirley Williams, were keen advocates of membership. There were two main areas of concern: first, it was felt that integration into a supranational community would restrict national sovereignty and the freedom of action of a Labour government; and second, the EC was seen as a 'capitalist club' with market-based purposes that offered little to working people. Arguments over EC membership were symptomatic of a creeping malaise within the Labour Party that saw the leadership frequently at odds with the membership, and which culminated in a grass-roots move to the left, with right-wingers splitting to form the Social Democratic Party (SDP) in January 1981.

In February 1975, the Conservatives replaced Edward Heath as leader with Margaret Thatcher. Thatcher had opposed the 1975 referendum, describing it, in a phrase that would come back to haunt her in her eurosceptical retirement (when she called for a referendum on the Maastricht Treaty), as a 'device for demagogues'. She argued for a 'Yes' vote on the grounds that Britain needed to foster economic links with the European markets on its doorstep.

Callaghan's pragmatism and Atlanticism meant he held no truck with the lofty rhetoric of European union. He had a poor reputation in EC circles as a result of his dogged pursuit of national interests during the British renegotiation, and failed as premier to ease tensions caused by Britain's entry to the Community.

From March 1977, Callaghan relied on support from the Liberals to sustain his administration. This support was conditional upon the insertion of a clause introducing proportional representation as the method of voting in direct elections to the EP. Such a clause was duly inserted into the European Assembly Elections Bill of 1977. However, it provoked a Cabinet revolt and, on a free vote in the House of Commons, was defeated. It also delayed direct elections, which, to the irritation of other member states, were put back from 1978 to 1979.

The British Presidency of the EC in the first six months of 1977 did little to enhance Britain's reputation. Callaghan was hamstrung by a eurosceptical party and by domestic economic problems. In a letter to the General Secretary of the Labour Party at the start of the British Presidency, he outlined three basic principles that informed the Labour government's stance on the EC:

- maintenance of the authority of nation states and national parliaments, with no increase in the powers of the EP
- emphasis on the necessity for national governments to achieve their own economic, regional and industrial objectives
- reform of the budget procedure.

Contained within these policy principles is a clear restatement of Britain's suspicion of supranationalism and continued concern over the high level of budget contributions. Margaret Thatcher shared these concerns when she became prime minister in May 1979. Thus, while she became well-known for battling for a budget rebate and opposing extensions of supranational authority, Britain's reputation as an awkward partner both preceded and survived her.

British membership of the EC was advocated on pragmatic economic grounds. Many British people seemed to think that they were joining a Common Market, an economic organization that was little more than a glorified free trade area – although the political intent of the European Community had been clear since its foundation in the 1950s. The idea that the EC was essentially designed as a glorified free trade area was not true. Suffice to recall that Britain's alternative to the EC in the form of EFTA was just such an organization, but this largely failed. Yet, the pragmatic acceptance of membership by Britain and the understanding propagated by some of the original purposes of the 'Common Market' meant that Britain has tended to judge the EC by utilitarian standards: what does it have to pay and what does it get out of it? Britain was paying a lot in the late 1970s and early 1980s, and seemed to be getting little in return. Not surprisingly, enthusiasm for the EC did not run deep.

1979–84: The Budget rebate

When Margaret Thatcher took office in 1979, the Conservatives were seen as a pro-European party. In her 1981 speech to the Conservative Party conference, Thatcher reflected on British membership of the EC and noted that:

> it is vital that we get it right. Forty-three out of every hundred pounds that we earn abroad comes from the Common Market. Over two million jobs depend on our trade with Europe, two million jobs which will be put at risk by Britain's withdrawal [Labour's policy at the time]. And even if we kept two thirds of our trade with the Common Market after we had flounced out – and that is pretty optimistic – there would be a million more to join the dole queues. (Harris, 1997: 147)

But Thatcher's pro-Europeanism was distinct from that of her predecessor, Heath. While Heath 'lived and breathed the air of Europe', Thatcher tended to depict European unity as desirable in terms of Cold War politics and anti-Soviet policy (H. Young, 1989: 184). From the mid-1980s onwards, Thatcher began to take a more populist line on Europe and viewed the EC, its institutions and other European leaders with much suspicion.

Europe was, however, not a central political theme of the first two Thatcher governments (1979–83 and 1983–87), which focused on domestic economic policy, the miners' strike and external events such as the Falklands War (1982–83) and the US bombing of Libya (1986). Probably the most pressing issue was the British contribution to the EC budget. By the end of the 1970s, Britain was the second largest contributor to the budget and was in danger of becoming the largest – paying over £1 billion a year, even though it had the third-lowest GDP per capita of the nine member states.

A series of often acrimonious negotiations – 'patient' and 'a little impatient diplomacy' as Thatcher put it in her speech to the 1984 Conservative Party conference – was held between 1979 and 1984. The Commission president at that time, Roy Jenkins, writes in his memoirs of long hours spent discussing the BBQ: the British Budget

Question (or, as he preferred to put it, the Bloody British Question). He notes how Thatcher made a bad start at the Strasbourg Summit in 1979 when she had a strong case but succeeded in alienating other leaders whose support she needed, if a deal were to be struck. Britain's partners in the Community were unwilling to receive lectures on the issue from Thatcher and were alienated by suggestions that the budget mechanisms were tantamount to theft of British money, particularly as Britain had known the budgetary implications when it had joined (Jenkins, 1991: 495). The issue was finally resolved at the Fontainebleau summit in June 1984, when a rebate was agreed amounting to 66 per cent of the difference between Britain's value added tax (VAT) contributions to the budget and its receipts (for further discussion of the budget, see Chapter 6). The Fontainebleau agreement was important, as it meant that EC leaders could lift their sights from interminable squabbles over the budget and begin to think strategically about the future of the Community. 'More generally, the resolution of this dispute meant that the Community could now press ahead with the enlargement [to Portugal and Spain] and with the Single Market measures which I wanted to see', as Thatcher put it (Thatcher, 1993: 545). The British government's preferences had been clearly stated in a paper, entitled 'Europe: The Future', circulated at the Fontainebleau summit (HM Government, 1984). The paper called for the attainment by 1990 of a single market within which goods, services, people and capital could move freely. It very clearly reflected the deregulatory zeal that Thatcher brought to domestic politics. The legacy of these ideas about deregulation and liberalization have also been strongly felt in British government preferences towards European integration in the administrations that have come since Margaret Thatcher left office in 1990. Buller (2000) argues that the single market project was seen as a way of enshrining core Thatcherite principles at EC level. The fact that this Thatcherite vision of a liberalized, deregulated EC was not widely accepted by other member states can help to explain the development of Conservative euroscepticism in the late 1980s and through the 1990s.

There is another point here, too. Thatcherism also changed the rules of the game of domestic economic and social policy, and shifted ideas about the respective roles of the state and market. Even though they may not have been widely accepted by other member states and at EU level, they have had major effects on British domestic politics with implications that can be traced through to more recent dilemmas, such as New Labour's debate on replacing the pound with the euro (discussed more fully in Chapter 4).

1984–87: Towards the single market

In Britain, Thatcher sought to 'roll back the frontiers of the state', and allow free enterprise and market forces to flourish. Thatcherism embodied what has been characterized as the uneasy amalgam of the free economy and the strong state (Gamble, 1988). For Thatcherites, the EC was a stultifying bureaucracy that could do with a dose of Thatcherite free market vigour, whether it liked it or not.

In order to secure the single market promoted in the Fontainebleau paper, Britain needed allies amongst its EC partners. There were potential allies at both the national and supranational levels:

• The two key member states, France and West Germany, were amenable to single market reforms. The French Socialist government elected in 1981 had abandoned its reflationary economic policies in 1983 (under Finance Minister, Jacques Delors), and the Christian Democrat-led coalition of Chancellor Kohl in West Germany supported the creation of a single market.
• The new Commission President, Jacques Delors, took office in 1985 and seized upon the single market as his 'big idea' to restart integration and shake off the 'eurosclerosis' of the 1970s and early 1980s. The Commissioner responsible for the internal market, the former Conservative Cabinet minister, Lord Cockfield, assisted Delors in his ambitions.

A White Paper prepared by the Commission put forward 300 legislative proposals for the single market. These were later whittled down to 282. Heads of government at the Milan summit in June 1985 accepted the proposals. In the face of objections from the Danes, Greeks and British, an intergovernmental conference was convened to consider reform of the EC's decision-making process to accompany the single market plan.

While Britain was hostile to strengthening Community institutions, France and West Germany asserted that attainment of the single market necessitated increased powers for supranational institutions such as the EP, in order to ensure that decision-making efficiency and a measure of democratic accountability followed the transfer of authority to the supranational level. The British did not see it that way and thought the single market could be achieved without reform of the EC's institutions. In her memoirs, Thatcher recalled that, 'it would have been better if, as I had wanted originally, there had been no IGC [intergovernmental conference], no new treaty and just some limited practical arrangements'. The British government compromised on some issues, such as increased use of QMV, in order to secure more prized single market objectives. The resultant SEA had two main features (the first of which was actively supported by the British government, while the second was not):

- establishment of a target date, the end of 1992, for completion of the internal market and attainment of the 'four freedoms': freedom of movement of people, goods, services and capital
- strengthening of EC institutional structures, with QMV.

The British government hoped that the Commission's single market White Paper would push the EC in the direction of the more minimal, regulatory type. The Commission identified three kinds of barriers to trade that needed to come down if the single market were to be attained:

- physical barriers (mainly customs and border controls)
- fiscal barriers (indirect taxes vary in the Community and constitute a barrier to trade)
- technical barriers; these were very significant because member states had developed their own product standards which differed widely and formed a substantial barrier to free trade.

The removal of these barriers was far from being the limit of the Commission's ambition, or that of other member states, and, as we see, this helps to explain why the single market programme and ideas about what it should involve were to provide a backdrop for Conservative euroscepticism. For Thatcherites, the single market was an end in itself that could raise to a European stage the liberalizing and deregulatory elements of the Thatcherite project. For many other member states, the SEA was a means to an end, that end being deeper economic and political integration, with the EC taking a bigger role in flanking areas such as social and regional policy, while also moving towards far more ambitious projects such as EMU. This gap between many other member states and the Thatcher governments centred on the respective roles of the state and market. This gap grew in the 1990s because of the acceptance among eurosceptics that European integration would bring with it an EU-imposed re-regulation of the UK economy.

1987–90: Thatcher's last hurrah

The final years of Margaret Thatcher's premiership were characterized by an almost incessant battle against post-SEA plans for deeper integration. This coincided with the birth of euroscepticism within the Conservative Party (which is analysed in Chapter 9). For the French and Germans, who had been key single market allies, adoption of a plan to complete the single market was a new beginning for integration. They sought to consolidate the success of the SEA by promoting integration in other areas. Plans were hatched for EMU and for Community social policies to ensure minimum rights for workers in the wake of the freedoms given to capital by the SEA.

Thatcher firmly set herself against the integrative consequences of the SEA. This was particularly evident in her response to questioning in the House of Commons following the Berlin summit meeting of EU heads of government in October 1990. During her responses, she departed from the pre-arranged and carefully worded text to launch into an attack on the integrative ambitions of other EC member states and the docility in front of this threat (as she saw it) of the opposition Labour Party. A section of Thatcher's off-script response went as follows:

> Yes, the Commission wants to increase its powers. Yes, it is a nonelected body and I do not want the Commission to increase its powers at the expense of the House, so of course we differ. The President of the Commission, Mr. Delors, said at a press conference the other day that he wanted the EP to be the democratic body of the Community, he wanted the Commission to be the Executive and he wanted the Council of Ministers to be the Senate. No. No. No.
> Perhaps the Labour party would give all those things up easily. Perhaps it would agree to a single currency and abolition of the

pound sterling. Perhaps, being totally incompetent in monetary matters, it would be only too delighted to hand over full responsibility to a central bank, as it did to the IMF. The fact is that the Labour party has no competence on money and no competence on the economy – so, yes, the right Hon. Gentleman [referring to opposition leader Neil Kinnock] would be glad to hand it all over. What is the point of trying to get elected to Parliament only to hand over sterling and the powers of this House to Europe? (*Hansard*, 1990)

This statement exposed divisions within the Conservative Party and was the breaking point for the Leader of the House of Commons (as well as the ex-Chancellor of the Exchequer and Foreign Secretary), Sir Geoffrey Howe. Moreover, as the Conservatives languished in the opinion polls in 1990 and the disastrous 'poll tax' prompted massive civil disobedience across the country, many Conservative MPs began to see Margaret Thatcher as an electoral liability (Watkins, 1991). The final straw for Howe was Thatcher's response (see extract above) to questioning after the Berlin summit. He resigned from the cabinet and used his resignation statement as a bitter criticism of her leadership style. Howe's speech was the beginning of the end for Thatcher's premiership. Howe (1995: 667) stated that 'the Prime Minister's perceived attitude towards Europe is running increasingly serious risks for the future of our nation. It risks minimizing our influence and maximizing once again our chances of being once again shut out.' Howe's statement prompted the long-standing opponent of Thatcherism, Michael Heseltine, to launch a leadership challenge, although he was unpopular amongst many Conservative MPs who remained attached to Thatcherite ideas, even after she had left office. This allowed John Major to come through the middle as the candidate who could apparently maintain the Thatcherite legacy of neo-liberal deregulation while bringing a more emollient style to domestic politics and international relations – or, at least, that was the thinking of many Conservative MPs. Major was perceived as the inheritor of the Thatcherite mantle, not least by Thatcher herself. Major had enjoyed a rapid ascent in the government hierarchy, including a remarkably brief stint as Foreign Secretary (July–October 1989), but his views on Europe were unclear. They remained so for much of his premiership.

1990–93: Major, the Exchange Rate Mechanism and Maastricht

Within the EC, John Major adopted a more conciliatory tone than his predecessor and expressed the intention of placing Britain 'at the heart of Europe'. In particular, there was an attempt to improve relations with Germany that had become frosty, not least because of a seminar organized by Margaret Thatcher when Prime Minister at her country residence, Chequers, to 'analyse' the German character. In a summary of the meeting that was strongly disputed by some participants (see, for example, Urban, 1996), the following were identified in the minutes of the meeting as aspects of the German character: 'angst, aggressiveness, assertiveness, bullying, egotism, inferiority complex, sentimentality', accompanied by 'a capacity for excess' and 'a tendency to over-estimate their own strengths and capabilities' (Urban, 1996: 151). These conclusions, drafted by Thatcher's foreign policy adviser, Charles Powell, outraged many of those present who had actually focused during the meeting on the remarkable transformation and stability of the Federal Republic.

Much of the fear among Conservative eurosceptics was based on the power of the German economy and reunified Germany's key role as the largest EU member state. This was the sub-text for development of the plan for EMU in the late 1980s. France, in particular, was a keen advocate of EMU because it was seen as securing Germany within the EU and thus, as Chancellor Kohl once put it, giving Germany a European roof, rather than Europe a German one. The British Conservative government was deeply divided about the plan for EMU and its forerunners, the European Monetary System (EMS) and the ERM. Thatcher was growing more sceptical about European integration and opposed EMU as a threat to national sovereignty, while her Foreign Secretary (Sir Geoffrey Howe) and Chancellor (Nigel Lawson) supported ERM membership. At the June 1989 Madrid summit, Thatcher was pressured by Lawson, and Howe to set a date for ERM membership. She resisted, but was forced to set a series of conditions that were to be met if Britain was to sign up to ERM (although these were not met when the UK did join a year later).

Chancellor Lawson saw ERM as strongly related to domestic anti-inflationary policy. As he put it in his resignation statement to the House of Commons on 31 October 1989:

Full UK membership of the EMS ... would signally enhance the credibility of our anti-inflationary resolve in general and the role of exchange rate discipline in particular ... there is also a vital political dimension ... I have little doubt that we [Britain] will not be able to exert ... influence effectively and successfully provide ... leadership, as long as we remain outside. (Cited in Balls, 2002)

Lawson and Howe both left their high offices for reasons linked to these divisions over Britain and Europe, but their successors (Major in the Treasury, and Douglas Hurd in the Foreign Office) were equally strong advocates of British participation in the ERM. By June 1990, Thatcher was forced to concede because, as she put it in her memoirs, 'I had too few allies left to resist and win the day' (Thatcher, 1993: 772). ERM membership tied sterling to the Deutschmark at a rate of £1 to DM2.95 and required market interventions to maintain exchange rate parities at levels 6 per cent below or above this central rate. A crucial reason for membership was the attainment of domestic economic objectives and to add external credibility to anti-inflationary policies. The downside was that it was far from clear that these external commitments would tally with the domestic economic situation. There was little direct evidence to suggest that the ERM would necessarily bring stability. Moreover, the enormous economic consequences of German reunification were high German interest rates and a strong Deutschmark. These placed unsustainable pressure on sterling's ERM parities. While German interest rates remained high, then so, too, would British interest rates, even though the UK economy was struggling to emerge from recession and required lower interest rates. Stephens (1996: 259) argues that the main mistake was 'the elevation of exchange rate parity into a badge of pride ... ensuring that when defeat came it was devastating'. As will be discussed in Chapters 7 and 9, the ERM fiasco was to shatter the reputation of the Conservative Party for economic competence and impel Tory eurosceptic rebellion (discussed in more detail in Chapter 9).

Major also faced the issue of the IGCs convened to discuss deeper economic and political integration. Despite Major's softer style, there were within the British government's negotiating position at Maastricht in December 1991 a number of continuities linking Thatcher and Major:

- an opt-out from the Social Chapter – the Secretary of State for Employment, Michael Howard, had said that he would resign if the Social Chapter were accepted (Lamont, 1997: 133)
- the right for the British Parliament to decide whether Britain would enter the third stage of the plan for EMU when a single currency would be introduced
- promotion of the notion of subsidiarity – meaning that power should be exercised at 'the lowest appropriate level' – which, in the eyes of the Conservative government, was a way of reinforcing national perspectives on Community decision-making
- advocacy of intergovernmental cooperation, rather than supranational integration, as the basis of cohesion in foreign, defence and interior policy; intergovernmental 'pillars' were incorporated into the Maastricht Treaty.

Unconstrained by high office after her replacement by Major in 1990, Thatcher remarked that she would never have signed the Maastricht Treaty. However, the treaty Major negotiated and signed could be seen as reflecting inherited policy preferences. In addition, Major also reaped the integrative whirlwind which Thatcher had helped initiate when she signed the SEA in 1986.

Major's deal at Maastricht temporarily assuaged Tory divisions over Europe and actually helped to lay the foundations for his April 1992 general election victory. A conspicuous feature of the election campaign was lack of debate about Britain's place in the EU. Both Conservative and Labour Party managers knew their parties to be divided on the issue, and tacitly conspired to keep silent about it. Eurosceptics later complained that the British people had not, in fact, endorsed Maastricht at the 1992 general election, and that they should therefore be allowed a referendum on the issue.

Safely returned to government, Conservative divisions over Europe could no longer be hidden and were to be exposed by a series of calamities in the summer and autumn of 1992. An important point in relation to the Europe in Britain theme is that the Major government was hamstrung by domestic divisions and unable to formulate either a clear or effective policy towards European integration. Major had to straddle the pro- and anti-EU wings of his Party, and was unable to provide strong leadership. Thus, while there were clear continuities in British preferences (intergovernmentalism and free trade with a Thatcherite twist), the capacity to achieve these preferences was chronically undermined by domestic political turmoil within the Conservative Party. Other member states became rather like rubberneckers observing a car accident: they would slow down and swerve to avoid the wreckage, but would continue with their own journey towards ambitious forms of economic and political integration. The 'Britain in Europe' and 'Europe in Britain' themes were connected by a rudderless government pre-occupied with domestic divisions; a series of set-piece confrontations at which Major would draw a 'line in the sand' only to see it swiftly washed away; and Britain weakened in Europe because not only did it fail to articulate a clear stance, but also because fundamental questions about British membership were being asked.

Chapter 9 discusses more fully the ways in which a determined and well-organized band of eurosceptics frequently defied the government by calling for a referendum on Maastricht and trying to block the passage of the Maastricht Bill through the House of Commons. Major was forced into a complex balancing act because he also had pro-European cabinet ministers such as Kenneth Clarke and Michael Heseltine in prominent government roles. The eurosceptics' rebellion culminated in July 1993 when they contributed to a government defeat on a Labour amendment incorporating the Social Chapter into the Maastricht Treaty. This was a mischievous move by the Tory euro-rebels who hated the Social Chapter, but loathed the Maastricht Treaty even more. Major's response was to 'go nuclear' and turn the issue of Maastricht into one of confidence in the government. In the face of near-certain defeat in a general election and the return of a pro-European Labour government, most of the Tory rebels returned to the party fold. This did little to ease divisions within the Conservative Party, which reached into the cabinet. For a participant's insight into the in-fighting, loathing, bitterness and acrimony that descended on the Conservative Party, see Gardiner (1999).

During the 1997 general election campaign, the deep divisions within the Conservative Party became all too evident. Even government ministers distanced themselves from the Party's policy to 'negotiate and decide' (more commonly known as 'wait and see') on EMU. Major felt powerless to dismiss the dissenting ministers because of the effects he feared such action would have on an already damaged Party (Geddes, 1997). In 1992, after Major had left the Maastricht negotiating chamber, one of his advisers unwisely claimed 'game, set and match' for Britain. With hindsight, this appears a rather rash judgement. Instead, the Maastricht deal lit the blue touch paper beneath the Conservative Party, which ignited to cause great conflict within the Party and played an important part in Labour's landslide victories of 1997 and 2001.

British pragmatism in Europe?

This chapter has examined the preferences and motivation of British governments between accession in 1973 and the devastating defeat for John Major's Conservative Party in 1997. It explored their capacity to attain these objectives and the reasons for the shifts in these preferences that have occurred over time, while also looking at what could be called the 'normative vision' that underpinned these objectives. The argument is that Britain's relations with Europe were shaped by views about the relationship between state, market and society that informed domestic political reform under Thatcher, and also by a view about Britain's place in the world. Neither this domestic normative vision, nor that of the international realm, were compatible with European integration as it was to develop from the 1980s onwards.

The chapter also showed important shifts in alignment on the EU issue, which is a theme that is also developed in Chapter 4. The Conservatives went from being a pro-European integration party, albeit based on a pragmatic acceptance of the EC as good for business, to hostility towards European integration that was strongly based on the Thatcherite legacy. Labour also fundamentally re-evaluated its stance on European integration and moved from advocacy of outright withdrawal in the early 1980s to a pro-integration stance by the early 1990s. Yet, even this apparent shift from Conservative hostility to Labour pro-Europeanism contains some elements of continuity. Thatcherite concern about the direction of European integration was informed, at least in part, by dismay that other EC member states were unprepared to accept Thatcherite strictures and that, for these other member states, the single market was a means to an end (that end being deeper economic and political integration), rather than an end in itself (i.e. Thatcherite deregulation and liberalization). New Labour, too – following a brief flirtation with European social democracy – has defined its relationship to core EU economic objectives around the attainment by the EU of certain economic reform prerequisites. New Labour's engagement was highly conditional and also somewhat ambivalent. When it came to power in 1997, New Labour seemed prepared to engage with important developments such as EMU but, in fact, New Labour between 1997 and 2010 maintained a long-standing British preference for conditional engagement with the EU and stood aside from key developments such as the creation of the euro.

Chapter 4

From New Labour to the Cameron Coalition

This chapter assesses British relations with the EU during the three New Labour governments led by Tony Blair (between May 1997 and June 2007) and Gordon Brown (between June 2007 and May 2010), and during the Conservative–Liberal Democrat coalition government led since May 2010 by David Cameron. The focus is mainly on relations with the EU (the 'Britain in Europe' theme), while Chapter 9 pays close attention to debates within and between the main parties about the EU (the 'Europe in Britain' theme). It could be asked whether New Labour's 1997 landslide victory heralded a new, more positive era in Britain's relations with the EU. Alternatively, the return to power – albeit within a coalition – of the Conservative Party could mean that Britain has moved closer to the exit. For a political system within which change tends to be slow and incremental, both positive engagement and/or exit would be radical departures. To assess these issues, it is important to consider the criteria that would be used. If we were to expect some kind of step-change or radical overhaul of previous approaches, then the overall assessment may well be negative because, as this chapter shows, British governments have not fundamentally changed the nature of British relations with the EU in a country which, Daddow (2011: 1) contends, is 'deeply mired in its nationalist past'. This chapter shows that New Labour did not – and probably did not intend to – induce a step-change in relations while, despite eurosceptic voices in the cabinet and on the Conservative backbenches, the coalition government has affirmed its commitment to Britain's EU membership.

Europe, political leaders and voters

This chapter does not search for radical change or overhaul of previous approaches as the benchmark for its evaluation of British policy to the EU between 1997 and 2010. Instead, it addresses a broader question about the relationship between intergovernmental negotiation at EU level and British domestic politics. This is achieved by factoring into the analysis both the normative visions of domestic and international politics espoused by British political leaders, and also the important changes in the relationship between voters and parties in Britain on the European (and other) issues. As already discussed in this book's Introduction, a prevailing view between the 1950s and 1980s was that the public would take their cues on Europe from political parties and that a 'permissive consensus' could give political leaders the space they needed to strike deals at EU level (Lindberg and Scheingold, 1970). Evans and Butt (2007) observe that the permissive consensus allowed political parties to structure debate about Europe and send cues to their supporters, who then played a key role in driving attitudes. They call this the 'party-driven' model and contrast it with a 'voter-driven' model: 'the party-driven model implies that the Labour government's powerful electoral mandate since 1997 should have enabled it to promote the integrationist agenda regardless of voter preferences, while the voter-driven model implies that room for manoeuvre over integration would be more limited and even a popular government could not expect to obtain a pro-integrationist response from the electorate' (Evans and Butt, 2007: 174). The point here echoes one made at the beginning of this book. The past might not be a reliable guide to contemporary and future challenges. The nature of the debate about Europe has changed since the 1990s, as, too, have the ways in which citizens engage with politics. This was also a time of flux as party positions on Europe changed, which meant that 'signals' from political leaders could be unclear. Labour moved in the 1980s and 1990s from an anti- to a pro-EU stance, while the Conservatives moved in the other direction. There was turmoil during the 1990s when signals to voters, particularly from the Conservative Party, would have been very unclear. If party signals on Europe have become less powerful in generating permissive consensus, then it would be unrealistic to expect a Labour government to have been able to mobilize its support to deliver a 'Yes' in a referendum on euro-membership. This did not mean that Labour pursued a eurosceptic strategy designed to align it with public opinion. Labour knew that Europe was a strong issue for the Conservative Party but, as we see, were keen to ensure that it did not become an issue on which there was a clear distance in the respective positions of the two main political parties. Labour tried to neutralize the issue by mimicking key Conservative positions (e.g. a referendum on the euro), trying to represent itself as a staunch defender of the national interest and, eventually, by kicking the euro debate into the long grass. In this attempt to neutralize the issue, New Labour was effective, in that Europe was a low salience issue throughout the 2000s (Oppermann, 2008). This did not mean that voters were enthusiastic about European integration but, rather, that they had other priorities – such as the economy, health and education. While New Labour's EU rhetoric was, at times, grand and ambitious (as it was on many issues), the reality was a pragmatic approach to the EU contextualized by domestic and international factors (including the US-led invasion of Iraq), by an intensification of EU developments, and by public euroscepticism.

In May 2010, there was little hope or expectation on the part of pro-Europeans that David Cameron's election as Prime Minister would herald some kind of new, more positive era in British relations with the EU. The Conservative Party pledged in its 2010 election manifesto that:

> We will be positive members of the European Union but we are clear that there should be no further extension of the EU's power over the UK without the British people's consent. We will ensure that by law no future government can hand over areas of power to the EU or join the Euro without a referendum of the British people. We will work to bring back key powers over legal rights, criminal justice and social and employment legislation to the UK. (Conservative Party, 2010: 113)

The government elected in 2010 is, of course, not a Conservative government, but a coalition with the Liberal Democrats. We thus also explore EU policy under the Conservative-Liberal Democratic coalition and analyse how the issue has been managed within government and the two parties.

'Modernization' under New Labour?

By the 1990s, Labour was more pro-European than the Conservatives and sought a stronger relationship with key EU partners. There was a more positive approach on issues such as economic reform, enlargement and defence policy. This engagement occurred in the context of a domestic political climate that was not conducive to bold pro-EU policies, or a re-making of the debate about Britain's role within the EU. This keen eye on domestic politics was evident even before New Labour took office in May 1997. In an article for *The Sun* newspaper on 5 April 1997, Tony Blair invoked St George when he noted that he 'would have no truck with a European superstate. If there are moves to create that dragon, I will slay it' (cited in Daddow, 2011: 9). This nationalistic language in Britain's best-selling newspaper and representation of the EU as a dragon to be slain hardly seems to be that of an instinctive pro-European. It was the language of a Labour leader fearful, after 18 years in opposition, of being outflanked on the EU issue by a eurosceptical Conservative Party. During New Labour's time in office, scepticism and anti-EU sentiment amongst the British public actually hardened and the kind of language deployed by Blair in this *Sun* article played to it.

This representation of the EU as an external threat points towards continuities in Britain's relations with the EU. However, it is not sufficient simply to argue that these past events and decisions determine contemporary choices. Governments and political leaders can – and do – call upon particular interpretations of past events, and are influenced by previous decisions and patterns of behaviour, but they are not completely constrained by them. There could be scope for attempts to embed a different kind of debate about the EU, or to engage in different ways with the European project. The key point is that political leaders in the UK have, in the main, chosen not to do so.

Two reasons for this can be identified. The first relates to Britain's idea of its place in the global economy, and to ideas about the best way to organize the economy and welfare state. Rosamond and Wincott (2005) refer to this factor as 'normative political economy', and find quite significant divergence between Britain and other member states. New Labour's engagement was dependent on transposition to EU level of an economic reform agenda that was strongly focused on deregulation and liberalization. For example, even before its election in 1997, Labour's 'Business Agenda for Europe' (published in May 1996) was strongly focused on the single market 'and indicated that [Labour's] pro-European policy was not following traditional social democratic concerns' (Bulmer, 2008: 599).

The second set of factors can be labelled as 'strategic'. There was a very straightforward imperative informing the action of New

Labour as a governing party: re-election. As soon as Blair was elected prime minister, he set his sights on a second term. A radical shift to a pro-EU policy would not contribute to the attainment of this over-riding strategic imperative. Relations with the EU were to be managed and, if possible, engagement could be positive. At the same time, domestic electoral fallout needed to be minimized. The advantage for New Labour between 1997 and 2010 was that it was not riven by internal party divisions over Europe as the Conservatives were until 1997. There were, however, serious divisions between Blair and his Chancellor of the Exchequer, Gordon Brown, which had major implications for Britain's EU policy, particularly for the euro.

Labour's route to pro-Europeanism

When Labour took office in 1997, after 18 years of opposition the Party had changed from advocating outright withdrawal from the EC at the 1983 general election to an ostensibly more pro-EU position. Labour fought the 1983 election on the basis of a manifesto that developed an Alternative Economic Strategy that would involve large-scale state intervention and controls over the economy. These were incompatible with continued EC membership. By the end of the 1980s, Labour was the more pro-European of the two main parties. Two factors explain the shift, one ideological and the other strategic. In ideological terms, Labour underwent a dramatic shift in its EU policy after the catastrophic 1983 defeat. The new party leader, Neil Kinnock, had been a staunch and eloquent left-wing opponent of the EC throughout the 1970s. He was now to begin a personal and political odyssey that would see him advocate the 'modernization' of the Labour Party, endorse positive engagement with the EC, and conclude with him moving to Brussels to become a European Commissioner.

Almost as soon as Kinnock became party leader, the commitment to outright withdrawal was watered down to a commitment to withdraw, if satisfactory renegotiated terms could not be secured. By the 1989 EP elections, Labour was advocating active engagement with the EC at a time when Conservative euroscepticism was beginning to emerge. The intellectual ballast for this pro-European ideology was provided by examples taken from other EU member states (particularly West Germany), whose economies and social welfare systems had performed better than those of the UK, and who offered the prospect of a more consensual form of capitalism with a stronger emphasis on welfare and social protection. Labour's modernization in its early stages was thus linked to mainstream aspects of European social democracy, although this changed under New Labour.

This domestic ideological shift by Kinnock's Labour Party in the late 1980s was reinforced by supranational developments that saw the EC develop its 'social dimension'. No longer could the EC be represented as a capitalist club that offered little to working people. Indeed, Thatcher's strong opposition to the social dimension sustained the left-wing view that perhaps Europe could offer new opportunities for progressive politics (at least, on the basis that my enemy's enemy is my friend). This was particularly so for the beleaguered trade unions that Thatcher labelled as the 'enemy within' and that experienced a legislative onslaught through new employment legislation. The opportunities presented to trade unions by European integration was a point made by the Commission President, Jacques Delors, in a 1988 speech to the TUC annual conference – much to Thatcher's annoyance, as she was not happy to see the Commission President being so supportive of her opponents (Rosamond, 1998).

The second reason for Labour's shift to a more pro-European stance is linked to the strategic concerns of an opposition party facing a Conservative government that was becoming more vocal in its opposition to European integration. The case for European integration had been a powerful feature of the political centre ground in British politics, with a broad measure of agreement between centrist elements in all three main parties that Britain's place was within the EC. As the Conservatives appeared to abandon this centre ground, then Labour could occupy it (facilitated by the ideological shifts outlined above: pp. 70–7) and portray themselves as a reinvented, moderate and mainstream party that had ditched the extremist policies which had been damaging in 1983. To be European was to be modern, and to be modern was to be European.

Tony Blair and Europe

The shift in Labour's stance under Kinnock – and, briefly, (between 1992 and 1994) John Smith – could suggest that the New Labour government elected in 1997 and re-elected in 2001 with overwhelming majorities would be more positive in its European policies. There were some early signs that it might be. In 1994, during his first speech as Leader to Labour's annual conference, Blair indicated that he wanted to take a different approach when he stated that:

> We should show courage too, over a quite different sphere of international relations: Europe. Britain's interests demand that this country is at the forefront of the development of the new Europe. Of course Europe should change. Of course we should stand up for British interests, as others stand up for theirs. Indeed we should be taking on the CAP costing the average British family 20 pounds a week and about which the Tories do nothing. But, the Tories are playing politics with Europe and the future of this country. Let them. Under my leadership, I will never allow this country to be isolated or left behind in Europe.

New Labour modelled itself on Bill Clinton's new Democrats in the USA and actively sought advice from Democratic Party strategists. The intellectual influences on New Labour were more US than European.

Labour's 1997 election manifesto stated that:

> We will stand up for Britain's interests in Europe after the shambles of the last six years, but, more than that, we will lead a campaign for reform in Europe. Europe isn't working in the way this country and Europe need. But to lead means to be involved, to be constructive, to be capable of getting our own way.

The manifesto did, however, commit New Labour to a defence of the British veto in areas such as immigration, taxation and social security.

Expectations were excessively high when Blair entered Downing Street. *The Observer* newspaper even felt moved to herald the New Labour approach to foreign policy with the headline 'Goodbye Xenophobia'. So, while the mood music and rhetoric suggested a new era of constructive engagement with the EU and a break from the past, the reality was a little more complex. On a personal level, Blair seemed much more comfortable with other European leaders than had his two Conservative predecessors. More substantively, the Labour government announced that it would sign up to the Social Chapter. In the final stages of negotiation of the Amsterdam Treaty (signed in June 1997), Labour accepted some key legislative and institutional changes – such as the addition of a new employment chapter to the Treaty, the inclusion of a new Article 13 within the Treaty that extended antidiscrimination provisions, as well as agreement to increase the use of QMV in some areas (but not for issues such as tax and social security) and an enhanced role for the EP. The UK had a more ambivalent relationship to the centrepiece of the Treaty, which was the definition of the EU as an Area of Freedom, Security and Justice (AFSJ). Many of the provisions made by the Maastricht Treaty for what was the JHA pillar were now moved into a new Title IV that was located within the main Treaty and, thus, subject to Community decision-making methods. The UK reserved the right to opt out of these Title IV provisions, which included policy areas such as immigration and asylum (Geddes, 2008).

Even in these early stages, there were some continuities in New Labour's EU policy compared with previous governments. The British government maintained a line consistent with that pursued by its predecessors on border controls (the Title IV provisions), as well as CAP reform, and the role of NATO in European defence and security policy (Hughes and Smith, 1998; Fella, 2002). New Labour also hedged its bets on the euro by not ruling out membership, but making any decision dependent on a referendum. Furthermore, as New Labour's enthusiasm for the German model of social capitalism faded, that of Blair and Gordon Brown seemed to grow for market liberalization. Divisions became apparent between Blair's 'third way' and European social democracy (Clift, 2001; Gamble and Kelly, 2000). New Labour expounded a vision of Europe that saw the central role of the nation state as the key building block of international politics but also saw the need for states to respond to the challenges of globalization. 'Open' EU regionalism within a global economy was to be encouraged, rather than more 'closed' and regulated EU regionalism. This was reinforced by a continued emphasis on transatlantic ties and the UK's self-positioning as the USA's closest ally in Europe. In a speech to the Foreign Office conference of British Ambassadors on 7 January 2003, Blair (2003) stated what the principles of British foreign policy should be:

> First, we should remain the closest ally of the US, and as allies influence them to continue broadening their agenda. We are the ally of the US not because they are powerful, but because we share their values. I am not surprised by anti-Americanism; but it is a foolish indulgence. For all their faults and all nations have

them, the US are a force for good; they have liberal and democratic traditions of which any nation can be proud ... it is massively in our self-interest to remain close allies. Bluntly there are not many countries who wouldn't wish for the same relationship as we have with the US and that includes most of the ones most critical of it in public.

Blair then added that:

Britain must be at the centre of Europe. By 2004, the EU will consist of 25 nations. In time others including Turkey will join. It will be the largest market in the world. It will be the most integrated political union between nations. It will only grow in power. To separate ourselves from it would be madness. If we are in, we should be in whole-heartedly. That must include, provided the economic conditions are right, membership of the single currency. For 50 years we have hesitated over Europe. It has never profited us. And there is no greater error in international politics than to believe that strong in Europe means weaker with the US. The roles reinforce each other. What is more there can be no international consensus unless Europe and the US stand together. Whenever they are divided, the forces of progress, the values of liberty and democracy, the requirements of security and peace, suffer. We can indeed help to be a bridge between the US and Europe and such understanding is always needed. Europe should partner the US not be its rival.

This intention to be a bridge between Europe and the USA illustrates the ways in which British politics remains between Europe and the USA (Gamble, 2003). The gap between Europe and the USA became more difficult to bridge in the run-up to, and aftermath of, the invasion of Iraq, when major divisions emerged between the UK government and the French and German governments. Tony Blair showed himself to be at least, if not more, pro-US than any of his postwar predecessors in Number 10 Downing Street, and this indicates strong transatlantic continuities in British foreign policy.

Blair's first term, 1997–2001

The key dilemma of Blair's first term was succinctly summarized by Philip Stephens (2001: 67) when he argued that, while Tony

Blair – 'the most instinctively pro-European Prime Minister since Edward Heath' – had been able to make Britain's case in Europe, he had been unable to make the case for Europe in Britain. Even here, a note of caution can be added, Blair succeeded John Smith as Labour leader following the latter's death in May 1994. Smith was a confirmed European. Blair had pro-European instincts and saw it as a necessary facet of a modernized Labour Party, but, as Seldon (2005: 316) notes, 'Blair's thinking about the EU ... lacked the long pedigree of visceral commitment of the true Europhile'. In terms of formative experiences, Heath had been present at the Nuremburg rally and seen Nazism at first hand. Blair was from a different generation and had not had such powerful formative experiences. He had worked in a bar in Paris during his gap year before going to study at Oxford University. Blair was also acutely conscious of the need for EU policy to be consistent with the broader objective of securing re-election. Simon Bulmer (2008) has developed this point in terms of what he calls New Labour's 'utilitarian supranationalism'. By this, he means that there was significant 'upstream' engagement at governmental level on issues such as economic reform and defence policy, but 'downstream' domestic constraints grounded in public hostility to the EU. This also connects with analysis of voters and parties. Evans and Butt (2007) argue that voters are now less likely to take their cue on Europe from political parties and that upstream engagement cannot rely on a permissive consensus in domestic politics.

In a speech delivered (in French) to the French National Assembly in October 1998, Blair noted that his first ever vote had been cast in favour of Britain's EC membership in the June 1975 referendum (although in 1983 he stood as a candidate for a Party committed to withdrawal). In government, after 1997, Blair could expect far fewer EU-related problems than his predecessor because of his crushing parliamentary majority and because of the broad agreement on a pro-EU policy within the Parliamentary Labour Party. Yet, controversial and potentially divisive issues still lingered, particularly membership of the euro. As we shall see, this was an issue that was to be assessed on the basis of the five economic tests by Gordon Brown's Treasury team. This does not mean that EU policy was entirely Brown's domain, but it does mean that tensions simmered and occasionally boiled over during Blair's time as Prime Minister, and that these had effects on British EU policy. It is probably plausible to argue that, during a honeymoon period soon after the 1997 general election, it may have been possible to make a successful case why Britain should join the euro. This would probably have been a political (not an economic) case. This would, however, have run strongly counter to the caution that characterized New Labour's first term in office. To this can be added that the Treasury was scarred by the ERM experience, while Gordon Brown as Chancellor of the Exchequer was not a committed pro-European. This meant that the Treasury would be a voice of caution, particularly if arguments for membership were political, rather than economic.

Within the government and beyond the Blair-Brown axis, there were no other prominent pro-EU voices within the cabinet able to challenge Brown's more sceptical position. The more pro-EU Robin Cook was replaced as Foreign Secretary by Jack Straw, while the europhile Peter Mandelson spent only two relatively brief periods in the cabinet during New Labour's first term, served in the European Commission and did not return to British government until the dying days of the Brown administration. During New Labour's 13 years in office, there were 12 Europe ministers. The longest serving of these was Dennis McShane, who had the job between October 2002 and May 2005. In contrast, Glenys Kinnock was in post for less than five months between June and October 2009. Geoff Hoon did the job twice, but for a combined total period of less than 18 months. The European brief in the Foreign and Commonwealth Office (FCO) was low profile and low priority. Policy was effectively run from the Treasury and Number 10, and strongly depended on Blair's working relationship with Brown.

New Labour and the euro

In the run-up to the 1997 general election, a key issue that needed to be dealt with was Labour's position on the euro. In its 1997 election manifesto, Labour pledged a referendum on the euro. This effectively neutralized the issue as a campaign theme by mimicking the Conservative stance. Management of Britain's policy towards the euro remained firmly in the hands of Gordon Brown and the Treasury. It was also the cause of early skirmishes within the government between Blair and Brown. A press briefing carried out by Brown's spokesman, Charlie Whelan, in the Red Lion pub just off Whitehall on October 18th 1997 spun the line to the press that Brown was ruling out euro-membership for the lifetime of a

Parliament. This was not government policy and caused confusion within and outside government when reported (Daddow, 2011: 49; Rawnsley, 2001: 72–88). On 27 October 1997, Brown announced a 'prepare and decide' policy to the House of Commons. He stated that, in principle, a successful single currency within a single European market would be of benefit to Europe and to Britain. He also announced that there was no constitutional impediment to British membership of the euro. If Britain were to join, then five economic tests were specified that would need to be satisfied. Interestingly, these did not replicate the criteria developed by the EU to assess whether a member state was ready for membership. If these had been used, then it has been argued that, aside from the question of exchange rate stability, the UK probably was ready for membership (Temperton, 2001). Brown concluded his statement to the House of Commons with the following rhetorical flourish: 'the time of indecision is over. The period of practical preparation has begun' (cited in Daddow, 2011: 49). We explore these five tests, and British policy on EMU and the euro, more closely in Chapter 7, but can note at this stage that, when Brown reported back to the House of Commons on 9 June 2003, he noted that only one of his five tests had been satisfied. After this negative assessment, membership of the euro was effectively off the domestic policy agenda, where it has remained ever since.

The broader EU policy agenda: economic reform and defence

Even though Britain was to be outside the euro, New Labour was keen to promote a liberalizing economic reform agenda at EU level that matched its domestic approach. Some progress was made in the form of agreement in March 2000 on the so-called 'Lisbon Agenda', which aimed to develop measures that would make Europe the world's leading knowledge-based economy by 2010, combining employment growth in the knowledge economy with social cohesion and environmental sustainability. Lisbon relied on 'soft governance' measures such as benchmarking and peer review through use of the Open Method of Coordination, rather than 'hard' law such as directives and regulations. This may have accorded with UK preferences in that it did not emphasize Commission-led harmonization, but the voluntary approach made it difficult to secure progress (Bulmer 2008: 608–9). By 2010, the EU was a long way from attaining the ambitious objectives it had set for itself and was actually mired in an economic crisis that threatened the very future of the Union itself. A further point to note is that the context of 'modernization' had changed. No longer was Germany heralded as a model. Instead, New Labour found also itself aligned with centre-right governments and leaders such as José Maria Aznar in Spain and Silvio Berlusconi in Italy. This division was to be further confirmed by alignments on foreign policy and relations with the USA.

It is also important to note the way in which New Labour sought to do business with the EU. While public attention is often focused on set-piece occasions such as summit meetings, particularly if there is a row or bust-up, much of the EU's work is done behind the scenes and is based on systematic and routinized contacts between minister and officials. The way to win an argument, or make a case, is not through compelling oratory in European Council meetings – which would, any way, lose its effect as it was translated into other languages. Influence depends on the strength, quality and degree of integration into the networks that support and sustain the EU. As we discuss in Chapter 8, Britain has a much admired civil service but, to be effective, these officials rely on a clear steer from government. In 1998, Blair announced that he wanted to see more interaction between ministers, officials and their counterparts in other member states (Smith, 2005: 708).

There did seem to be a clearer direction to EU policy, and there were not the attempts at deliberate obstructionism that had been seen during the Major administration. During Labour's first term, there were signs of a more European approach to defence and security policy, and the attempt to build strong bilateral relations. On defence policy, the obvious member state to work with was France – Europe's other leading military power. While Blair made it clear that NATO remained the cornerstone of UK defence policy, he also came to the view that that a stronger and more coordinated European role was needed, if it were to attain its own objectives as well as to deal with European conflicts, such as that which arose in Kosovo in 1999. The St Malo summit meeting of the British and French governments in December 1998 led to a Franco-British attempt to inject new leadership to EU defence and security policies. Article 2 of the St Malo Declaration stated that: 'the Union must have the capacity for autonomous action, backed up by credible military forces, the means to decide to use them and a readiness to do so, in order to respond to international crises'. This development is analysed in Chapter 7. At this stage, it is important to note that this was a significant achievement for the Labour government. Indeed, at the time, Howorth (2000: 33) described it as a 'revolution in military affairs'. However, divisions within the EU over Iraq between the UK, France and Germany were to undermine British efforts in this area. This does not mean that the British were isolated in Europe, but key allies were Aznar in Spain (until his replacement by a Socialist government led by José Luis Rodriguez Zapatero in April 2004), Berlusconi in Italy, and pro-US new member states in central and eastern Europe that joined the EU in 2004.

Blair's second term, 2001–05

In June 2001, Labour secured a second landslide victory against a weakened Conservative Party led by William Hague. The Conservative campaign was strongly – almost obsessively – focused on the EU issue and the perils of economic integration. Hague toured the country urging the electorate to 'save the £'. While this was a theme that struck a chord for many voters, it was not a sufficiently salient issue for it to help the Conservatives break out from their core support. To do so would require a Conservative campaign that appealed more broadly on issues that were of more importance to voters, such as health and education. The strong EU focus made the Conservatives seem like a single-issue party (for further discussion, see Chapter 9). Labour's 2001 general election manifesto stated that: 'Labour has negotiated successfully for Britain in Europe. Our rebate is protected, enlargement is being taken forward. We have led the debate on European economic reform and on the development of a European defence capacity rooted in NATO structures' (Labour 2001 election manifesto, cited in Smith, 2005: 713).

During its second term, the New Labour government closely aligned itself with the USA in its 'war on terror', and actively supported military interventions in Afghanistan and Iraq. By 2003, the euro was effectively sidelined as an issue in British politics following Brown's negative assessment of the attainment of the five economic tests. There were, however, important developments within the EU and a decided quickening of the pace of treaty reform. The Nice Treaty 2000 had not generated major controversy in the UK, but eurosceptic suspicion was aroused when the EU turned its attention to development of a new 'Constitutional Treaty'. The initial intention behind the constitutional convention was, in many ways, laudable. The EU's three founding treaties (Paris, 1951, and the two treaties of Rome, 1957) provided the legal basis for EU action. The SEA in 1986, Amsterdam in 1997 and Nice in 2000, together with other instruments (such as the 1970 Treaty establishing the budget procedure), amended these founding treaties. This meant that the legal base of the EU was potentially confusing. The idea was to try to consolidate this diffuse legal base and simplify the treaties, while also exploring new areas for development. A Convention on the Future of Europe, from February 2002 until July 2003, was led by former French president Giscard D'Estaing and was tasked with drawing up proposals for a constitution and then presenting these to IGCs of the member states for approval.

The constitutional convention

Labour's approach to the Convention on the Future of Europe cannot simply be characterized as defensive or negative. Initial positive engagement was replaced in early 2003 by a more defensive approach as the Convention reached its conclusion but, even in its final form, the Treaty was actually viewed as a favourable outcome for the British government. The Constitutional Treaty was described by the French constitutional expert Robert Badinter as a 'British constitution', in that he thought it mirrored British priorities and was distinctly 'Anglo-Saxon' (cited in Kassim, 2004: 268). Even if the Treaty did have a British hue, the British government was, by 2003, less enthusiastic about it. The British government had not initially favoured the creation of the Constitutional Convention but, once it was established, did specify clear objectives and was more positive in its approach than had been the governments of Thatcher and Major at the times, respectively, of the IGCs on treaty reform in 1985 (prior to the SEA) and 1991 (prior to Maastricht).

Blair's vision of Europe that informed Britain's approach to the Constitutional Convention was outlined in a speech to the Polish Stock Exchange in October 2000. The speech was a response to the overtly federalist vision expounded by the German foreign minister, Joschka Fischer, and to calls by French President Chirac for a group of pioneer states to move ahead more quickly (Smith, 2005: 712). Indeed, other member states were actually concerned about stronger collaboration between Britain, France and Germany on issues such as economic reform and relations with Iran. Member states such as

Italy and Spain were worried that the 'big three' could form an inner core or *directoire*. This fear was unfounded, in the sense that the 'big three' fractured over the Iraq issue and did not challenge the traditional dominance of the Franco-German relationship.

In his Warsaw speech, Blair reaffirmed Britain's commitment to the EU and stated his strong support for enlargement to central and eastern Europe. He outlined a pragmatic vision of an EU attuned to the need to develop policies to deal with transboundary issues such as competitiveness, climate change and immigration. He also rejected notions of a European superstate and reaffirmed the centrality of nation states because to do otherwise would be to 'fail the test of the people'. Blair argued that:

> Europe is a Europe of free, independent sovereign nations who choose to pool that sovereignty in pursuit of their own interests and the common good, achieving more together than we can achieve alone. The EU will remain a unique combination of the intergovernmental and the supranational. Such a Europe can, in its economic and political strength, be a superpower; a superpower, but not a superstate.
>
> We should not therefore begin with an abstract discussion of institutional change. We begin with the practical question, what should Europe do? What do the people of Europe want and expect it to do? Then we focus Europe and its institutions around the answer. How we complete the single market. How we drive through necessary economic reform. How we phase out the wasteful and inefficient aspects of the CAP. How we restore full employment. How we get a more coherent foreign policy. How we develop the military capability we require without which common defence policy is a chimera. How we fight organised crime, immigration racketeering, the drugs trade. How we protect an environment that knows no borders. And of course, how we stop Europe focusing on things that it doesn't need to do, the interfering part of Europe that antagonises even Europe's most ardent supporters. (Tony Blair, speech to the Polish Stock Exchange, 6 October 2000)

It is worth exploring the Convention because it helps to demonstrate the workings of inter-state bargaining and because 'the treaty that never was' (the EU constitution) ended up being recycled in the form of the Lisbon Treaty.

The British government was well-prepared for the Convention. Britain's lead representative – the Europe Minister, Peter Hain MP – was widely seen as effective, while the former Foreign Office Permanent Secretary, Lord Kerr, served as Secretary-General to the Convention. The British government did face difficulties on some issues. A majority of member states favoured incorporation of the Charter of Fundamental Rights into the Treaty, which the UK opposed. There was wide support for stronger cooperation on foreign policy, which the British advocated, but with use of QMV, which the British opposed. Similarly, on tax policy, the UK opposed use of QMV, but was again in a minority. On institutional questions, British calls for a permanent Chair of the European Council found favour, as, too, did calls for a stronger Commission able to meet the challenges of a wider Europe. There was less support for the British idea to create second chamber of the EP (Kassim, 2004).

Towards the end of 2002, the dynamics of the Constitutional Convention began to shift. Most notably, France and Germany began to engage much more seriously and dispatched their foreign ministers, Dominique de Villepin and Joschka Fischer, respectively. It was reported that Peter Hain was greeted by German foreign minister Fischer at his first meeting at the Convention with the words: 'I hear you Brits are running the Convention, that's why I'm here' (Kassim, 2004: 272). Hain also found considerably more pressure on his time when he was appointed Secretary of State for Wales while also maintaining his role on the Convention. The French and German governments were soon to play a key role in shaping the Convention's agenda, underpinned by more than 40 years of close and systematic cooperation on Europe based on the Elysée Treaty of 1963. The French and German governments called for stronger EU foreign, defence and internal security policies, as well as stronger economic governance for the eurozone and a more developed EU role in tax policy. From January 2003, draft Treaty articles began to appear. The UK suggested amendments to 15 of the first 16 (Kassim, 2004). By May 2003, as the Convention moved towards its conclusion, the UK found itself boxed into a corner. At a meeting with Giscard, Blair threatened use of the UK veto if the word 'federalism' appeared, and if references to use of QMV for tax policy and social security were not expunged. This threat was taken seriously, as the final version did not contain any of these features (Kassim, 2004: 273).

The Labour government also faced a domestic dilemma with the Constitutional Treaty. New Labour would seek an unprecedented

third term in office – but there was euroscepticism amongst the electorate, while sections of the press were fiercely sceptical. Although
the European issue did not have a high salience, there was little to
suggest that a pro-EU stance would reap electoral dividends for New
Labour. In such circumstances, it could be argued that that the best
strategy for Labour would be to neutralize the EU issue. This was
done by mimicking the Conservative position and stating that there
would be a referendum on the Constitutional Treaty. So, while in
France, the Constitutional Treaty was seen as a victory for the British
because of the limited vision it expounded, it was also the case, as
Smith (2005: 717) puts it that: 'the British press and the opposition
Conservatives continued to see it as a federalist document, likely to
undermine British sovereignty'. This semantic conundrum aside, the
key point is that the referendum tactic neutralized the issue, but did
not challenge sceptical representations of the Treaty as a federalizing
document. New Labour dodged the issue, rather than confront the
sceptics' arguments. This returns to the point made earlier: that Blair
may have made some headway in making the case for Britain in
Europe, but did not make the case for Europe in Britain.

New Labour's third term, 2005–10

In June 2005, New Labour secured an unprecedented third term,
albeit with a much reduced majority (65) in the House of Commons.
The internal pathologies of the New Labour government became
particularly clear during this third term. While in the early days of
New Labour in the 1990s, Brown had appeared to share Blair's EU
enthusiasm, this ardour had seemed to diminish. Brown's intellectual influences had always been more US than European, with his
idea of a good holiday apparently being a trip to the East Coast of
the US with a bag full of the latest heavyweight economic tomes
from US thinkers. His key advisers – such as Ed Miliband and Ed
Balls – shared this orientation to US society and thinking. As
Chancellor, Brown did not appear to enjoy EU meetings. He was
renowned for allowing the UK to be represented by more junior
Treasury ministers at meetings of the finance ministers (ECOFIN)
Council. Bulmer (2008: 618) quotes a Treasury official who, as
early as 1998, noted that Brown 'is not comfortable with the
European process, he is not comfortable with his colleagues, he
doesn't like the cosying up that needed to be done and all that sort
of thing, he loathes travelling'.

The dysfunctional relationship between Brown and Blair, and the key role played by the Treasury at the heart of British government, do need to be recognized as key issues during the New Labour governments. For example, earlier we noted the call from Blair to build stronger relations with other EU member states and to help the British government build the networks of influence that could help make the case for Britain in Europe. The importance of this day-to-day work within the EU's internal governance structures should not be under-estimated. In his account of managing EU policy, Scott James (2011) describes how the Treasury control of the five economic tests effectively presented Blair with a *fait accompli* when it came to assessment of whether or not the UK had satisfied these criteria. Blair's special advisor on European affairs, Roger Liddle, argued that this Treasury veto prevented Blair from being able to develop any kind of road map or plan for future entry, while the power of Brown and the Treasury within Whitehall largely excluded other cabinet ministers from this debate (James, 2011: 134).

Brown succeeded Blair on 27 June 2007. Amongst his first major EU-related duties was to sign the Lisbon Treaty on 13 December 2007. However, Brown preferred to appear before a House of Commons committee rather than travel to Lisbon for the official signing ceremony with other heads of government in the splendour of the fifteenth-century Jerónimos Monastery. David Miliband, the foreign secretary, stood in for Brown – who arrived later to append his signature. There was, in fact, significant overlap between the content of the Constitutional Treaty and that of the Lisbon Treaty, although, in line with earlier treaties, Lisbon was an amendment of previous treaties, rather than an attempt to create an EU constitution. Brown argued that, for this and other reasons, Lisbon was different to the constitutional treaty and did not require a referendum. The other main reason was that Brown declared that British 'red lines' had been secured (on issues such as border controls) and, thus, the British national interest has been protected. Box 4.1 shows that the Lisbon Treaty maintained many of the provisions that were present within the Constitutional Treaty.

Lisbon marked a further significant stage in the EU's development, but the British government did seek to limit some of its effects. For example, the Charter of Fundamental Rights was incorporated into the EU's legal framework, although the UK has an opt-out which means that it cannot be used by domestic courts in rights cases. Lisbon also extended the CJEU's powers by allowing for

Box 4.1   Key provisions of the Lisbon Treaty

- The Lisbon Treaty came into effect on 1 December 2009. It amended previous Treaties. It was, thus, in line with revisions made by the SEA and Maastricht Treaties and was not the constitutional convention that had been initially envisaged.
- The EU's main legal document, the Treaty establishing the European Community (TEC), was renamed as the Treaty on the Functioning of the European Union (TFEU).
- The Charter of Fundamental Rights became a part of the EU's legal framework. The UK, Poland and the Czech Republic secured derogations that meant that citizens of these countries could not use the Charter in rights cases before domestic courts in these countries.
- The role of the European Council was strengthened as it became an official EU institution with a President of the European Council.
- A High Representative for Foreign Affairs and Security Policy to manage EU foreign and security policy, including the creation of an External Action Service (EAS).
- The rotating Council presidency changing every six months was replaced by a trio of countries working together in order to ensure greater continuity. The Foreign Affairs Council will be chaired by the High Representative, not the country holding the presidency.
- The application of the OLP gave the EP equal powers with the Council in most areas of legislation except taxation and foreign policy.
- The European Central Bank became an official EU institution.
- The role of the CJEU was expanded to include scope for preliminary rulings from lower courts on migration and asylum cases. Previously, these had to come from the highest courts in member states, which significantly slowed the procedure.
- The Treaty established a procedure for a member state to leave the Union.

preliminary references from lower courts in member states to be made to the Court on migration and asylum issues. However, the UK can opt out of EU measures on migration and asylum and so, if it has opted out, will not be subject to the CJEU's jurisdiction.

Despite the major changes made by the Lisbon Treaty, the Brown government argued that Lisbon was an amendment of previous treaties, rather than a new constitutional framework, and thus did not require a referendum. The leader of the Opposition, David Cameron, issued a 'cast iron guarantee' that a Conservative government would hold a Lisbon referendum. By the time he came to power, the Treaty had been ratified by the UK and all the 26 other member states. A referendum was no longer feasible.

Brown, Britishness and the financial crisis

With Lisbon signed, Brown argued that the EU needed to focus on policies that mattered to people, such as climate change and economic reform. The intellectual ballast for Brown's domestic agenda came through a focus on 'Britishness'. It is very difficult to articulate a coherent notion of Britishness when set against a variety of factors that call into question the continued resonance and relevance of British identity, or even whether it was particularly meaningful in the first place. These factors include European integration, but also the British multi-national state encompassing England, Scotland, Wales and Northern Ireland, as well as the effects of immigration and multiculturalism. The debate about Britishness that Brown hoped to lead did not have Europe as its main focus, but Britain's place in the world would necessarily be a central component of it. A problem was that Brown's emphasis on Britishness actually ran counter to European integration. Three weeks before he became Prime Minister on 6 June 2007, Brown made a speech in which he promised to train thousands of British workers to offset the need for migrant workers. However, as many as 80 per cent of migration to Britain in the first decade of the twenty-first century came from other EU member states and was by people who had a right to move to the UK as EU citizens guaranteed by EU law (in the same way that British citizens can move to other EU member states). Britain had been one of only three member states that, in May 2004, had allowed immediate access to the UK labour market by nationals of what were known as the A8 states in central and eastern Europe. This right of free movement is protected by EU laws in the same way as it is for British citizens who want to work in another member state. Other member states did impose a transitional period on citizens of new member states that restricted these rights for a maximum of seven years. In his first speech as leader at the party conference in September 2007, Brown began by noting – uncontroversially – that he wanted Britain to be a 'world leader' in science, business, creativity and manufacturing. More controversially, he said he would be 'drawing on the talents of all to create British jobs for British workers'. This is the language of the far right, not social democratic governments. The words came back to haunt him. In early 2009, a series of wildcat strikes broke out after a contract to extend the diesel refining capacity of the Lindsay refinery in Lincolnshire was awarded to a US company that, in turn, subcontracted its labour recruitment to an Italian company that brought in workers from Italy and Portugal. At a time of recession, trade unions argued that unemployed British workers should have access to these job opportunities and were very keen to emphasize Brown's point about 'British jobs for British workers' in the face of EU free movement rights, Brown was powerless to act because EU law guaranteed the rights of EU workers to move to the UK in the same way that British companies and workers were free to operate in other member states.

The final two years of Brown's time as prime minister were dominated by the effects of the economic crisis, which had huge implications for the UK and eurozone economics, and also demonstrated that the fortunes of the UK economy were closely tied to those of eurozone states. Chapter 7 looks at the origins of EMU and Labour's stance on the issue between 1997 and 2010. At this point, it can be noted that Brown did try to play a central role in developing and leading a European response. He did so from a position of relative strength as an experienced finance minister, but he also did so from outside the eurozone and from a position of domestic weakness, with constant talk of plots amongst his colleagues to replace him and an alarming drop in Labour support in opinion polls, culminating in the 2010 general election defeat.

The EU and the coalition government

We now assess the approach to the EU of the coalition government elected in May 2010. We look at the coalition agreement, the European Union Act of 2011, and the 'veto that never was' of the

EU's 'fiscal compact'. This section complements the analysis in Chapter 9 of party politics and euroscepticism that looks more closely at debates about the EU within and between the main parties.

There were clear indications that the Conservatives would, at the very least, adopt a 'this far and no further' approach with opposition to the ceding of more powers to the EU. One question was whether this would lead to Cameron drawing 'lines in the sand', as John Major often claimed he was doing, only to see them washed away. Another was whether Cameron would be able to quell back-bench eurosceptics who were keen to head for the exit door and leave the EU altogether. The first key test for Cameron was the EU's so-called 'fiscal compact'. The British government did not necessarily disagree with the compact's content, given its pursuit of domestic budget discipline and austerity (which led some to call it the 'pact of pain'), but did oppose its inclusion within the Treaty framework and the consequent empowerment of EU institutions.

Following Cameron's election in 2005, the Conservatives distanced themselves from their traditional allies in Europe in the centre-right European People's Party (EPP). The EPP was seen by Conservatives as a federalist party. In strategic terms, it meant that the Conservatives distanced themselves from the leaders of centre-right parties. Fearful of being outflanked on the right by his eurosceptic opponent, David Davis, Cameron had, during his leadership campaign, pledged to take the Conservatives out of the EPP. He said that he would seek to create a new group. After some delay, this new group was formed four years later in the aftermath of the June 2009 EP elections. The new grouping comprised the Conservatives and parties mainly from new member states in central and eastern Europe. The result was that the Conservatives distanced themselves from centre-right parties in key member states such as France, Germany, Spain and Italy that remained within the EPP and, instead, grouped together with smaller parties from mainly newer member states. The Conservatives were in a grouping that was more consistent with their ideological stance on European integration, but at the cost of diminished influence within the EP.

The EU was not a key focus of the Conservatives' 2010 general election campaign. In both 2001 and 2005, the Conservatives had made issues such as the EU and immigration central components of their national election campaigns. The lesson they drew from defeats in 2001 and 2005 was that they needed to focus on issues that mattered more to voters than the EU, such as the economy and welfare state. While the Conservative stance on the EU did not fundamentally alter, this topic was far less apparent within their campaign strategy. Given the economic crisis, the 2010 general election was dominated by debate about the economy and deficit (Geddes and Tonge, 2010).

The Conservative 2010 general election manifesto called for a 'positive relationship' with the EU, but said that there would be no further extension of powers without the consent of the British people, i.e. a referendum. The election outcome was, of course, indecisive and the main parties entered into discussions about coalition government. Opposition to increased powers for the EU was a 'red line' issue for the Conservatives during coalition negotiations, i.e. one on which they would not compromise (Fox, 2010; Quinn *et al.*, 2011).

The Liberal Democrats were ostensibly the most pro-European of the three main parties, but the EU was not a key issue for them in the negotiations. Under the leadership of Nick Clegg, the Liberal Democrats had developed a more critical stance on European integration, albeit one that could certainly not be labelled as 'eurosceptic'. It is worth bearing in mind that Liberal Democrat voters have been as eurosceptic as other sections of the electorate. Liberal Democrat strongholds on the 'Celtic fringe' in the south-west of England and northern Scotland were also areas where euroscepticism, driven by EU agriculture and fisheries policies, could be very strong. The more critical stance of the Liberal Democrats was evident in the so-called 'Orange Book' published in 2004, with contributions from those on the economically liberal wing of the party. The chapter on Europe was written by Clegg himself. Clegg had worked within the Commission as a member of the 'cabinet' of former Conservative minister Leon Brittan during his time as a European Commissioner in the 1990s. Clegg had also been a Member of the EP between 1999 and 2004 before taking the Sheffield Hallam seat in the Westminster Parliament in 2005. In his Orange Book chapter, Clegg expressed his support for European integration as the best response to fragmented sovereignty and cross-border issues where economic and political integration could help to resolve collective problems. He was, however, critical of the EU as constituted. He argued that the EU did not need more debate about institutional reform once the Constitutional treaty had been ratified (although this was to take somewhat longer and eventually

Box 4.2   The Coalition Agreement – Section 13: Europe

- The Government believes that Britain should play a leading role in an enlarged European Union, but that no further powers should be transferred to Brussels without a referendum. This approach strikes the right balance between constructive engagement with the EU to deal with the issues that affect us all, and protecting our national sovereignty.

- We will ensure that the British Government is a positive participant in the European Union, playing a strong and positive role with our partners, with the goal of ensuring that all the nations of Europe are equipped to face the challenges of the 21st century: global competitiveness, global warming and global poverty.

- We will ensure that there is no further transfer of sovereignty or powers over the course of the next Parliament. We will examine the balance of the EU's existing competences and will, in particular, work to limit the application of the Working Time Directive in the United Kingdom.

- We will amend the 1972 European Communities Act so that any proposed future treaty that transferred areas of power, or competences, would be subject to a referendum on that treaty – a 'referendum lock'. We will amend the 1972 European Communities Act so that the use of any *passerelle* would require primary legislation.

- We will examine the case for a United Kingdom Sovereignty Bill to make it clear that ultimate authority remains with Parliament.

- We will ensure that Britain does not join or prepare to join the Euro in this Parliament.

- We will strongly defend the UK's national interests in the forthcoming EU budget negotiations and agree that the EU budget should only focus on those areas where the EU can add value.

- We will press for the European Parliament to have only one seat, in Brussels.

- We will approach forthcoming legislation in the area of criminal justice on a case-by-case basis, with a view to maximising our country's security, protecting Britain's civil liberties and preserving the integrity of our criminal justice system. Britain will not participate in the establishment of any European Public Prosecutor.

- We support the further enlargement of the EU.

occur only when Lisbon was finally ratified in 2009). He also called for a realignment of the 'mishmash' of EU powers 'in a more open, decentralised accountable direction' (Clegg, 2004).

The upshot of this is that, while in theory the EU issue could have been a cause of trouble between the eurosceptic Conservative Party and the ostensibly more pro-EU Liberal Democrats, in the context of the hurried negotiation of the coalition agreement, it was not a bone of contention. On the day after the general election, Cameron stated that he was prepared to make a 'big, open and comprehensive offer to the Liberal Democrats'. This offer, he stated, would allow the Liberal Democrats to attain many of their manifesto objectives on issues such as the 'pupil premium' and taxation. The Conservatives would not, however, countenance further powers being extended to the EU without the express consent of the British people (meaning a referendum).

In their analysis of the coalition agreement and the way that it reflected the manifestos of the two coalition partners, Quinn *et al.* (2011: 305) characterized the EU section of the coalition agreement as 'weakly right [wing]'. As Box 4.2 shows, the section on Europe expresses the intention to develop a positive relationship with the EU and identifies some issues on which the coalition government would seek to see a stronger EU response, such as climate change, global poverty and competitiveness. The section does strike one or two positive notes but is, in the main, defensive. Much of the document seeks to empower a coalition government to protect Britain from the further development of EU powers, and also effectively to constrain the government by requiring use of referenda if EU proposals for increased powers are made. This idea of a 'referendum lock' is particularly important, as, too, was the European Union Act of 2011 that gave it effect, which we now analyse.

The European Union Bill 2011

The thinking behind the European Union Bill 2011 introduced in Parliament in October 2010 was quite straightforward. It sought to realize the idea in the coalition agreement of a referendum lock on any future extension of EU powers. At the 2010 Conservative party conference, the Foreign Secretary, William Hague, proclaimed that: 'A sovereignty clause on EU law will place on the statute book this eternal truth: what a sovereign parliament can do, a sovereign parliament can also undo ... this clause will enshrine this key principle in the law of the land'. This could imply unpicking previous agreements with the EU, although the coalition government seemed to focus its attention on future Treaty changes. Presumably the referendum lock could be abandoned by any future government in a way that is entirely consistent with what Hague calls 'this eternal truth'.

The European Union bill contained three key provisions:

- A referendum would be held before there could be any further transfer of power to the EU. The bill thus addressed a lingering resentment that major constitutional changes such as the Lisbon treaty had not been subject to a vote. The government argued that the provisions for a referendum lock within the European Union bill would help reconnect politicians with the people that elected them.
- Acts of parliament would be required before EU *passerelle* clauses could be used. These clauses apply when the Council decides (acting by unanimity) to replace unanimous voting in the Council on a Treaty provision with QMV. They could be seen as a treaty change by the back door, as they can move sensitive issues such as immigration and asylum to majority voting and thus end national vetoes.
- Clause 18 of the bill stated that EU law has effect in the UK only through an act of Parliament.

In evidence to the House of Commons European scrutiny committee, Professor Phillip Allott wrote that 'the Bill has a whiff of revolution about it. It is a Boston Tea Party gesture against *creeping integration*. As such, one might say, it is twenty years too late'. (House of Commons European Scrutiny Committee, 2010: Ev 8, emphasis in original).

The coalition agreement had already made it clear that the government did not intend to support any treaty change or transfer of powers in this Parliament. This appeared to mean that the government was seeking to constrain the actions of future governments, but under the principle of legislative supremacy this is not possible, as no parliament can bind its successors. If it could, then this would be contrary to the principle of parliamentary sovereignty that was supposedly being protected.

A further question is the definition of major or important issues requiring a referendum. The government stated that it would not extend to whether or not new member states could join the EU.

Former French President Sarkozy had said that he would hold a referendum on whether Turkey should join the EU. The government's stance during the debate on the European Union bill would seem to rule out such referenda in the UK. This would seem sensible, as it is hard to imagine the British people flocking to the polls on the question of whether or not Macedonia should join the EU. The European Union Bill provided that a minister would make the decision about whether or not a power is being transferred that would require a referendum, although this decision could be challenged in the courts.

The Bill became law in July 2011. It symbolized the apparent intention to stop what has been seen as the creeping effect of European integration, but this can be questioned on two counts. First, fairly soon after the bill became law the EU moved towards a far more integrated fiscal policy, developed to complement existing EU economic and monetary policy competencies. The UK opted out of these provisions, but they went ahead anyway; they will have implications for Britain and there is little the British government can do to offset the will of the vast majority (25 out of 27) of other member states. Second, the European Union Act was unlikely to appease harder-line eurosceptics on the Conservative benches, who were less concerned with the scope to prevent further Treaty change than by the question of whether Britain required a far more fundamental re-evaluation of its relationship with the EU. This could include either exit or, at least, a renegotiation on issues such as social and employment law. As noted earlier, if the European Union Act was a Boston Tea Party moment for Conservative eurosceptics, it was probably 20 years too late and raised as many questions as it answered.

Anatomy of a 'veto'

When is a veto not a veto?: presumably when the thing being opposed goes ahead anyway; albeit with Britain looking in from the outside by use of an opt-out. This was the eventual outcome of the attempt by David Cameron to block new EU fiscal rules unless certain 'British safeguards' (largely related to the City of London) were secured. The Conservative-Liberal Demcrat coalition was – by choice – a spectator in debates about eurozone governance. The running was made by the French and Germans. The German Chancellor, Angela Merkel, had hoped that Britain, together with Scandinavian member states and the Netherlands, could be a potential liberalizing ally for the Germans and help to counterbalance the

French. At his first meeting as prime minister with Merkel in May 2010, Cameron made it clear that, while he wished them well, eurozone governance was a matter for eurozone countries. This contrasted with the position of Brown, who had tried to secure a place for the British government inside the eurozone discussions. For ex-French President Sarkozy, the crisis had actually been caused by lax regulation of financial services and tougher rules were needed to rein in 'Anglo-Saxon capitalism'. This pointed to the need for tighter regulation of the banking and finance sectors. For Cameron, financial services were a vital national interest that needed to be protected from EU regulation. There was never to be a meeting of minds between Sarkozy and Cameron.

Prior to the December 2011 summit, Sarkozy and Merkel had agreed to proposals for treaty changes in the form of what was to be known as the 'fiscal compact'. This would impose much tougher rules on member states, including requiring budgets that were balanced, or in surplus, with member states open to sanctions if they did not. Would other states agree to such a deal? The summit began on 7 December with a dinner that dragged on until 5.00 am. Cameron was determined to protect the City of London and asked for a series of 'British safeguards' that would require the use of unanimity in the Council of Ministers on a range of measures related to financial services. These would include fiscal rules and any attempt to impose, at EU level, maximum harmonization rules that could, for example, override national provisions on levels of bank capitalization. Britain also sought exemption from EU rules for non-EU financial institutions based in Britain but not operating in other EU member states (such as major US banks), and also wanted the new European Banking Authority to be based in London.

There was actually some reluctance amongst member states to pursue the Treaty reform requested by France and Germany; not least because such changes could be very difficult to sell to their own citizens and, in some member states, would require a referendum. Was a compromise available? Into the debate stepped European Council President Van Rompuy. He had been asked by the member states at their summit meeting on 25–26 October 2011 to come up with ideas for new rules on economic governance. He proposed a technical solution that would involve using the existing Protocol 12 of the Treaty covering what was known as 'the excessive deficit procedure'. Into Protocol, 12, he argued, could be imported new fiscal rules. He argued that the advantage of this technical solution would be that it would not amount to a major treaty change and, thus, would not raise the kinds of ratification headaches that referenda could induce. In one way, this argument is quite staggering, as it would mean introducing hugely important policy decisions that would have major implications for the livelihoods of EU citizens inserted via a technical 'back door'. However, in the atmosphere of high-level and high pressure EU negotiations could a deal be done? The key player was Cameron. Would he continue to insist on his 'British safeguards', or would he be prepared to compromise in order to agree to allow the other member states to use Protocol 12? He made it clear that he would not drop any of his 'British safeguards'. Other member states saw his stance as being paradoxical, as his insistence on maintaining unanimity rules in relation to financial services could actually jeopardize the single market (a key British interest) because QMV had been the *modus operandi* since the SEA came into force in 1987.

 If Treaty reform involving all member states was off the table because of the threat of a British veto, and Britain was also not prepared to make any concessions to ease the path to the Protocol 12 fix, then the only remaining alternative was to append a new Protocol to the Treaty enshrining the fiscal compact. The UK made it clear that it would not participate, so the fiscal compact would apply to the 17 eurozone countries and to those non-eurozone countries that wanted to sign-up. To enter into force, the agreement would require ratification from only 9 states. Would this mean a two-speed Europe, with 17 eurozone and 10 non-eurozone countries? This would be misleading. Many of the 10 non-eurozone countries are committed to seek entry and actually want to move towards full membership. The Polish government expressed the view that it did not want to be part of an outer core or slow lane. However, the Czech, Hungarian and Swedish governments all expressed some misgivings about the fiscal compact. The specific features of this, which was to be known as the Treaty on Stability, Coordination and Governance in the EMU, are shown in Box 4.3.

The summit created a new structure for eurozone governance which Germany and, to a lesser extent, France are likely to dominate. The British government would be at the table, but only as an observer. For the French, this could herald a move towards their preferred vision of a more closely integrated inner EU core, as France had feared that a wider Europe would be a more Anglophone and less integrated Europe.

Box 4.3   The Treaty on Stability, Coordination and Governance in the Economic and Monetary Union

The commitment agreed on 9 December 2011 by eurozone governments at the Brussels summit was as follows:

- General government budgets shall be balanced or in surplus; this principle shall be deemed respected if, as a rule, the annual structural deficit does not exceed 0.5% of nominal GDP.
- Such a rule will also be introduced in Member States' national legal systems at constitutional or equivalent level. The rule will contain an automatic correction mechanism that shall be triggered in the event of deviation. It will be defined by each Member State on the basis of principles proposed by the Commission. We recognise the jurisdiction of the Court of Justice to verify the transposition of this rule at national level.
- Member States shall converge towards their specific reference level, according to a calendar proposed by the Commission.
- Member States in Excessive Deficit Procedure shall submit to the Commission and the Council for endorsement, an economic partnership programme detailing the necessary structural reforms to ensure an effectively durable correction of excessive deficits. The implementation of the programme, and the yearly budgetary plans consistent with it, will be monitored by the Commission and the Council.
- A mechanism will be put in place for the ex ante reporting by Member States of their national debt issuance plans.

Source: Statement by the Euro Area Heads of State or Government, Brussels, 9 December 2011.

The election of François Hollande as French President in May 2012 created uncertainty about the future of the fiscal compact and its strict budget rules. During his election campaign, Hollande had said that he would offer an alternative to the politics of austerity, even if this created tension within the Franco-German alliance, because Chancellor Merkel had been to the fore in pursuing national level retrenchment and debt reduction. It would create serious political difficulties for Merkel – herself facing national elections in 2013 – if she were seen to back down from these tough fiscal rules and concede ground to countries seen as profligate by many Germans. Hollande sought measures to promote growth within the fiscal compact alongside those that sought to enforce budget discipline.

Immediately after the December 2011 summit, opinion polls suggested as much as 62 per cent support for Cameron's supposed veto. Cameron also seemed quite sanguine about British isolation by noting that Britain remained a full member of the EU and that this exclusion from the fiscal compact was merely another instance of variable geometry in line, for example, with the Schengen agreement. However, by 30 January 2012 Cameron had agreed to allow the Treaty on Stability, Coordination and Governance in the Economic and Monetary Union to be established as an intergovernmental agreement with the UK and Czech Republic outside. The Czechs did indicate that they might seek to join later. In effect, the British government was the only EU member state that set its face against the fiscal compact and the attempt to develop fiscal and budget rules that some had seen as the main weakness of the EMU as developed post-Maastricht (see Chapter 7, for discussion of the EMU system). The aim was that the fiscal compact Treaty would enter into force on 1 January 2013, provided that 12 of the 17 eurozone states had secured ratification. In February 2012, the Irish Attorney-General announced that there would be a referendum in Ireland on the Treaty. This was held on 31 May 2012, with the people of Ireland endorsing the Treaty, although they had little alternative but to hold tight to the eurozone. Once they agreed to its provisions, participating states would have one year (until 1 January 2014) to introduce a balanced budget rule into national legislation. Such a rule was one of the first acts of the technocratic Italian government led by Mario Monti, who replaced Silvio Berlusconi as Italian Prime Minister. Berlusconi was one of 12 EU leaders who had, by May 2012, fallen victim to the political fallout of the financial crisis.

Signals of Cameron's thinking on the issue of the fiscal compact were given in his speech at the Davos meeting in January 2012, when he argued that Europe needed not just austerity, but also measures to stimulate growth. However, if such measures were to occur within the eurozone, then they would require active intervention by the German government, which was sitting on a large fiscal surplus. However, the German government insisted on the disciplines associated with the fiscal compact and continued to seek its incorporation into the Treaty structure. Cameron was ultimately prepared to agree to this, so long as assurances were received that measures would not be taken that threatened the City of London. Cameron effectively backtracked from his blocking manoeuvre at the December 20112 summit, because he was well aware that the issue that would determine his chances of being re-elected in 2015 would be economic recovery and this, unquestionably, would be tied to the future of the eurozone. Cameron will, however, have to manage dissent from his backbenches and also from within his Conservative colleagues in cabinet with Work and Pensions Secretary Iain Duncan Smith (a veteran Maastricht rebel) and the Environment Secretary, Owen Patterson, making it clear that they expected the government to steer a eurosceptic course. These voices will be countered by more pro-EU Liberal Democratic voices. The balancing that Major sought in the 1990s between pro- and sceptical wings of the Conservative Party has now become much more complex for Cameron, who must balance degrees of scepticism within his own party with the views of his Liberal Democrat coalition partners.

It is strongly in the interests of the British government that these new eurozone structures succeed, not least because of the trade and financial interdependencies linking the British economy to that of other EU member states. However, if it does succeed and does mean a higher level of economic integration within the eurozone, then Britain will only be an observer at the forum within which key decisions about EU economic governance are likely to be made, and its advocacy of liberalizing reforms could be marginal to discussions. The insistence on 'safeguards' was a representation and exemplification of the British government's lack of confidence in its ability to make its case and win arguments in Europe. We saw an early representation of this in the essentially defensive language that suffused the 2010 Conservative general election manifesto and the coalition agreement.

Conclusion

This chapter has surveyed the EU policies of the four British governments since 1997. The purpose has not been to search for radical departures or step-changes in British relationships with the EU because these are unrealistic criteria. Under New Labour, there was some positive engagement on issues such as single market integration, and defence and security, but New Labour government did not move Britain to the 'heart of Europe'. Such a move was always unlikely, given the factors conditioning British relations with the EU and the quickened pace of integration during the 2000s. Similarly, we should be more sanguine when assessing the coalition. The coalition has maintained a commitment to UK membership, but the European issue still retains potential to ignite fervent debate within the Conservative Party where significant numbers of MPs have severe reservations about UK membership and would, at least, like to see the issue put to a referendum.

The underlying argument within this chapter is that the EU issue needs to be discussed in the context of the changed relationship between voters and leaders in Britain. Not only has the EU become more unstable as a political issue (most recently because of the eurozone crisis), but also political leaders have become more nervous about confronting it. The key factor is the strength of the 'constraining dissensus' in British domestic politics. There is, of course, a 'chicken and egg' situation here. Which came first: weak leadership on the EU, or popular opposition to the EU? The argument in this book is that the late and ambivalent choice for Europe made in the 1960s continues to exert its effects on contemporary debate, even though the world has changed markedly since Britain joined the EC in 1973. By 2012, Britain had effectively located itself in the 'outer core' or 'slow lane'. The point is that, for many in the Conservative Party, this was the right place to be. Indeed, as we shall see in Chapter 9, this is precisely the position argued for by the more pro-EU (or less eurosceptic) strand of thinking within Cameron's Conservative party, i.e. pro-EU or less eurosceptic only in the sense of its position relative to those within the Conservative Party who would actually rather see Britain head for the exit door.

If we then think about the conclusions of this chapter in the broader sweep of British relations with the EU since 1973, then we can begin to see this as a consistent pattern of ambivalence on the part of British governments that has been accommodated since the

1990s within more 'flexible' forms of integration. Other member states have moved more rapidly on issues such as free movement within the Schengen area and on eurozone governance. Britain has been accommodated within a slow lane or outer circle. Other member states find themselves outside the core too, but the key point is that they do not do so by choice but because they aspire to the core and are seeking to satisfy requirements for membership. The outer core is not an alternative sphere for British leadership, but is a position on the outside looking in.

Chapter 5

Britain, EU Institutions and Decision-Making Processes

The EU is a political system in its own right with processes of debate, decision and implementation within which UK political institutions play a part, but within which power is shared. The chapter analyses EU institutions and their impact on British politics. It also opens a series of broader questions not just by looking at the role of EU institutions, but by thinking about representative politics in the EU through formal routes such as the EP, and also through interest representation and lobbying. By doing so, the chapter aims to go beyond the formal mechanics of EU institutional processes and explore some wider implications for British politics. Through the analysis of EU institutions and associated processes contained in this chapter, we see a key aspect of power sharing. This can be understood as a practical manifestation of a sometimes arcane and abstract debate about 'sovereignty'. EU institutions represent the quest to create common decision-making procedures in areas of shared interest. The EU is a complex system of power sharing across levels of governance. British governments have tended to prefer intergovernmental structures, with an underlying understanding of the EU as an association of sovereign states, while harbouring some reservations about grand designs and ambitious projects concerning the EU's *finalité*, such as a European constitution that might stress a 'federal vocation'.

The Brussels empire?

The spring 2011 EU-wide opinion polls conducted by Eurobarometer showed a comparatively low level of knowledge of EU institutions in the UK, as shown by Tables 5.1 and 5.2. These tables show responses in the UK compared with the EU average when people were asked whether they had heard of the main EU

114

TABLE 5.1   *Knowledge of European Union institutions in Britain compared with EU average (%)*

Institution	UK	EU27 average	Top of the form
European Parliament	83	90	Finland: 99
European Commission	70	80	Finland: 97
Council of Ministers	44	66	Slovenia: 89
European Central Bank	63	80	Finland: 98

Source: Data from *Eurobarometer Standard Report No. 75* (Spring 2011).

institutions and the level of their trust in these institutions. Tables 5.1 and 5.2 show that UK respondents declared relatively little knowledge about, or confidence in, EU institutions. In such circumstances, the impression that there is some vast Brussels monolith issuing directives and regulations can take hold. There are important EU-level developments, but the picture is more complex and nuanced than a vast monolithic organization. EU governance is more fluid than such a perspective would suggest, and also a more finely balanced mix of both intergovernmental and supranational elements.

EU institutions operate within a system within which powers are shared between the member states and EU institutions, and exemplify the ways in which supranational integration challenges a vocabulary of political analysis based on nation-state centred forms of political organization. As already noted, Britain is the only

TABLE 5.2   *Trust in European Union institutions compared with EU average (%)*

	Tend to trust		Tend not to trust	
	UK	EU27	UK	EU27
European Parliament	23	45	57	38
European Commission	20	40	51	37
Council of Ministers	17	36	45	35
European Central Bank	22	40	46	38

Source: Data from *Eurobarometer Standard Report No. 75* (Spring 2011).

political system in the EU that has a principle of legislative supremacy, although this is challenged by the movement of powers 'up' to the EU, 'down' to sub-national government and 'out' to private actors. The production of EU laws through a common institutional system that can override acts of the UK parliament is an obvious challenge to this principle, but one that has been accommodated within the British legal system. The other challenge is to state sovereignty and to the capacity of British governments to secure their objectives through common institutions.

Analyses of political systems tend to focus on the allocation of legislative, executive and judicial authority. In the EU political system, we see that legislative authority in many key areas is now shared between the directly elected EP and the Council of Ministers, on which sit representatives of member state governments. Political direction is provided by the European Council, which now has a President appointed by the member states. The Commission has executive authority for the management and implementation of policy, but shares this responsibility with institutions and agencies in the member states. The Commission is also responsible for making policy proposals, which gives a more 'political' edge to its activities and belies the idea that it is simply a bureaucracy. Finally, judicial authority is exercised by the CJEU. As EU competencies have expanded, then so, too, has the CJEUs jurisdiction.

There are five main EU institutions:

- The Commission comprises 27 members of the College of Commissioners, including one from Britain, Baroness Cathy Ashton, who was appointed in 2009 as a Commission Vice President and High Representative of the Union for Foreign Affairs and Security Policy. In June 2011, there were also a total of 32,949 people employed by the Commission. Of these, around 23,000 were employed in the key organizational units, the 33 Directorate-Generals and 11 Service departments. Neofunctionalist theories of European integration attributed great significance to the European Commission as an agent of 'spillover'. The argument was that, through its role making policy proposals, the Commission could push forward European integration by instigating 'spillover' processes. For example, integration in one area would draw in other associated areas, which was labelled as 'functional spillover'. A result of functional spillover would be the relocation of political activity to reflect the changed locus of policy-making, which was labelled as 'political spillover' (Rosamond, 2000). Under the Presidency of Jacques Delors, between 1985 and 1995, the Commission entered the political demonology of British eurosceptics. Since then, the Commission's reputation was dented by fraud and mismanagement in the 1990s, and by the more general difficulties and mood of europessimism in the 2000s. The Commission is, however, central to the EU's political and economic development.

- The Council of the European Union (or, as it is more commonly known, the Council or Council of Ministers), within which national governments are represented and which combines both legislative and executive functions. British governments have tended to see the Council as the most legitimate basis for collective decision-making, rather than increased powers for either the Commission or EP. A key issue is the voting procedure. Since the Lisbon Treaty and the application of the Ordinary Legislative Procedure (OLP) to almost all areas of policy (except for taxation and foreign policy), QMV is the decision-making norm within the Council.

- The EP is the only Community institution which is directly elected and which is acquiring increased legislative authority alongside the Council. There are 736 MEPs elected from 27 countries, of which 72 are returned from the UK. In Britain, low levels of turnout in its elections (34 per cent in 2009) and a low level of public awareness plague the Parliament. However, the EP is now a co-decision-maker in most areas of EU law. This means that it shares power with the Council, and exercises real power and authority in the EU's political system.

- The CJEU interprets the growing body of Community law, rules on the acts of institutions and, thus, plays an important role in shaping the parameters of an integrated Europe.

- The European Council, set up in 1974 to provide high-level political leadership, comprises heads of government who meet for two-day summits at least once every six months. The Lisbon Treaty crested the office of European Council President in a bid to bolster political leadership at the core of the EU system.

The Commission

British eurosceptics have often portrayed the Commission as an agent of integration by stealth and as the bastion of a monolithic

'Brussels bureaucracy'. For pro-Europeans, it is necessary that the Commission has a central role within the Union, not least to ensure effective attainment of EU objectives.

The Commission holds the power of policy initiative, implements policies and exercises executive responsibilities in pursuit of agreed objectives. It also manages the EU's finances and exercises external responsibilities in policy areas, most notably international trade negotiations where the member states have ceded authority to the Union to act as their representative. The Commission also guards the legal framework and reports breaches to the CJEU. In addition, the Commission also performs two other important, but more informal, roles as a mediator and conciliator between member states and EU institutions in cases of dispute, and as the conscience of the Union committed to the goal of deeper European integration.

There has been some continuity in the preferences of British governments towards the Commission. In October 1998, the then Minister for Europe made it clear that, from the point of view of the British government, the Commission was not a 'big political leader', but was necessary to ensure the EU's smooth running and efficient administration. British governments including the Conservative-Liberal Democrat coalition have been keen to emphasize the need for the Commission to focus on the delivery of existing tasks, rather than the ambitious search for new roles. If we probe beneath the surface of this observation, we also encounter a British perspective on the role of public officials and administrators, albeit not one that is shared by all member states, or necessarily evident within the Commission itself.

The 27 Commissioners appointed between 2009 and 2014 were nominated by the member states and ratified by the EP. While they have the general responsibility to 'organize Europe', there is no guarantee of a shared conception of what this organization of Europe should involve, or how it should evolve. When appointing the Commission president, there is the requirement that the member states take account of the results of EP elections, but the Commission does not need to reflect the political majority within the Parliament.

The President of the Commission, currently the former Portuguese Prime Minister, Manuel Barroso, is proposed by the European Council, approved by a majority of members of the EP and appointed for five years. He – the Commission President has always been male – is responsible for the allocation of portfolios (which must be approved by the Council), although larger and more powerful member states would expect to see Commissioners from their country in the more prestigious posts. Each Commissioner is supported by a personal cabinet, which supports his or her tasks and liaises with other Commissioners' cabinets. Upon appointment, Commissioners are meant to forswear their national loyalties, but this is unrealistic: Commissioners cannot wipe their national political memory banks clean upon moving to Brussels and, anyway, it is seen as no bad thing if Commissioners are in touch with political developments in their country of origin.

Commission officials come from member states with different administrative traditions, which can mean rather different understandings of roles and responsibilities. There is no agreed model of European public administration. Stevens (2002) contrasts a 'public authority' model that is rule-based and stresses the independence of senior officials in pursuit of their responsibilities with a 'service provision' model that pays close attention to delivery. The latter model would be recognizable in the UK context (as well as Denmark and the Netherlands), but not in those member states where a public authority model continues to hold sway (Austria, Belgium, Greece and Italy and, to a lesser extent, France, Spain and Sweden, according to Page and Wright, 1999: 273). An illustration of the potential for clashes between different administrative traditions was provided by a report prepared by a British official within the Commission's personnel department. The report argued that 'The first shock of many staff recruited into the European institutions is to find that many of their underlying assumptions about behaviour, often barely made explicit in their own country since they seem so obvious, are not necessarily shared by colleagues' (cited in Stevens, 2002: 10).

There can also be tensions and rivalries within the Commission. Stevens and Stevens (2000: 196) identify three sources of conflict: turf wars for influence and control over particular policy areas; ideological conflict over policy and solutions; and conflict over the distribution of resources. In such terms, it is better to think of the Commission as a 'multi-organization', rather than a monolith (Cram, 1994). This is illustrated by Hooghe's (1997: 95) interviews with senior Commission officials about their perceived roles: 'Actors were often motivated by a number of issues: more or less supranational control, more or less Europe of the Regions, the prevalence of one DG [Directorate General] over another, the need for a mobilizing idea for the Commission versus running things efficiently, public intervention versus free market, and career concerns.'

In the aftermath of the corruption and mismanagement scandals that led to the resignation of Jacques Santer as Commission President in 1999, there were renewed efforts to focus on the Commission's management capacity. For example, a Committee of Independent Experts (CIE) found that: 'It is becoming difficult to find anyone who has even the slightest sense of responsibility ... The temptation to deprive the concept of responsibility of all substance is a dangerous one. The concept is the ultimate manifestation of democracy' (CIE, 1999a, point 9.4.25; see also CIE, 1999b). Reform attempts were led by former Labour leader Neil Kinnock in his role as a Commissioner. Kassim (2008) argues that, prior to the Kinnock reforms, the Commission was not a complacent organization unwilling to reform but, rather, it lacked external impetus and internal drive to reform. This was provided in 1999 following the crisis caused by Santer's resignation. The Commission then seized the opportunity of a 'once in a generation' opportunity for reform.

A key constraint on the Commission's policy implementation role is its relatively small size when compared with national bureaucracies. The notion of a 'Brussels Empire' administered by a vast Commission is rather absurd. The more important issue is that cooperation with national bureaucracies creates a 'dual executive', with responsibility for implementation and oversight shared by the Commission and the member states. This is a practical response to the scale of the tasks but can lead to problems of fragmentation that make management and supervision of policy implementation difficult. The result is that whether or not EU law is properly implemented depends to a large extent on how efficient national bureaucracies are in taking account of the various directives and regulations that emanate from Brussels. The British track record has been good because a Whitehall ethos of collective responsibility and information sharing has enabled a relatively smooth adaptation by the British core executive to the requirements of membership (Bulmer and Burch, 2009; James, 2011). In this regard, the UK is not particularly 'awkward'.

Since the 1990s, there has also been a shift in emphasis from creating institutional structures and establishing policy priorities to attempting to ensure that policy objectives are actually attained. Policy implementation is a key EU challenge, with a more general emphasis on developing patterns of European governance that mesh with more general state, social and market changes in Europe and the rest of the world. There has been discussion of new forms of

European governance that seek to move beyond what were seen as the inflexible and hierarchical structures put in place during the 1960s to more network-based patterns of interaction that reflect the complex multi-level interactions between and within member states that now characterize the EU (Metcalfe, 2000).

The Council

For British governments, the Council representing national governments has tended to be seen as the most legitimate basis of EU decision-making. This rests on a conceptualization of the EU as an association of sovereign states that have agreed to pool sovereignty. According to this thinking, the member states are the building blocks of the international political order. The idea of 'multi-levelledness' introduced at the start of this chapter does challenge this state-centred view, but it does not write states out of the equation. Multi-levelledness suggests more complex systems of power-sharing as powers move 'up' to the EU, 'down' to sub-national level and 'out' to the market and the private sector.

The Council adopts legislative acts (Regulations, Directives and so on) typically using the OLP within which decision-making power is shared with the EP. It also helps coordinate member states' policies (e.g. in the economic field and the CFSP), and can conclude international agreements on behalf of the Union. It also adopts the EU's budget together with the EP. The Council could actually be characterized as the dignified element of a more complex process that predominantly occurs at official level rather than ministerial. National ministers are unlikely to have the time to involve themselves in the minutiae of policy proposals.

For the UK government, a key point of engagement with the Council, other EU institutions and other member states is the UK's Permanent Representation (UKRep) in Brussels. UKRep highlights 'beneath the radar' aspects of European integration and everyday interactions between the British and EU political systems. We assess UKRep later in this chapter and, in Chapter 8, look at its role within the core executive of the British political system.

Some UK ministries are more Europeanized than others (Chapter 8 develops this point more fully). Areas such as agriculture and fisheries have become intensively Europeanized, while the EU has had less effect on areas such as education. Some ministers encounter their European colleagues on a regular basis, others less so. The

FCO has been seen as more pro-European, while other departments of state, particularly the Treasury, are seen as more 'sceptical'. However, under New Labour the Foreign and Commonwealth Office (FCO) was seen as more marginal, as EU policy was driven by Blair and Brown. Other factors contributed to the FCO's diminished role including the growing technicality of much EU business, a reduction in FCO capacity on European matters in Whitehall, and the ability of government departments to interact with the EU without FCO guidance (House of Commons Foreign Affairs Committee, 2011). Chapter 8 takes this point forward by looking at the EU issue within the coalition government since 2010 and shows there to have been a renewal of the FCO's central role in Britain's EU policy, albeit led by a distinctly eurosceptic Foreign Secretary in William Hague.

A key point is that the UK's conditional and differential engagement is also reflected in the way that Europe has not become fully embedded within the preferences, interests and identities of some key departments of state, such as the Treasury. Nevertheless, routine trips to Brussels are a key part of the job description for national ministers and many departments now have long-established experience of dealing with the EU. When they reach Brussels, officials encounter a rather different form of politics from that experienced in Whitehall and Westminster.

The Council in action

There is no public gallery from which the Council of Ministers can be observed. If there were, then viewers would see a room containing around 150 people with ministers from the 27 member states and their officials, the Commission's representatives, members of the Council's secretariat and legal service. Also, seated in glass boxes surrounding the room, are the translators needed to ensure that the ministers actually understand events. The whole event can seem rather chaotic as officials scuttle in and out of the meeting. The Council works in all 23 of the EU's official and working languages with simultaneous translation, together with rapid translation of important documents into the official languages.

Until the Lisbon Treaty came into force in 2009, the role of the Council presidency was of great importance as, for a six-month period, a member state would chair meetings of the Council and also of the European Council. However, the role of the presidency has been downgraded and, in effect, divided into four new roles. This is because of the need to ensure greater continuity in planning and policy development, and also to try to attach greater political weight to EU action in key policy areas. First, to develop greater political weight at EU level, the Lisbon Treaty created the role of President of the European Council, held since 2009 for an initial 30-month period by the former Belgian Prime Minister Herman Van Rompuy (see the section on the role of the European Council: pp. 134–5). Second, there is the role of High Representative of the Union for Foreign Affairs and Security Policy (Baroness Ashton, appointed to the role in 2009), responsible for chairing the Foreign Affairs council. Third, the eurozone (with 17 members in 2011) had a separate eurozone group chaired by the Prime Minster of Luxembourg, Jean-Claude Juncker. Finally, the old six-month presidency has now been replaced by a trio of presidencies with three countries working together on a common programme. This system was introduced in 2007.

Martin Westlake (1999: xxiii) contends that a caricatured view of the Council has developed as 'a monolithic institution, negative in instinct, labouring in confidentiality, forging secretive deals, restrained by unanimity and blinkered by notions of national sovereignty'. Westlake argues that this is a misrepresentation, and that the Council is both more complex and less negative: more complex because it combines legislative and executive roles, lacks a standard decision-making procedure, and has developed its own idiosyncratic processes in particular issue areas; less negative because it has 'organically developed a series of – sometimes very delicate – mechanisms'.

There are two key points to grasp about the Council's role in EU decision-making. The first is the operation of the OLP. Co-decision-making between the EP and Council was introduced by the Maastricht Treaty. The essence of this procedure is that it is an effort to move to a system within which the EP and the Council share decision-making power. Since Maastricht came into force in 1993, there has been a steady growth in issues subject to the co-decision. The Lisbon Treaty further extended the EP's role through application of the OLP. The procedure can be summarized as follows:

- The Commission makes a policy proposal to the Council and EP, which both consider the proposal without time limits. If the Council approves the EP position, then the proposal is adopted.

- If the Council rejects the EP's position, then it adopts its position at first reading and submits it to the EP for a second reading. If the EP approves this position, the legislative act is adopted. If the Council position is rejected, the proposal can then only be resumed on the basis of a new proposal from the Commission. If the EP proposes amendments to the Council's position, the Council's second reading is conducted. If all the amendments are approved, the act is adopted; in the event of rejection, a Conciliation Committee is convened.
- The Conciliation Committee is comprised of equal representation from the EP and Council, and has six weeks in which to try to reach agreement.

The second key issue is the extent to which issues should remain reliant on a unanimous vote, or should be subject to a majority voting system. The system of QMV has evolved over the years. The Council can make a decision if it is supported by 14 of the 27 member states (18, if the proposal is not made by the Commission), has at least 255 of the 345 voting weights and represents at least 311 million people of the total EU population (although this third condition is more effectively guaranteed by application of the voting weights). Voting weights distribute more votes to larger member states and fewer votes to smaller member states, as shown in Table 5.3.

The UK was not a keen advocate of QMV but realized that, if EU objectives were to be attained in areas such as single market integra-

TABLE 5.3   *Voting weights in the Council of Ministers (2012)*

Member state	Weighted votes
Germany, UK, France, Italy	29
Spain, Poland	27
Romania	14
Netherlands	13
Greece, Czech Republic, Belgium, Hungary, Portugal	12
Austria, Bulgaria, Sweden	10
Denmark, Finland, Ireland, Lithuania, Slovakia	7
Latvia, Slovenia, Estonia, Cyprus, Luxembourg	4
Malta	3

tion, then it is necessary to move towards QMV and not risk one country having the power to block. This was one reason why other member states were surprised at the December 2011 summit meeting when, in pursuit of 'British safeguards', David Cameron called for unanimity on issues relating to financial services.

Disputes about Council decision-making induced one of the EC's first crises in the mid-1960s when de Gaulle blocked plans for the use of QMV. The use of the national veto to protect vital national interests was enshrined by the Luxembourg compromise of January 1966, but the problem was that reliance upon unanimity was a block on decision-making. The difficulty of securing unanimous agreement among member states could make it near impossible to achieve substantive action. The shift towards QMV that has occurred since the SEA of 1986 has been central to the resurgence of integration, and has been seen as a way of unblocking decision-making procedures and ensuring attainment of EU goals, particularly single market integration.

There have been important changes in the Council's role since the 1990s as the EU has developed responsibilities for foreign and security policy, and for internal security matters such as policing, judicial cooperation, immigration and asylum (see Chapter 7, for an analysis of the EU's move into areas of 'high politics'). These are areas in which decision-making has been strongly focused on the Council, and where the EP, Commission and CJEU have all developed stronger roles. For example, the Commission, EP and CJEU are all now fully associated with EU migration and asylum policy, which is largely subject to the OLP.

UKRep: the bridge between domestic and EU politics

UKRep plays a particularly important because it is the British government's voice in Brussels, where it deals every day with the Commission, other EU institutions and other member states' permanent representations. However, UKRep is not only the British voice in Brussels, but also plays a key role in coordination of EU relations within British government. Chapter 8 looks more closely at UKRep's position within the core executive. This section analyses UKRep's role in Brussels and assesses what is being 'represented'. UKRep is an important means for the projection of 'British interests' to EU level. An obvious point is that these interests have become more complex as a result of devolution to Scotland, Wales

Box 5.1   The UK in Brussels: the role of UKRep

- The UK's Permanent Representative has overall responsibility for the work of UKRep and represents the UK on the Committee of Permanent Representatives (COREPER).
- In 2011, this role was held by Kim Darroch, supported by a Deputy Permanent Representative and a UK Representative on the Political and Security Committee.
- The UK Permanent Representative sits on COREPER II, which deals with issues of 'high politics' such as foreign and defence policy, economic and financial policy, and internal security.
- The Deputy Permanent Representative sits on COREPER I, which deals with other social and economic issues such as the single market, consumer rights, environment and social affairs. Eight thematic teams cover key areas of EU policy. There is also specific representation for the devolved administrations in Scotland, Wales and Northern Ireland.
- UKRep staff are intensely involved in undertaking the preparatory work for the British government as it prepares to engage with the EU on a wide range of institutions. UKRep staff serve on COREPER I and II, but also a plethora of Council working groups within which legislation is developed.
- UkRep staff also play a key role in preparing ministers for Council meetings, as they are the eyes and ears of the UK government in Brussels. Indeed, many of the issues with which ministers deal may actually have been resolved at official level. Whitehall career paths for high-flying civil servants often now contain a period in Brussels within COREPER, learning about the mechanics of the EU system.

and Northern Ireland. This is not to suggest that there is automatic tension between these different representations. For example, the Scottish Government Office in the European Union (SGOEU) assists with 'intelligence gathering' and works closely with UKRep 'rather than provid[ing] an alternative or rival means of inputting the

Scottish dimension to EU policy (Smith, 2010: 219; see also Wright, 2005: 103–4). Bulmer *et al.* (2006: 83) note that: 'great care was taken to stress that these [Scottish, Welsh and Northern Ireland] offices were part of the overall 'family' of the UKRep, rather than being independent agencies advocating a specific Scottish, Welsh or Northern Irish view of EU legislative proposals' (see also Murphy, 2011).

UKRep thus maintains a key role in the coordination of all UK interests. Murphy argues that, counter to the claims of MLG that the central state would be weakened by European integration, the formalization of representation for Northern Ireland has actually limited regional autonomy by affirming the key role of UKRep. De Maillard and Smith (2012) analyse European cooperation on policing and show UKReps's role in the projection of British interests. They also show that, even though policing has become more complex, the key relationship is the Home Office, as the key domestic institution, liaising with UKRep in Brussels. Box 5.1 outlines the organization and roles of the UK's Permanent Representatives.

The European Parliament

The EP is the only directly elected institution at EU level. Since the accession of Bulgaria and Romania in 2007, there have been 739 members. The EP's role should not be underestimated. It possesses shared budgetary authority with the Council and has seen increased legislative authority as the OLP has developed as the standard decision-making procedure. The EP has six main roles:

- to scrutinize and amend legislation, and to act as a co-decision-maker. This role has grown in importance as the range of issues subject to the OLP has increased
- since the Maastricht Treaty, to endorse the appointment of the Commission president and the other Commissioners (*en bloc*, not individually)
- to decide, together with the Council, the EU's budget
- to scrutinize the Commission
- to question the Council and Parliament
- to convene committees of inquiry.

Since 1979, the EP's powers have increased, but turnout in elections has declined. The EP claims to represent the peoples' of

Europe, but the people demonstrate only limited interest in its activities. Moreover, when EU citizens participate in EP elections, they tend to do so in national political contexts and on national political issues; i.e. the 'second order' elections problem (Reif and Schmitt, 1980). The extension of powers to the EP through use of the OLP could be a double-edged sword. The EP does have a much more significant legislative role; but, to exercise this role, the EP must often retreat into processes of conciliation and negotiation with the Council that reduce, rather than increase, the EP's ability to reach out to groups and organizations within the EU that could be affected by the legislation (Lambert and Hoskyns, 2000; Warleigh, 2003).

Since 1999, elections in Britain to the EP have used proportional representation. In 2002, the EU agreed to 'Uniform Election Procedures' for elections to the EP. These are very broad and did not actually require adjustment in any member state. They did, however, affirm that proportional representation would be the method for election to the EP, using either a list system or single transferable vote (STV).

There were British 72 MEPs returned to the EP by the June 2009 EP elections, using a single transferable vote system in 11 multi-member regions with 'closed' party lists. This number would have been 73, if the Lisbon Treaty had been ratified in time. Elections to the EP have been understood as 'second order', in that they do not change national governments and, thus, can be a useful vehicle for protest votes (Reif and Schmitt, 1980). This has given opportunities for representation to smaller political parties (such as the Greens, UKIP and the BNP) that have not secured representation in the House of Commons by the first-past-the-post system (although the Green Party did secure their first MP at the 2010 general election). In the 2009 EP elections in the UK, the Conservatives were the largest party; the eurosceptic UKIP came second, receiving 16.5 per cent of the vote. Labour trailed in third on 15.7 per cent of the vote. Table 5.4 provides full results.

Between 2004 and 2009, the combined share of the Conservative and Labour parties at the 2004 and 2009 EP elections fell to below 50 per cent. The Greens have traditionally done well in EP elections, dating back to their 1989 breakthrough when they secured nearly 15 per cent of the vote. Since 1999, support for UKIP has grown strongly, while the extreme-right BNP secured a breakthrough with two MEPs elected at the 2009 elections.

TABLE 5.4 *Results in the United Kingdom of the 2009 elections to the European Parliament*

Party	Votes	Votes (%)	MEPs
Conservative	4,198,394	27.7	26
UK Independence	2,498,226	16.5	12
Labour	2,381,760	15.7	13
Liberal Democrat	2,080,613	13.7	11
Green	1,223,303	8.6	2
BNP	943,598	6.2	2
Scottish National	321,007	–	2
Plaid Cymru	126,702	–	1
Sinn Fein	126,184	–	1
Democrat Unionist	88,346	–	1
Conservatives and Unionists	82,892	–	1

Source: Adapted from easily available data sources – see europa.eu/scadplus/constitution/doublemajority_en.htm

Despite the continued strong national component in EP elections, political parties within the EU are coalescing into transnational groupings. This has proved a troublesome issue for the Conservative Party which, as noted in Chapter 4, left the main centre-right grouping, the European People's Party (EPP), after the 2009 elections to form the European Conservatives and Reformists Group (ECRG), comprising mainly of parties from central and eastern Europe. Labour MEPs are members of the Party of European Socialists, Liberal Democrats form part of the Alliance of Liberals and Democrats for Europe. The SNP, Plaid Cymru and the Green Party all form part of the Green/European Free Alliance group, while UKIP align with the Europe of Freedom and Democracy group. The two BNP members elected in 2009 were not attached to a party grouping and, following bitter party in-fighting, were not particularly attached to each other either.

Direct representation in the EU

Until 1979, British MEPs held a dual mandate as members of both the Westminster and European parliaments. This changed after the introduction of direct election to the EP in 1979. Initially, elections to the EP were by the first-past-the-post system used for Westminster elections. A significant change occurred in 1999, when the UK moved to a proportional system for elections to the EP. One result of this was a change in ballot structure, with movement to party lists, and also in district magnitude, as large multi-member constituencies were created. Changes in ballot structure and district magnitude could then be expected to have an impact on the representative role played by MEPs. Farrell and Scully (2003) analyse the impact of these changes on British MEPs with regard to how they understand their role, the priorities that MEPs pursue, and their organization of both time and resources. A key difference between 1994 (when a modified version of first-past-the-post was used) and 1999 (when PR was introduced) was an increase in the number of parties with seats in the EP from 4 to 7. The number of women MEPs increased from 19 per cent to 25 per cent (although this was still below the EU-wide average of 33 per cent), and the number of MEPs from ethnic minority groups increased from 1 to 4. The shift to PR also has other implications for representation. The regions that were created were very large and also very diverse when compared with smaller, more territorially focused constituencies for Westminster parliament elections. Multi-member constituencies change the link between the MP and their constituents. The downside may be that the bond between representatives and constituents is broken (at least, in the sense that it is traditionally understood). However, constituents may be able to 'choose' an MEP whose political alignment is more in line with their own. In terms of the impact of this new system on the role of MEPs, Farrell and Scully (2003) find some evidence that relatively less attention is paid to constituency work and greater emphasis is placed on legislative and oversight roles within the EP. In later work, Farrell and Scully (2010: 51) find evidence of a distinct 'British effect' that they characterize as a continued focus on geographical representation by British MEPs, despite its apparent weakening by the creation of large multi-member constituencies after 1999. They argue that this 'anomaly' is likely to erode over time, which would mean greater attention being paid by British MEPs to their roles in the EP.

There is a puzzle when the formation of these transnational party groupings is assessed. Low levels of public awareness of what actually happens within the EP mean that parties are unlikely to be punished for divisions and splits. MEPs are also selected, and depend for re-selection, on national political parties. These mean that the sanctioning effects of European political groupings are limited, which raises the question of why relatively coherent transnational party groupings have formed when the incentives for doing so appear to be weak? The behaviour of MEPs has been found to be far more closely related to their party grouping than to their national origin. Noury and Roland (2002) show that there is a 90 per cent likelihood of knowing which way an MEP will vote on any particular issue as a result of their party affiliation, while their national origin gives only a 10 per cent likelihood. Put another way: 'a British Labour MEP is far more likely to vote with a French or German Social Democrat than with a British Conservative or British Liberal Democrat' (Hix *et al.*, 2009: 821). An explanation for this is that, in a complex setting such as the EP, with a wide range of policy issues under consideration, a 'division of labour contract' is established within which MEPs who share policy preferences form party groupings within which their collective expertise is shared and, thus, the costs of collecting information can be reduced (Hix *et al.*, 2009). The leadership of the party grouping can then distribute roles within the EP, issue voting instructions and seek to enforce party discipline. This type of division of labour contract reduces transaction costs for MEPs arising from complexity of the EP issue agenda and, thus, addresses a collective action problem. MEPs are likely to maintain discipline within the grouping because, if they deviate from the group's preferences on particular issues, then other group members may well no longer trust them on the issues on which they have specialist knowledge and will look to other group members instead. This means that the costs of defecting from the group's position could be high for an MEP, who may lose the benefits of group membership regarding the collecting of information and the distribution of roles within the EP.

The Court of Justice of the European Union

The CJEU has been viewed by eurosceptics in a similar light to the Commission, as an agent of integration by stealth pursuing a federalizing agenda. In contrast, pro-Europeans see the CJEU as a vital institution securing adherence to key EU goals, such as single market integration.

Supranational European integration involves the creation of a body of law at European level that overrides national law. The EU legal system and the role of the CJEU have been central to the process of supranational integration that has seen treaties agreed in public international law between states turned into laws that bind these states. This has *constitutionalized* relations between EU member states (Stone Sweet and Sandholtz, 1998). One result of this is that relations between European states have become hierarchical and rule-based. This intensive system of rule-based multilateralism is a key feature of the European legal and political order (Caporaso, 1996).

Following the rejection of the proposed Constitutional Treaty (see Chapter 4), the EU 'constitution' resides in the treaties and the legislation produced since the 1950s. There is thus a well-established legal framework at EU level stemming from the core EC purposes, which have been primarily economic and concerned with economic integration. The CJEU in Luxembourg has, therefore, been primarily involved with economic and commercial issues. This contrasts with the European Court of Human Rights (ECHR) in Strasbourg, which is an entirely separate institution attached to the intergovernmental Council of Europe. It is not uncommon for the CJEU and ECHR to be confused, but they have very different remits and exist within different kinds of legal order.

The shift towards greater competencies for the EC/EU since the 1980s has placed increased strain on the CJEU. The Court consists of 27 judges, one from each member state, and eight advocates-general. Judges are appointed by agreement of member states for a period of six years, with partial replacement every three years. The advocates-general assist the judges by analysing the arguments of parties in dispute. The increased CJEU workload led to the creation by the SEA of a Court of First Instance (renamed the 'General Court' by the Lisbon Treaty), with the power to hear and determine on points of law only and with a right of appeal to the CJEU. The General Court is not competent to hear cases brought by member states or Community institutions.

The CJEU has the following responsibilities:

- the interpretation of the Treaties through use of preliminary rulings
- to determine whether any act or omission by the European Commission, the Council or any member states constitutes a breach of EU law
- to decide on the validity and meaning of Community legislation.

There are a number of core principles of Community law.

Direct effect and supremacy
The most significant cases in this respect were van *Gend en Loos* (1963), *Costa v ENEL* (1964) and *Simmenthal* (1978). These provided that it was possible for national law to be overridden, if it conflicted with Community law. In English law, it was confirmed in 1974 by *Aero Zipp Fasteners v YKK Fasteners (UK) Ltd*. In making the judgment, Mr Justice Graham noted that, 'This [European Communities] Act to put it very shortly enacted that relevant Common Market Law should be applied in this country and should, where there is a conflict, override English law.' The *Factortame* case in 1991 affirmed the supremacy of EU law. A House of Lords ruling acknowledged that a decision of the CJEU could deny effect to an Act of Parliament. Lord Bridge noted that: 'whatever limitation of its sovereignty Parliament accepted when it enacted the European Communities Act 1972 was entirely voluntary. Under the terms of the Act of 1972 it has always been clear that it was the duty of a United Kingdom court, when delivering final judgment, to override any rule of national law found to be in conflict with any directly enforceable rule of Community law ... Thus there is nothing in any way novel in according supremacy to rules of Community law in those areas to which they apply (*R. v Secretary of State for Transport, ex parte Factortame (no.2) [1991] 1 AC 603*; see also Turpin and Tomkins, 2007).

Member state liability
Francovich (1991) established that where member states breached Community law resulting in damage to individuals, then the member state was obliged to compensate individuals for damages incurred. In *Hedley Lomas* (1996), the CJEU ruled that this was the case when member states' restrictions in breach of Community law harmed an exporter of live animals.

Rights of individuals
The CJEU has, for instance, made rulings on equal pay provided for by Article 119 of the Treaty of Rome. In *Defrenne* (1971), the CJEU ruled that all courts of member states should apply a direct effect of this principle so that all citizens could benefit from it. In the case of *Barber* v. *Guardian Royal Exchange* (1990), the CJEU extended the application of Article 119 to occupational pension schemes, and ruled that differences between men and women in

access to occupational pensions were a breach of Article 119 (this decision did not apply to state pensions).

EC freedoms

The key decision in the matter of EC freedoms was *Cassis de Dijon* (1979), which established the principle of mutual recognition and, as such, was central to the creation of the European single market. Cassis is a French liqueur, but was denied access to the German market because its alcohol content was too low, at 20 per cent, to make it a liqueur by German standards (25 per cent being the required figure). The CJEU ruled that if Cassis was legally manufactured and sold in France as a liqueur, then it could be legally sold in other member states, too. This is known as the 'principle of mutual recognition'. The importance of mutual recognition is that it removes the need for a mountain of regulations to specify product standards for all goods traded within the EC.

The CJEU has also acted to ensure that the EU's four freedoms (free of movement for people, capital, goods and services) apply to all EU citizens. This has led to action against member states and companies that have tried to circumvent Community law. *Binsbergen and Reyners* (1974) provided for the freedom to provide services and freedom of establishment. *Nouvelles Frontières* (1986) provided that EU deregulation should also apply to the air industry, and helped give rise to the low-cost airlines that have transformed air travel within the EU.

The European Council

The Lisbon treaty recognized the European Council as an official EU institution, which was confirmation of the important role played by meetings of heads of government in sketching out the Union's future direction or responding to crises. It is, in fact, this latter role that has been far more prominent as EU leaders have tried to respond to the eurozone crisis.

The European Council comprises heads of state or government, the President of the Commission and the Union's High Representative for Foreign Affairs and Security Policy. It meets at least twice a year, although in practice meets more often. The European Council was established in 1974 to provide political leadership at the highest level. The European Council is central to the 'history-making decisions', to the grand declarations, to the photo opportunities and, more recently, to the protests and massive operation that accompany any high-level political gathering. The Lisbon Treaty created the new post of President of the European Council in an attempt to impart greater political leadership. There was talk of Tony Blair taking on this job, although there was reluctance amongst some national leaders to have such a high profile politician as a potential rival at EU level. Instead, the little-known former Belgian Prime Minister Herman Van Rompuy was appointed to the role for a 30-month period, renewable once

The European Council was institutionalized in Paris in 1974, formalized by the SEA in 1986 and, with the entry into force of the Lisbon Treaty in 2009, became an official EU institution. It meets twice a year, although extra meetings can be held in the event of exceptional circumstances. The Maastricht Treaty outlined the European Council's role to: 'provide the Union with the necessary impetus for its development and shall define the general political guidelines thereof'.

Democracy and interest representation

Chapters 3 and 4 of this book looked at the representation of British interests at EU level between the 1950s and 2012. There was recognition that these interests are sometimes diffuse and that subnational government is represented in Brussels within UKRep. Party political interests are represented in the EP.

This section takes this discussion forward by looking at two key debates that are central to discussion of representative politics in the EU. The first of these is the EU's 'democratic deficit', which is the idea that power has shifted to EU level without a similar shift in scrutiny and accountability of those that exercise this power. The second is representation of non-state interests in the EU, such as agricultural interests, environmentalists, business groups and trade unions. This involves analysis of the strategic setting at EU level within which such interests are represented. Both the democratic deficit and the representation of non-state interests are key issues in British relations with the EU. Perceptions of a democratic deficit can fundamentally weaken the EU in the eyes of its citizens. Interest representation can provide provides channels for representation of non-governmental interests, such as business, trade unions and other important societal interests.

The democratic deficit

In its 'standard' version, the EU's democratic deficit is seen as having five components (Follesdal and Hix, 2006: 535–7):

- an overly powerful executive, evident through the power of the Council of Ministers
- a weak EP with only limited consultative powers
- no genuinely European elections on which EU issues are debated; instead, there are national elections joined together to elect the EP
- a lack of knowledge of and interest in the EU amongst EU citizens
- 'policy drift' at EU level as governments pursue policies, such as massive subsidies to farmers, that they would not easily be able to pursue at national level.

Since the 2000s, there has been a lively academic debate about the democratic deficit. There has been a growth in EP powers that has led to a rebalance of the legislative and executive relationship. There has also been great effort to make the EU system more transparent, with vast tracts of information now made available through the EU website and other sources. There is, however, little sign of an increased knowledge of the EU, or of greater participation in EU elections that still tend to be fought on national bases.

Challenging the conventional wisdom about the democratic deficit have been arguments that the EU is actually already as democratic as it could and should be (Majone, 2002; Moravcsik, 2002). One reason for this advanced by Majone (1996, 2002) is that much EU activity is essentially a regulatory state devoted to the correction of market failure. This gives rise to technical tasks that, in the member states, would tend to be managed by regulatory agencies, rather than be the subject of legislative scrutiny and broader public debate. Others argue that the EU has now moved into areas of greater political significance, such as economic, financial and internal security issues, that do require 'contestation for political leadership and argument over the direction of the policy agenda' (Follesdal and Hix, 2006: 534).

When the Council is in negotiating mode, secrecy could have some advantages: 'Ministers and their officials build coalitions, exercise leverage and do deals benefiting from the veil of secrecy that mostly cloaks their actions, as do ministers within national governments' (Hayes-Renshaw and Wallace, 1997: 7). When the Council is legislating, then this confidentiality can appear anomalous and, at worst, can breed suspicion or hostility. Hayes-Renshaw (1999: 40) argues that quite significant steps have been taken towards greater openness with the post-Maastricht provisions for disclosure of information and public access to Council meetings. But some core EU legislative and executive processes do remain shrouded in secrecy. In sensitive areas, such as internal security, there has been a reluctance to disclose information, although it must be said that national governments are not prone to openness in these areas either, so it is unfair to pillory the EU for failing to attain standards of which national governments also fall short.

Interest group politics

We now move on to assess interest representation and its relationship to representative politics in the EU. To use a market analogy, there is likely to be a *supply of* interests coupled with a *demand for* interests from EU level to facilitate the development of policy, as well as other policy and institutional agendas (Coen, 1997). There was an important role for interest group mobilization within neo-functional accounts of European integration because it was thought that a re-focusing of interest group activity could contribute to 'political spillover' and a consequent reinforcement of EU action. This somewhat simple mechanism does, however, need to account for the strategic institutional context at EU level and the high level of variation in interest group strategies. The EU is not a level playing field. Some groups are stronger than others and, unsurprisingly, the strongest tend to be those that are resource rich, such as in business interests. However, the point made earlier about the demand for interests can lead to the sponsoring of interest group development by the European Commission through funding. EU institutions need interlocutors, and have been prepared to fund them.

Interest group activity increased dramatically after the extension of regulatory competencies arising from the SEA (Greenwood, 2003). Specific growth areas have been enterprise and the environment, while there has also been growth in other policy areas, such as health. This extension of interest group activity also led to a focus on the Europeanization of lobbying and interest group activity (Coen, 2007). There are various arenas at EU level within which interests can be represented, and EU institutions such as the Commission are very active in creating forums or venues for dialogue with key interests (as well as deciding which interests or groups are 'key').

We have already analysed the role played by the EP in direct, electoral representation, the development of party groupings within the EP, and in changes in the representative role of British MEPs. However, there are also other ways in which interests are represented at EU level. For example, the Committee of the Regions is a basis for sub-national representation within the EU system. There is also extensive lobbying of the EU system by a wide range of private- and public-sector organizations. It is in this context that we can assess the representation of 'British interests', but also begin to see that such a term actually disguises a far more complex situation of interaction between a wide range of actors within and beyond the British political system, and actors and institutions at EU level. In fact, to talk about 'British interests' may well miss the point, as not only does the British government extensively engage with the EU, but so, too, do key interests such as business, farmers, trade unions and a vast array of other groups. (The sub-national dimension is analysed more closely in Chapter 8.) In the remainder of this section, we look at other forms of interest representation.

The EU had, from its foundation, a strong corporatist element. The Economic and Social Committee (ESC) created by the Treaty of Rome was a way of securing the representation of key societal interests – particularly business and trade unions – into a supranational body at Community/Union level with consultative powers. Farmers were also a powerful voice at EU level, with a very strong relationship with the Commission's Agriculture DG. This replicated patterns in many member states, including Britain, where the old Ministry of Agriculture was seen as the voice of the National Farmers Union (NFU). The EU is an intensely lobbied organization. In the European quarter of Brussels are offices housing all kinds of groups that are seeking to influence the EU policy agenda. The EU also provides a distinct setting for this kind of interest group mobilization. For example, the Commission has long been central to the EU policy process, although as we have also seen there have been major changes in recent years that have affected its role. However, policy proposals still largely emanate from the Commission. It makes sense for interest groups to seek to influence the Commission agenda. However, a key issue is how such groups could influence the Commission's agenda? Or, put another way, what kinds of strategies in pursuit of influence are more likely to be successful. An obvious need is to ensure that the particular interest that is being represented is one in which the EU actually has competence but, related to this, it is also important to develop a strategy that combines with key EU themes. So, for example, the EU has long sought greater competitiveness for business and industry. The Lisbon agenda sought to develop the EU as a knowledge economy, while the 2020 agenda has similar ambitions for development of the European economy. These kinds of declarations and statements of general political intention issued by EU leaders can then provide a hook for interest group campaigns as they seek to persuade the EU that their particular interest is a good way to advance the broader EU agenda. The question then becomes the kind of strategy to pursue. A key point here is the Commission's relatively small size and reliance on outside expertise, such as academic research. The Commission often depends very heavily on the highly specialized contributions to the EU policy process that may, for example, involve very detailed scrutiny of existing legal frameworks, with suggestions for their further development. One result of this is that the 'mobilization of expertise' can be a particularly useful strategy. This, then, favours groups and associations with the resources to mobilize this expertise, such as academic research in pursuit of their own interests. The result, unsurprisingly, is that rich and well-resourced groups tend to be present and relatively effective at getting their voices heard. They are also likely to 'cover the bases' by ensuring that an EU strategy is matched by similar efforts at other levels, particularly at the member state level.

A caveat can be introduced at this point. It is the case that well-resourced groups have an advantage over less well-resourced groups. However, the Commission does also play a role in stimulating interest representation that might suit its own policy plans and intentions. For example, there was debate in the 1990s about a worrying rise of racism and xenophobia in some EU member states and a need to ensure effective action to protect the rights of migrants and ethnic minorities in EU member states. The Commission funded an EU Migrants Forum (EUMF) to represent migrants and minorities (including Roma) from across the Union. It also worked closely with a broader civil society initiative, the Starting Line Group (SLG), which was created in 1991 to campaign for comprehensive anti-discrimination legislation covering measures to tackle racism and associated discrimination. Ultimately, the SLG was the more effective of the two groups. The EUMF faced difficulties aggregating highly diverse interests that were often more focused on subnational and national issues. The SLG was very closely focused on the EU level and directed its attention at the provision of the kinds of specialist expertise that the Commission valued. There was a string influence of SLG proposals in two anti-discrimination directives agreed by the Council in June and November 2000 (Geddes and Guiraudon, 2004; Geddes, 2008). There was also a distinct 'British' influence on the content of these EU measures, because they brought into EU law an emphasis on civil law remedies to tackle both direct and indirect forms of discrimination. This reflected the efforts not only of British organizations such as the Commission for Racial Equality (CRE), but also the work of UK specialists, such as academic lawyers working within European networks such as the SLG. In this case, particular interests within the British political system were mobilized at EU level and, through a targeted and quite lengthy campaign that involved the mobilization of expertise, were able to help to shape the EU policy agenda. These cannot be simply boiled down to 'national interests' because the strategies that were involved were quite issue-focused and did depend on working with like-minded groups in other member states.

Similarly, while the British government will take a generally pro-business line, the representation of business interests cannot be labelled under the heading of 'British interests'. Business interests will be sectorally focused on particular areas of the economy. They may be more or less multi-national in the scale of their operation. They may also conflict with other important societal interests, such as consumer groups or environmental interests. Coen (1997: 92) analyses the evolution of the large firm as a political actor at EU level, and shows how they have constructed alliances between each other that cross national borders and thus create a form of European identity as a basis for lobbying. Coen (1997: 96) also shows how the Commission was able to regulate access by creating various kinds of forum or club within which it was able to regulate participation and thus create 'an élite pluralist arrangement between institutions and policy actors, where a number of political channels are utilized to develop political credentials and achieve insider status'. Within this framework, the Commission must seek to maintain its credibility, while interest groups must seek to build a reputation that helps to secure their access to consultation.

This discussion of interest representation in the EU is designed to complement the discussion of formal institutional roles. It looks at how the supply of and demand for interests creates a new strategic setting at EU level that has been characterized as 'elite pluralism'. There is also high variation in levels of activity, with particularly intense engagement around well-established areas of EU competence such as enterprise and the environment. This section has also qualified the discussion of 'British interests'. It is obviously the case that British business, farmers, trade unions, environmental groups and a wide range of other groups will seek to influence the EU agenda. However, these cannot simply be represented as national interests. They are also indicative of a Europeanization of interest group activity within the EU's new strategic setting.

Conclusion

At the beginning of this chapter, two visions of the EU were contrasted. One was a state-centred view that focused on the role of national governments and the centrality of intergovernmental decision-making. Key institutions from this perspective are the Council and European Council. The other vision was of a multi-level EU within which powers are distributed across levels of governance and with the result that the EU becomes a complex arena for power-sharing among a wide range of political actors. Our assessment of the role of EU institutions allows us to contrast these visions, to see how they relate to the development of the EU institutional system and to think about their implications for British politics. There have clearly been some very important developments. The role and power of EU institutions has grown. This can be seen through increased application of the OLP and co-decision, and which changes the dynamics of decision-making in the Council through greater use of QMV. It can also be seen through the growing CJEU role linked to the developing body of EU law. However, these changes do not mean that we write national governments and member states out of the equation and focus only on 'multi-levelledness'. Member states remain core actors in the EU system, but they are not the only actors; they share power with each other and with other institutions. For a political system such as that in Britain, that was understood as unitary and centralized, it could be quite a challenge to grasp these new dynamics, although the British system has, of course, become more multi-level.

To ask whether the EU can be understood as state-centred or as multi-level may be missing the point that the EU's institutional structures are 'hybrid', in the sense that they contain both intergovernmental and supranational elements. The discussion becomes even more complex when interest representation within the EU's system of elite pluralism is factored into the analysis. While British governments have long preferred to highlight the centrality of intergovernmental institutions such as the Council and European Council, and be wary of increased powers for the Commission and the EP, it is also the case that institutional changes have contributed to the consolidation of supranational decision-making processes that could be seen to run counter to this British preference. These political and legal entanglements have developed progressively over time and are difficult to roll back. The EU institutional system has evolved into a more advanced form of supranational governance that has become part of an EU political system which also reaches into domestic politics.

This chapter has shown that British engagement with processes of institutional design and development reveals a particular and self-consciously pragmatic understanding of the limits of European integration, and a preference for intergovernmental cooperation. At the same time, analysis of these institutions also demonstrates the ways in which supranational decision-making has evolved above the nation state with law-making powers that bind participating states. This changes the nature of policy debate, as Chapters 6 and 7 now discuss.

Chapter 6

Britain and Core European Union Policies

This chapter analyses what could be called 'core', or well-established, EU policies. Some (such as the budget, CAP, the common market and social policy) were established before Britain joined. Others (such as regional development and the environment) were not in the Treaty of Rome but have become key aspects of the EU policy agenda. The chapter will assess Britain's variable role in policy design and development, and analyse effects of these policies in Britain (which now vary because of devolution). The chapter thus combines both the 'Britain in Europe' and 'Europe in Britain' themes as we begin to explore the ways in which Britain has sought to pursue its interests at EU level, and also look at how Europe hits home by affecting domestic politics.

The chapter shows there to be no typical EU policy sector. Each is shaped according to particular circumstances; notably, the amount of autonomy member states have been willing to cede by Treaty to the Union, and the configurations of institutions and interests that then develop over time in particular policy areas. Key points for consideration are not only the ways in which British governments have sought to pursue their policy preferences at EU level through negotiation with other member states and with EU institutions, but also how this developing EU framework meshes with the basic practices of policy in Britain and the ideas that inform them.

The policy areas that we analyse in this chapter tend typically to be seen as matters of 'low politics', which means that they impinge less directly on state sovereignty. The argument is that integration can be more straightforward in such areas (Hoffmann, 1966). Integration in areas of high politics such as foreign policy is then more difficult because these relate more closely to state sovereignty. While helpful as an organizing device, we can also ask whether the high-low distinction is actually so clear-cut. Indeed, in the article that made this distinction, Hoffmann (1966: 29) actually noted that issues such as foreign policy, while usually seen as high politics, might not always be so; similarly, trade and economic integration tend to be viewed as low politics, which may well not be the case during economic recessions.

Understanding policy impacts

In a language that suffuses discussion of Europeanization but that will also be familiar to the technologically-minded, EU impacts are often assessed in terms of 'uploading' and 'downloading'. This terminology is helpful because it avoids the idea that the EU and national politics are separate domains detached one from the other. This would be a complete misunderstanding of the EU and its impacts. Through analysis of policy areas, we will see how member states working with each other and EU institutions can shape or affect the development of policies at EU level – uploading their policy preferences – and subsequent impacts these policies then have once they have been downloaded into domestic systems.

An obvious and frequently made point with regard to the UK was that it was not a founder member state, with the result that key policy priorities were decided without British influence and were not necessarily in its best interests. Even as a member state, Britain has had an ambivalent relationship to policy developments in areas such as the budget, social policy, employment policy, border controls and the single currency. If Britain has been a reluctant bystander, then we could expect its influence on policy development to have been low. If EU policies do not match British preferences, then this could be a reason why Britain has been a reluctant and awkward member state.

To discuss EU policy in terms of uploading and downloading creates an appealing image that helps the intuitive grasping of a core conceptual issue in British relations with the EU; i.e. that they centre on interactions with the EU. If we extend the metaphor a little further, we also know – often from bitter first-hand experience – that computer users not only upload and download, but also have to update hardware or software. This can be a relatively trouble-free, albeit sometimes time-consuming, process. At times, it can also require a much more fundamental reboot of the system; or, even worse, the system may crash. In political terms, this points towards the importance of focusing on the organization of domestic policy processes, the ideas that animate them and their receptiveness (or not) to EU influences. For example, British governments since 1979 have responded enthusiastically to a neo-liberal agenda of deregulation and liberalization that is seen to operate at a global, rather than regional, European level. British governments have been reluctant to support EU-level regulation in areas such as employment and social policy because they see EU regulation as inimical to global competitiveness. The Conservative Party under David Cameron's leadership announced its intention to repatriate aspects of social and employment law from the EU, but this is far easier said than done.

An additional issue can also be factored into analysis, if issues of time and timing are considered; i.e. asking why developments occurred at particular points in time, as well as the impact of the steady growth of EU responsibility on the shape of domestic debate in Britain about the EU. There have clearly been pretty powerful tensions at particular points in time linked, for example, to disjunctions between the speed and direction of European integration and the attitude to these developments of British governments. This was very apparent in both the mid-1970s and mid-1990s. A further dimension of this is to relate these tensions to the growth in EU responsibilities. Debates in Britain about Europe in 1975, 1985, 1995, 2005 and 2015 will be different because the referent object – the EU itself – changes and develops. There has been a significant growth in the range of policy areas that now fall within the EU's remit, including areas that are more clearly of high politics, such as economic and monetary policy, immigration and asylum, and some aspects of foreign and security policy. These cannot be represented as largely technical issues within a limited 'regulatory state', as Majone (1996) called it. The growth of EU competencies in these areas must necessarily challenge the ways in which we think about the EU, its competencies and its effects on British politics.

The budget

> We are not asking the Community or anyone else for money, we are simply asking to have our own money back. (Margaret Thatcher, Fontainebleau summit, June 1984)

Finances are the lifeblood of any political system. We need to know how a political system is structured, but also how it is financed and resourced. The EU has two main spending areas which, put simply are: subsidies for farmers and regional development aid. Together, they account for around 90 per cent of the total EU budget. Key areas that consume the bulk of national budgets such as health, education, social security and defence are not EU responsibilities. Attached to both agriculture and regional development are powerful national and sectoral interests that make changes in the budget difficult to secure. Consequently, when David Cameron talked in 2010 and 2011 about reining in EU spending and opposing increases in the EU budget, he encountered opposition from member states that currently benefit from the system and will also look to continuing EU support in years to come. On the budget, British allies have been the Germans, Scandinavians and Dutch. Many of the newer member states in central and eastern Europe, such as Poland, that can be UK allies on other issues, are unlikely to favour cuts in EU spending.

A typical refrain of eurosceptics is that British budget contributions are high, while Britain extracts very little benefit from this contribution. Irrespective of any assessment of costs and benefits accruing from EU membership, another way of representing the overall size of the UK's EU budget contributions is by noting that they amount to under 1 per cent of Britain's gross national income (GNI). Rather like the relatively small size of the European Commission, it is useful to put the EU system in context. In 2010, for all the EU member states taken together, EU budget payments amounted to 1.04 per cent of their combined GNI. Eurobarometer polling shows that people in Britain over-estimate the size of their country's contribution to the EU budget. Not surprisingly, given that this is a rather arcane issue, there was a considerable lack of knowledge, with 38 per cent of respondents saying they did not know the scale of the contribution. Of those that did venture an estimate, the average amount of British national income that was thought to go to the EU was 19 per cent. This is a vast over-estimate. Around 75 per cent of respondents also thought that the EU's budget was bigger than that of the British government. In fact, the British government's budget is around six times larger than that of the EU (Eurobarometer, 2011: 19).

While the EU is far from being a monolith, it does possess substantial resources and growing powers. The Commission has proposed to commit around €1 trillion of resources between 2014 and 2020 to support key EU activities, such as agricultural policy, and regional economic and social development. At a time of

economic crisis and austerity, these EU efforts have rightly come
under close scrutiny, with some member states seeking much slower
growth in the budget, or even a brake on EU spending. Others have
argued that growth is necessary if the EU is to emerge stronger from
the economic crisis and maintain its commitment to regions that are
less economically-developed.

In 2010, the total EU budget in 2010 amounted to just over €120
billion. This divides between four main areas of expenditure, plus
the payment for EU administration. Table 6.1 presents an overview
of the budget process, showing as it does – reading from left to right
– the spending ceilings specified by the multi-annual framework and
then the OLP involving the Council and EP on the basis of the
Commission's proposed budget.

If we now think about the meaning of these headings, we swiftly
see two very important areas of EU action. The largest area of
expenditure comes under the heading of 'the preservation and
management of natural resources'. In fact, under this heading, direct
payments to farmers accounted for 77.5 per cent of these payments.
Rural development then consumed a further 20 per cent. In 2010,
France was the largest recipient of payments under this heading,

FIGURE 6.1 *Estimates of the percentage of the UK's Gross
National Income that goes to the EU*

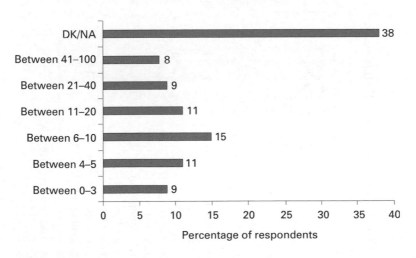

Source: Eurobarometer (2011b).

TABLE 6.1 *The EU budget, 2010 (€ millions)*

Commitment appropriations	Financial perspective ceilings	Preliminary draft budget	Council First reading, Draft Budget	EP First reading, Draft Budget	Council Second reading, Draft Budget	Adopted budget 2010	Budget 2009
Sustainable growth	63,555	62,152	62,052	64,255	63,734	64,249	62,202
Preservation and management of natural resources	59,955	59,004	58,640	59,808	59,450	59,499	56,332
Citizenship, freedom, security and justice	1,693	1,629	1,608	1,674	1,608	1,674	2,132
The EU as a global player	7,893	7,921	7,812	7,866	7,829	7,889	7,597
Administration	7,882	7,851	7,812	7,866	7,829	7,889	7,597
Compensations	0	0	0	0	0	0	209
Total commitment appropriations	140,978	138,557	137,994	141,745	140,555	141,453	136,576
Total payment appropriations	134,289	122,316	120,770	127,526	121,737	122,937	113,035
Payment appropriations as a percentage of EU GNI	1.14	1.03	1.02	1.08	1.04	1.04	0.98

Source: HM Treasury (2010: 12).

with just under €10 billion of support for its farmers. The French government – closely monitored by farmers' organizations that are quick to anger – has long opposed cuts in this area of EU activity.

The second main area of EU spending is sustainable growth, which is particularly directed towards economic and social development in Europe's poorer regions. The UK was the fifth-largest gross beneficiary in 2010, with payments of just under €4 billion. This heading does also include items such as support for research and development (€6.5 billion in 2010), but is dominated by what in EU parlance is referred to as 'cohesion' funding. Cohesion funding is aimed at stimulating economic growth and development in Europe's poorer and less developed regions. Since 2004, these resources have been increasingly directed towards newer member states in central and eastern Europe. The main beneficiary of these funds in 2010 was Poland, with nearly €8 billion. The UK was the eighth-largest net recipient of cohesion funds, with around €1.6 billion devoted to projects in less economically developed regions. To put this in perspective, these payments in the UK amounted to around 0.25 per cent of total GNI. In newer member states that joined in 2004 and 2007, their significance is far greater (e.g. 2 per cent of GNI in Lithuania and around 1.5 per cent in both Bulgaria and Latvia).

A key point in terms of the overall structure of the budget is that there has been a long-term re-balancing towards spending on regional development, or 'sustainable growth', as it is labelled. In the 1980s, agriculture consumed around 80 per cent of the total budget. It is now nearer 45 per cent – still far higher than the proportion of state budgets that would be accounted for by agricultural support, while funding on regional development (including research and development) has grown to around 40 per cent of the budget.

Having seen how the EU budget is structured, we now need to know how it is funded. Put simply, where does the EU get its money from? The obvious answer is from the member states, but it is not that simple, because the EU is not a club to which member states pay a subscription. Rather, it has a system of independent financing called 'own resources' (Laffan, 1997). This system of own resources is a key characteristic of the EU as a supranational system. A 1970 Treaty laid the foundations for the current system. The budget framework was determined before Britain joined the club and was not in the UK's interests because it favoured countries that traded more extensively with other member states (the UK had more extensive global trading links) and that had relatively inefficient agricultural sectors (the UK's was relatively efficient). The Prime Minister at the time of accession, Edward Heath, maintained that it would be better for Britain to join the EC and then try to shape it from within.

The sources of 'own resources'

A golden rule for the EU budget is that it must balance. The EU cannot run a budget deficit. Usually, it runs a small surplus. There are now three main sources of own resources. The first are labelled as 'traditional own resources' and comprise customs duty levies on imports to member states, levies on agricultural imports and sugar levies. Traditional own resources amounted to around 13 per cent of the total budget in 2011. The second source arises from a proportion of member states' sales tax (usually 0.3 per cent, although Austria, Germany, the Netherlands and Sweden contribute less). The total proportion accounted for by sales tax was around 11 per cent of the budget in 2011. A third source was added in 1988, when the EU was under pressure to make ends meet. This third source is an amount proportional to each member state's share in total EU GNI. This GNI resource amounted to 75 per cent of the total budget in 2011.

The Council and EP share decision-making authority over the budget. Until the Lisbon Treaty came into force in 2009, the Council had the final say on what was known as 'compulsory expenditure' related to original objectives set out in the Rome Treaty. This was predominantly agricultural expenditure. The EP had the final say on 'non-compulsory expenditure', in the main spending on regional development. Since 2009, the Council and EP decide together on the whole budget through negotiations that usually begin in April or May of each year, based on a proposal from the Commission.

Since 1988, the EU has also sought to put its budget system on a sounder footing by introducing longer-term financial perspectives called Multi-Annual Financial Frameworks. These are laid down in Inter-Institutional Agreements and last for seven years (e.g. 2007–2013 and 2014–20) and set out annual expenditure ceilings for each of the broad categories listed in Table 6.1.

The introduction of these multi-annual frameworks was designed to put an end to the disputes that plagued the EU budget process in the 1980s, as the institutions argued about the budget and, at times, failed to reach agreement. The 2007–13 framework, agreed during the British Council Presidency in December 2005, committed: to increase expenditure on research and development by 75 per cent; to simplify the management of cohesion funds; to stabilize spending on the CAP and rural development; to increase spending on freedom, security and justice by 15 per cent a year over the period; and that 90 per cent of the external action budget be dedicated to development assistance (HM Treasury, 2010: 5–6).

The British government and the EU budget

Figure 6.1 shows total UK contributions to the budget in 2009. These are calculated after the factoring in of Britain's budget rebate. The budget was a particular bugbear for Margaret Thatcher when she was prime minister. She was determined 'to get our money back', as she put it. In June 1984, at the Fontainebleau European Council, she secured a budget rebate. The UK is reimbursed by 66 per cent of the difference between its contribution and what it receives back from the budget. In 2010, the rebate amounted to about €4bn (HM Treasury, 2010). The UK compromised on an aspect of the budget rebate within the 2007–13 financial perspective by agreeing that it would be calculated on allocated expenditures for the EU15 (i.e. the countries that were member states prior to the 2004 and 2007 enlargements to central and eastern Europe). By 2011, expenditure in the remaining 'EU12' would be excluded from the British rebate. This effectively meant that newer, relatively poor member states would not be funding a budget rebate to a relatively rich member state.

Britain is a net contributor to the budget. Table 6.2 shows UK payments minus the rebate and the receipts from the EU budget. Although patterns can vary, Germany is the main contributor to the EU budget with Britain, France, the Netherlands and Italy also net contributors.

The British government position has two main elements: to protect the budget rebate; and to ensure tight control of EU finances, preferably with spending maintained at current or reduced levels. As noted, there was some compromise on the structure of the rebate within the 2007–13 framework. The rebate remains a UK 'red line' in EU negotiations. It is inconceivable that a British government, particularly a Conservative-led government, could concede on this issue without massive domestic political ramifications. In April 2011, David Cameron called for a freeze in the EU budget in the face

152

TABLE 6.2 *British payments, rebates and receipts from the EU budget 2004–10, € (million)*

	2004	2005	2006	2007	2008	2009	2010 (est.)
Gross payments	10,895	12,483	12,426	12,456	12,563	14,129	14,852
Less: rebate	–3,593	–3,572	–3,569	–3,523	–4,862	–5,392	–3,052
Less: receipts	–4,294	–5,329	–4,948	–4,332	–4,497	–4,398	–5,598
Net contributions to EU budget	3,008	3,581	3,909	4,601	3,294	4,339	6,272

Source: HM Treasury (2010a).

of domestic austerity and a Commission proposal for 4.3 per cent growth in EU expenditure for 2012. The *Daily Mail* was swift to report that this would take British contributions to more than £400 per household (without factoring in the rebate and receipts). The *Mail* fired a warning shot to by asking 'Was Cameron ever really a Eurosceptic?' (*Daily Mail*, 25 April 2011). The closest allies for the British on this issue were the Dutch government, but it is unlikely that budget cuts would be supported by newer member states that have benefited from EU funding directed towards their less economically developed regions. The election of François Hollande raised questions about the British rebate. Cameron had reportedly secured agreement with former President Sarkozy that Britain's budget rebate would remain in place, and that Britain would not lead attempts at CAP reform that could impact on French farmers.

Agriculture

The CAP is one of the most highly developed EU polices, while agriculture is one of the most Europeanized activities within the British government. The old Ministry of Agriculture, Food and Fisheries (MAFF) used, effectively, to conduct its own mini-foreign policy as it liaised closely with other member states on this key EU competence. Without the CAP, it is debatable whether the MAFF would have survived as long as it did (Marsh *et al.*, 2001). The BSE and foot-and-mouth disease crises dealt MAFF fatal blows and its activities were merged into the new Department for Environment, Food and Rural Affairs (DEFRA).

In the UK, the CAP has become a by-word for wastefulness and inefficiency, although significant reforms have been introduced. Domestically, the UK agricultural sector has experienced a series of crises linked, for example, to BSE and foot and mouth disease. There have also been high levels of political mobilization around a diverse array of environmental and 'countryside' issues that range from hunting to the power of the large supermarket chains. These are often not seen as EU issues; however, because agricultural policy is a core EU matter, the question needs to be asked whether the CAP is part of the solution or part of the problem for British agriculture?

CAP objectives

The CAP's establishment in 1962 and phased introduction by 1968 marked the establishment of a supranational decision-making process in an important area of economic activity. It was based on a *unified market* with free movement of agricultural products within the Common Market; *Community preference*, which means that EU agricultural products are given preference and a price advantage over imported products; and *financial solidarity*, which means that all expenses and spending that result from the application of the CAP are borne by the Community budget. Article 39 of the Treaty of Rome outlined five objectives for the CAP:

- to increase agricultural productivity
- to ensure a fair standard of living for the agricultural community
- to stabilize markets
- to ensure the availability of supplies
- to ensure reasonable prices to consumers.

These objectives were to be attained by institution of common prices for agricultural produce. Prices were decided annually by the Council of Ministers in the first half of the year, on the basis of proposals made by the Commission's agriculture Directorate General. The weakness of the system was that prices tended to be set too high, which presented farmers with a relatively inelastic demand curve (farmers effectively received the same price no matter how much they produced). This stimulated over-production, with the effect that agricultural surpluses built up and led to the infamous wine lakes, butter mountains and so on (for details, see Grant, 1997). Wastefulness, market-distorting effects, EU enlargement and the liberalization of world trade all led to pressure for change – as too did heightened consumer awareness of food safety and environmental issues, and the negative consequences of the CAP for global development, as it is essentially a protectionist and market-rigging arrangement that harms farmers in developing countries. For instance, subsidies on sugar exports by EU farmers have distorted the international terms of trade and have had negative effects on sugar producing countries such as Brazil, Malawi and Zambia.

There are, however, major difficulties with CAP reform because it is essentially an intergovernmental process within which national governments and agriculture ministries (often closely aligned with farming interests) are key players. British governments have sought CAP reform, but their efforts have been hindered by the absence of allies, as powerful member states with an interest in maintaining the CAP have worked with agricultural and farming interest groups.

The reform agenda

As the analysis of the budget showed, the proportion of the budget devoted to agriculture has declined, with more funds now devoted to social and economic development in poorer regions. There has also been pressure to stabilize the funds devoted to agricultural subsidies as it was increasingly hard to justify them, given their well-documented negative effects. However, opposition from some member states and from powerful agricultural interests have made it difficult to secure deep-seated changes. Rather, a series of measures can be identified since the 1980s that have sought to rein in agricultural expenditure and deal with some of the more serious problems. The perception of these problems has also changed. In the 1980s, over-production was top of the agenda. Now, environmental concerns, food safety and fair trade with developing countries are seen as equally, if not more, important.

The Commission's Agenda 2000 document called for a new decentralized model of agriculture that would, in theory, give member states the ability to settle issues for themselves by taking better account of a particular sector or local conditions, although the Commission warned that this should not go so far as to re-nationalize agricultural policies. Commission proposals of March 1998 sought further price cuts; increased use of direct payments to farmers managed by national governments; simplification of the rules; the reinforcement of action on the environment, with current aid linked to less-intensive farming methods; and rural development as a 'second pillar' of the CAP, backed by funding for rural development schemes. It was difficult for the member states to agree on substantive change to the CAP at the 1999 Berlin summit because of French sensibilities in light of the impending 2001 presidential elections. Discussion of substantive reforms was effectively postponed until 2005.

In its mid-term review of the Agenda 2000 reform agenda, the Commission proposed a further CAP makeover (CEC 2002). Key elements were 'decoupling' (which means cutting the link between production and direct payments) and better monitoring of compliance (which means that payments are made conditional on environmental, food safety, animal welfare and occupational safety standards). The key point with these proposals, as with all others, is that they are subject to the Council of Agriculture Ministers, from which it has been difficult to secure support for substantive reform. A quick look at the political context in the member states illustrates some of the broader problems with substantive change. President Chirac in France and the centre-right government elected in 2002 were unwilling to upset farming interest groups and opposed radical changes. Changes were also delayed prior to 2002 because of looming German federal elections that could have seen the return to power of the Christian Democrats, which has traditionally been linked to farming interests. The 2001 elections in Italy also saw a change from a green to an extreme right agriculture minister in the new Berlusconi government who moved the Italian government into the anti-reform camp. There was also some reduction in pressure on the EU to get its own house in order when US President Bush signed the Farm Bill, which greatly increased subsidies to US farmers.

Since 2005, there has been a major shift in the CAP. The old production model of subsidies created by the Treaty of Rome led to huge surpluses and has now been replaced by direct payments known as Single Farm Payments, distributed by member state governments that are not tied to production. The transition to this system began before the 2004 enlargement because the old production mode would have led to incentives to over-production in new member states that could have led to unsustainably high levels of CAP expenditure, as well as mountains of waste.

Britain and the CAP

British governments have long sought CAP reform but have met opposition from powerful vested interests. However, as noted, there has been reform motivated by a range of factors, including the economic and environmental unsustainability of the production model in an enlarged EU.

Sectoral woes in the UK have been compounded by major crises caused by the BSE crisis in 1996, and the outbreak in 2005 of foot-and-mouth disease. In March 1996, following the announcement of a possible link between a cattle disease (BSE) and its human equivalent (Creutzfeldt-Jakob disease), the Commission imposed a complete ban on the export from the UK of cattle and beef products such as gelatine. The British government took the Commission to the CJEU but, in May 1996, the Court upheld the Commission's ban. The Florence European Council of June 1996 put in place a timetable for lifting the ban, including the slaughter of an estimated 85,000 animals aged over 30 months and deemed at risk because of their association with infected cattle. The effects on the UK beef industry were substantial. In 1995, Britain exported beef worth £594 million and live calves (another very controversial issue because of the animal rights implications of transporting live animals) worth £73 million. It was reported that, between 1996 and 1998, some 1,000 jobs were lost and that the ban had cost £1.5 billion, including government eradication measures. In June 1998, the Commission recommended that the export ban be lifted for de-boned beef from cattle aged 6–30 months and born after 1 August 1996. Exports from Northern Ireland had been allowed to recommence from 1 June 1998, although the French authorities continued to block UK beef exports until October 2002. A further foot-and-mouth outbreak began in February 2001. The Commission imposed an immediate ban on the movement of animals susceptible to foot-and-mouth, which led to further devastation in the UK agricultural industry coupled with the effective closure of the countryside in large parts of the country, which hit tourism hard.

A report prepared for the government on the future of British agriculture by Sir Don Curry indicates important strands in official UK thinking on the CAP (Curry, 2002). The report was damning of the CAP, which it saw as dividing producers from their market, distorting price signals and masking inefficiencies (Curry, 2002: 20). The report proposed the removal of market price support and production controls, and called for a reduction in direct payments and 'decoupling', with direct payments untied from production. To promote the economic development of rural communities, the Curry report called for the transfer of resources from Pillar I of the CAP (subsidies to farmers) to Pillar II (support for rural development and environmental protection).

There has been CAP reform. It is also interesting to consider the ways in which the changing allocation of responsibility within the UK political system since devolution in 1999 has affected the CAP. The UK government represents British interests in Europe, but operational powers in the area of agricultural policy are devolved to Scotland, Wales and Northern Ireland. There were, for example, sharp divisions between the Scottish National Party (SNP) government in Edinburgh and the UK administration in January 2011, when the Scottish Rural Affairs Secretary, Richard Lochhead, sharply criticized UK government policy and argued for more direct support for farmers. The Scottish government commissioned the Brian Pack Inquiry to look at the future of the CAP and its implications for Scotland. The Pack Inquiry developed a very different vision of the future of the CAP to the one being espoused by the UK coalition government. Scotland, however, does not operate its own EU policy and must seek to influence UK policy, as must the Welsh and Northern Irish governments.

A key issue for the Conservative–Liberal Democrat coalition was the future of agriculture in the context of the 2014–2010 Multi-Annual budget framework. The financial framework proposes to reduce agricultural spending from 39 to 36 per cent of the total budget. In an October 2011 report, the Commission proposed a series of measures designed to promote greater income convergence between farmers in the pre-2004 EU15 and those from the 12 member states that joined in 2004 and 2007. This would include measures to limit payments to richer and larger-scale producers. In addition, around 30 per cent of direct payments would be linked to 'greening' measures, such as maintaining permanent pastures and diversifying production. The DEFRA Secretary of State, Caroline Spelman, argued that the measures did not go far enough in cutting back on direct subsidies and promoting environmentally-sustainable farming. She also argued that the UK needed to speak with one voice on these issues and made this point by attending the November 2011 Agriculture Council, meeting with ministers from the Welsh and Scottish governments and the Northern Ireland executive.

The Single Market

We now assess a policy area in which the UK has positively engaged with European integration. Single market integration meshes with UK preferences for deregulated, flexible and liberalized economies. Chapters 3 and 4 showed how Conservative governments of the 1980s, New Labour governments between 1997 and 2010, and the Conservative–Liberal Democrat coalition have all seen the single market as a key argument for British membership. In his Mansion House speech in November 2011, David Cameron argued that the single market was a key reason for British EU membership. He argued that, if Britain were to leave the EU, then it would lose the ability to shape the single market and perhaps see a retreat or roll-back from the kinds of liberalization that the British government wants to see. Cameron went on to say that:

> Outside, we would end up like Norway, subject to every rule for the Single Market made in Brussels but unable to shape those rules. And believe me: if we weren't in there helping write the rules they would be written without us – the biggest supporter of open markets and free trade – and we wouldn't like the outcome. (David Cameron, 2011, Speech at the Lord Mayor of London's banquet)

The organization of the single market

The Treaty of Rome provided for the creation of a 'common market' based on the free movement of goods, persons, services and capital. The creation of the single market after 1987 was a progressive extension of the idea of the common market, in the sense that the SEA provided for the creation of a single market defined as an area without internal frontiers within which the free movement of people, services, goods and capital would be assured.

The UK Conservative government led by Margaret Thatcher was favourable to the single market project, but did not agree that such measures would require major institutional changes or further policy integration. For the British government, the single market was an end in itself, not a means to an end. Figure 6.2 shows how an initial point of intergovernmental preference convergence around the terms of the SEA soon turned into divergence as the expansive post-SEA agenda developed, and the EC discussed ambitious plans such as EMU and a strengthened social dimension. The significant point is that this gap between more limited UK preferences and the plans of other key EC member states and EC institutions, particularly the European Commission, was filled by the development of Conservative euroscepticism.

Main features of the single market

The SEA contained both policy and institutional reforms. As well as putting in place a timetable for the realization of free movement, it also sought to establish more efficient decision-making processes. It did so by extending the use of QMV in the Council, with exceptions for sensitive areas such as taxation, free movement of people (affecting immigration policies) and the rights of employed people (affecting trade union rights). The White Paper also set a target date of 31 December 1992 for completion of the single market. Not all measures were attained by this date but there was substantial movement towards the completion of the single market.

The single market centres on the 'four freedoms': free movement for goods, people, services and capital, and these will now be considered in turn.

- *Free movement for goods* involves the abolition for trade within the single market of customs duties and charges. The CJEU has played an important part in ensuring that trade regulations in member states do not hinder, either directly or indirectly, intra-Community trade. The 1985 White Paper also proposed the removal of physical barriers (border and customs checks).
- *Free movement for persons* is a sensitive issue because, while allowing nationals of member states to live and work in other member states, the measure also affects national immigration policies. Nationals of other member states have a right to move freely within the EU, subject to only very limited restrictions.

FIGURE 6.2   *Preference divergence and the political space for euroscepticism in the late 1980s*

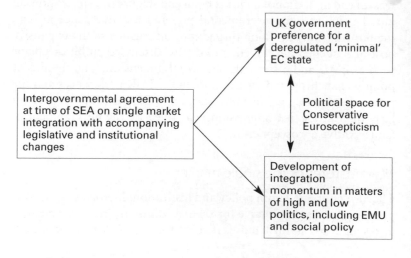

Article 39 of the Treaty of Rome provided that the 'freedom of movement for workers shall be secured within the Community'; this involves 'the abolition of any discrimination based on nationality between workers of the Member States as regards employment, remuneration and other conditions of work and employment'. The CJEU has been active in ensuring that Article 39 is applied broadly, and has extended the principle of freedom of movement to persons seeking employment – subsequently extended to other categories, such as retired people.

- *Free movement for services* is linked to the right of establishment; i.e. Community nationals or Community businesses are given equal treatment when operating in other member states. The right of establishment also allows self-employed persons and Community businesses to set up and perform their activity in another member state. UK governments have been keen to see deregulation applied to the banking and insurance sectors, too, because of UK strength in the financial services industry.
- *Free movement for capital* involves the prohibition of restrictions on capital movements (investments) and on payments (payment for goods or services).

A key issue that also needed to be dealt with was product standards. If there were differing standards in each member state, then how could there be free circulation of goods? The key development that resolved this issue was the *Cassis de Dijon* case of 1979. Cassis is a blackcurrant liqueur made in the eponymous French city. The German authorities argued that the alcoholic content was too low for cassis to be classified as an alcoholic drink in Germany. The CJEU ruled that, if cassis were lawfully made and sold in France, then the same should apply in Germany. So, rather than the EC having to specify standards for every conceivable product and then harmonize them across the single market, it was able to rely on the principle of mutual recognition. The same principle of mutual recognition has been applied to services, although this application of what is known as the 'country of origin' principle became a highly controversial component of the 2006 Services Directive, as discussed in the next section. A key point here is that mutual recognition has been 'managed' to contain its effects, meaning that 'regulatory competition did not lead to consumer confusion and a general downgrading of standards' (Nicolaïdis and Schmidt, 2007: 721).

Britain and the single market

British governments have continued to emphasize the benefits that business gains from the single market. From documents released by the Treasury in 2010 in response to a Freedom of Information request, it is possible to obtain estimates of the effects of single market integration on the British economy. The Treasury estimated that membership in 1973 boosted British trade within the EC by 7 per cent and that this outweighed any trade diversion effects. The creation of the single market in 1986 was calculated to have boosted British trade with the EC/EU by 9 per cent, although this was seen as a conservative estimate. The Treasury also calculated further beneficial effects arising from the removal of trade barriers, although these would be more difficult to quantify. The Treasury identified continued barriers to trade in services and agriculture as key areas in which they would like to see further liberalization.

The Department for Business Innovation and Skills (BIS) argued that the effects of the single market on the UK economy have been profound. In its submission to the House of Lords Inquiry into the Single Market, BIS argued that: 'EU countries trade twice as much with each other as they would do in the absence of the single market programme. Given that, according to the OECD, a 10 percentage point increase in trade exposure is associated with a 4 per cent rise in income per capita, increased trade in Europe since the early 80s ... may be responsible for around 6% higher income per capita in the UK'. BIS calculated that 3.5 million jobs in the UK were linked directly or indirectly to the UK's trade with the EU, based on the assumption that the share of UK employment linked to trade with the EU is equal to the share of total UK value added generated in the production of goods exported to the EU. BIS also calculated that around 31 per cent of regulations in the UK are EU-sourced and that this amounted to a 'cost' of between €8.6 billion and €9.4 billion (HM Treasury, 2011), although there would be debate about whether these are costs for business or protections for workers, the environment and so on. Generally, within the British government there is a more liberal approach to regulation that does not always tally with the EU approach. This means that British governments have often called for a lighter regulatory touch at EU level, but this has not found favour with other EU member states.

As the final point illustrates, these statistical estimates of the effects on the UK economy of single market regulation also become tied up with specific ideas and arguments about competitiveness, regulation and economic reform that are strongly related to domestic debate in Britain. The basic parameters of this debate were not questioned by New Labour between 1997 and 2010, which pursued market liberalization with the same vigour as its Conservative predecessors and Conservative-Liberal Democrat successor. Single market integration is one of the few areas in which British governments have maintained a consistent set of preferences and also been consistently positive about EU membership.

David Cameron has argued that there needs to be stronger EU effort to liberalize service industries such as telecommunication and energy, both of which were privatized by the Conservative governments in the 1980s. Ambitious plans for economic reform were part of the Lisbon Agenda agreed by Heads of Government in 2000. The aim of the Lisbon Agenda was to make the EU the world's leading knowledge-based economy by 2010. The difficulties developing an ambitious agenda of economic reform were illustrated by the Services Directive proposed by the Commission in 2004 and only agreed in a much watered-down form in 2006. Most controversial was the proposal to apply the 'country of origin' principle established by the *Cassis de Dijon* ruling to service provision. This had already caused controversy in the 1990s when, under free movement provisions for the self-employed, builders employed from Britain and Portugal in Germany were seen as under-cutting German workers. After the 2004 enlargement, the fear was that workers would be undercut by cheap labour from new member states able to move within the EU and take up employment opportunities. In France, the idea of Polish plumbers moving to France and stealing the jobs of French plumbers became a feature of debate about the Bolkestein directive, as it was named, after the Commissioner responsible for its development. The apparent onward march of the horrors of 'Anglo-Saxon' capitalism became part of French domestic debate about the EU constitution. This was the opposite of right-wing eurosceptic debate in Britain that preferred to cast the EU as an unwieldy vehicle for stultifying over-regulation. In its final watered-down form, the Services Directive stated that it did not affect national labour laws and also excluded a wide range of service industries including broadcasting, health care and postal services. The principle of mutual recognition had been 'managed'.

FIGURE 6.3   *British trade with the EU and the rest of the world (2010, £ billion)*

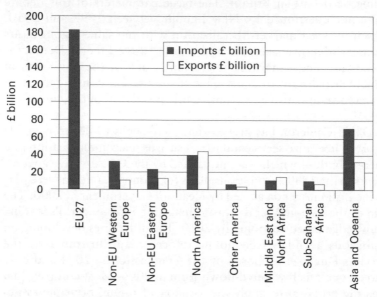

Source: HM Revenue and Customs information.

Eurosceptics argue that the advantages of the single market would accrue whether or not the UK was an EU member. A key issue is whether or not a credible alternative scenario can be identified, or whether going it alone Norway-style is a plausible option for Britain. Britain could remain in the European Economic Area (along with Norway), which is closely linked to the EU single market. Perhaps, too, as the world's seventh-largest economy (in 2012), the UK has nothing to fear from a go-it-alone strategy? The comparison with Norway and Switzerland as though they are free from the EU and its rules and regulations, but able to benefit from its key features such as the single market, is misleading. Both Switzerland and Norway are extensively engaged with the EU and subject to EU rules, but have no say in the rule-making. For example, Norway as a member of the European Economic Area does have access to the single market and is subject to a range of associated rules on, for example, social policy. It also makes a contribution to the EU budget. Switzerland, too, is integrated within the set of rules that constitute the EU single market and, unlike Britain, is also a member of the Schengen framework for passport-free travel. It is difficult to imagine the UK being able to exit the EU, retaining single market access but not being subject to the rules that govern the single market (Springford, 2012). Although within the EU, Britain is part of the world's most powerful economic bloc. It has also been argued that the UK could position itself as a low regulation, privatized economy on the edge of the EU and become a magnet for inward investment (Gamble, 1998). Despite the deep rift in Britain's relationship with other member states, caused by the veto exercised at the December 2011 European Council summit, David Cameron has argued that the UK cannot go it alone, that it cannot be compared to Norway and that British economic interests depend on trade with EU member states and being able to shape the EU single market from within. Cameron's argument is that more needs to be done, and that the EU needs to pursue further liberalization, particularly in services.

It is this wider debate about the appropriate balance between states and markets, and on the features of European models of capitalism – and their sustainability – that informs debate about single market integration. It would be wrong to reduce the single market to a narrow debate about legal and technical provisions. For example, the Services Directive 'meant different things to different people: a crucial test for the Commission's liberal agenda as well as for the left's "social Europe"; the promise of a better life for service workers from the East, the threat to a way of life for unions in the West' (Nicolaïdis and Schmidt, 2007: 717).

Structural funds to promote social and economic cohesion

We now analyse the EU role in economic and social development through what is known as 'structural funding'. Structural funds include regional economic development funding, as well as the European Social Fund (ESF) and some support for agricultural areas. Structural funding is designed to reduce disparities between regions within the EU. It is also based on a notion of distributive solidarity that crosses state borders.

The total allocated to structural funding across the EU in the Inter-Institutional Agreements for 2007–13 was €308 billion, of which the UK received €10.6 billion allocated across three objectives:

• Regional Competitiveness and Employment, with a total allocation to the UK for 2007–13 of €7 billion.

- Convergence objective (total allocation to the UK in 2007–13 of 2.7 billion) that seeks to improve growth and development in the least-developed regions where Gross Domestic Product (GDP) is below 75 per cent of the EU average – in the UK, Cornwall and the Isles of Scilly and West Wales and the Valleys had Convergence status.

- European Territorial Cooperation programmes (€722 million in 2007–13) to support cross-border, trans-national and inter-regional cooperation, and harmonious and balanced development of the European territory – an example of this is the Two Seas programme funded to the tune of €167 million to bring together the South West, South East and East of England, the coastal (Channel, North Sea) parts of France, Flanders and the Netherlands in a collaboration aiming at building an economically competitive, attractive and accessible area, promoting and enhancing a safe and healthy environment, and improving the quality of life.

The development of cohesion policy

There were no regional development provisions in the Treaty of Rome. The origins of regional development policy can be traced to the Paris summit meeting of 1972 and the decision to create the European Regional Development Fund (ERDF). The ERDF was activated in 1975 on a quota system, with Italy taking 40 per cent of the funding (the UK received 28 per cent). The principle of additionality also applied, which meant that national funds were required to match those coming from the EC (Bache, 1998).

From 1988 onwards, the EC began to play a much more active role in pursuit of social and economic development in less-developed regions, as marked by an increased allocation within the budget to structural funds, including the ERDF, from just over 10 per cent at the end of the 1980s to around 40 per cent at the time of writing. In the 1980s and 1990s, the bulk of regional and social structural funds was directed towards member states in southern Europe and to Ireland. In the early 1990s, a specific cohesion fund was created to fund programmes in Greece, Ireland, Portugal and Spain. Since 2004, there has been a redirection towards new member states in central and eastern Europe. The development of this regional dimension was seen to herald new forms of multi-level politics, perhaps within some kind of federal Europe with power and authority allocated across tiers of government (sub-national, national and supranational).

There has been much discussion of the ways in which the British political system did not fit with this vision of a multi-level EU (Bache, 1998). For beleaguered non-Conservative local authorities, the EU offered the prospect of influence denied to them in national politics. The Commission was keen to encourage local and regional involvement in EU politics, including the creation of the Brussels-based Committee of the Regions by the Maastricht Treaty. Sub-national mobilization at EU level is a normal feature of politics in countries with stronger sub-national and local government, such as Germany and Spain. There have also been important changes in the UK with devolution of powers to Scotland, Wales and Northern Ireland (see Chapter 8, for fuller discussion). However, the UK government still leads on EU policy, and will define the UK position on the budget and subsequent negotiation of spending priorities.

Devolution affects the delivery of structural funding in the UK. Overall management is the responsibility of BIS. Delivery of specific programmes occurs through the Department for Communities and Local Government (DCLG) in England, through the Scottish and Welsh governments and the Northern Ireland executive.

At UK level, the Department for Work and Pensions (DWP) has overall responsibility for the ESF, which supports both the Regional Competitiveness and Employment and Convergence objectives of structural funding. ESF programmes are managed in England by the DWP, by the Scottish and Welsh governments and the Northern Ireland executive.

While regional economic development has become more impor-tant, there is little to suggest that social policy has been a core EU priority. The EU is not a welfare state as we would recognize this term in the member states. It does not have responsibility for core welfare state functions such as education, health and employment-related benefits. Majone (1996) characterized EU social policy as a regulatory social policy designed to correct market failures. To the extent to which it has been evident in the Lisbon process and the more recent 2020 agenda, it is more in terms of a focus on 'produc-tive' (getting people back to work), rather than 'protective' (reduc-ing poverty), activities (Daly, 2006). Streeck (2001: 26) calls this 'competitive solidarity', which means that, rather than decommodi-fying – reducing people's reliance on the market – the Lisbon Process and associated EU actions create new opportunities for commodification. The various EU documents that often express their commitment to social policy tend to do so in ways that interchangeably refer to terms such as 'social cohesion', 'poverty' and 'social inclusion/exclusion' that, as Daly (2006: 468) puts it: 'are from different intellectual universes and spell quite different approaches to social policy'.

Despite this limited and market-serving role for EU social policy, debates on the eurosceptic right in Britain have sometimes seemed to represent it as one step removed from Leninism. After 1988, the development of EU social policy came to symbolize Thatcherite resistance to European integration. Thatcher characterized EU social policy as inspired by Marxist ideas about class warfare, while the Tory tabloids directed their ire at Commission president Jacques Delors as the harbinger of what they saw as an integrated EU economy suffocated by Brussels red tape. Even today, for Conservative eurosceptics, EU social and employment polices exemplify EU over-regulation and the need to roll back EU law through repatriation of powers to the EU, or even more drastic remedies such as withdrawal.

When the UK joined the EC in 1973, there were social policy provisions contained in Articles 118–23 of the Treaty of Rome to which Britain became subject. This included a commitment to gender equality and the creation of a European Social Fund. Plans to further develop these social policy competencies occurred after the SEA. The Social Charter of 1989 was a non-binding declaration but, even so, the British government refused to sign. The Charter crystallized divisions between the British Conservative government and other member states. The British Prime Minister, Margaret Thatcher, saw in the Social Charter not the moderation of mainstream European Christian Democracy, but remnants of Britain's old system of industrial relations with 'beer and sandwiches' for trade union leaders at 10 Downing Street. She was not prepared to invite union leaders in through the front door of Number 10 and was determined that they would not gain entry through a 'back door' opened by Brussels. For this reason, British trade unions cast off their previous hostility to European integration (understood as a capitalist club that offered little to workers) and, instead, began to extol the virtues of integration. This process was accelerated by a speech made to the 1988 Trades Union Congress (TUC) conference by the Commission's President, Jacques Delors, who called on British trade unions to be active in the construction of a more closely integrated Europe. Delors' presence at the TUC conference and his message to the assembled trade unionists enraged Margaret Thatcher, and damaged relations between her and the Commission President (Rosamond, 1998).

John Major followed the line of his predecessor by opposing any extension of Community social policy. Major secured an opt-out from Maastricht's Social Chapter. The result of British opposition to extended social policy competencies was that the Social Chapter, embodying many rights outlined in the non-binding Social Charter, became an agreement between the other 11 members.

The Amsterdam Treaty added a new Title VII covering employment to the Treaty of Rome, while the promotion of employment was added to the list of Community objectives as a 'matter of common concern' (Article 2 of the EC Treaty). The new objective consists in reaching a 'high level of employment' without undermining competitiveness. In order to attain this objective, the Community is given responsibility to complement the activities of the member states, involving the development of a 'coordinated strategy' for employment. The Amsterdam Treaty extended QMV, although social security remained subject to unanimity and levels of pay remained excluded from EU competence. The Nice Treaty made little substantive change to social policy. The Lisbon Treaty was more significant. Lisbon added four new objectives to the Treaty: full employment and social progress; the fight against social exclusion and discrimination; the promotion of justice; and the eradication of poverty. The Charter of Fundamental Rights was made binding (see Chapter 4, for discussion of how a British opt-out limits the Charter's domestic effects in the UK) and affects issues such as the freedom to choose an occupation and the right to engage in work, collective bargaining rights and protection from unfair dismissal. The UK government has secured a protocol to the Charter of Rights that greatly waters down its effects. The Labour government was concerned that application of the Charter by the British courts could force changes to labour laws. The protocol specifies that the charter does not extend the ability of the CJEU to find that UK laws are inconsistent with fundamental rights and does not create 'justiciable rights applicable to the United Kingdom' (House of Lords, 2008).

These developments help us to contextualize the decision by Tony Blair's Labour government to opt back into EU social policy following their election in June 1997. The extent and impact of EU social policy interventions had been considerably exaggerated during the 1980s and 1990s, and there has been little evidence that opting into the Social Chapter has sent the UK economy into a downwards spiral. Lax regulation of financial services was vastly more damaging. During its time in office, New Labour remained fixed on pursuit of an economic reform agenda for Europe that matched key components of UK 'modernization'. The 'productive', rather than 'protective', focus of EU social policy actually fitted well with New Labour's plans for 'modernization' of the British welfare state.

Environmental policy

While there was no mention in the Treaty of Rome of environmental policy, it has become a more 'mature' policy area, with QMV used for decision-making since the 1980s and six Environmental Action programmes forming the basis for policy. The environmental policy agenda is broad, ranging from water and air pollution to issues that have recently ascended the policy agenda, such as genetic modification and biofuels. Environmental policy is a classic 'trans-boundary' issue with interdependence between member states and where there is a strong argument for common policies. An average EU citizen uses four times more resources than someone in Africa or Asia, but half as much as someone in the USA, Canada or Australia. The location of the challenge is strongly focused on urban areas within which reside 75 per cent of the EU's population (projected to rise to 80 per cent by 2020).

An initially sceptical and defensive reaction from British governments in the 1970s and 1980s (Golub, 1996) has been subsumed by the sheer weight of EU policies and initiatives. This has meant greater emphasis on the codification of legal standards and the clearer formulation of national policy in response to EU standards, CJEU decisions and Commission enforcement. All have intensified the pressure to adapt to EU-wide standards, e.g. in areas such as water quality standards.

Environmental policy was an issue that ascended the EU agenda in the 1970s, reflective of the increased concern about 'post-material' quality of life issues. Environmental policy was formalized as an EU competence by the Maastricht Treaty, while Amsterdam enshrined the principle of sustainable development (Lenschow, 2001). This sustainability approach informed the Cardiff process (named after the European Council meeting at which it was agreed). This sought to integrate environmental concerns across a wide range of EU activities (e.g. trade, development and agriculture) so that sustainability was 'mainstreamed'. This pursuit of Environmental Policy Integration has become a cornerstone of green thinking, but has encountered operational difficulties putting it into effect in the complex EU system (Jordan and Lenschow, 2010).

The Sixth Environmental Action Programme (EAP) (2002–12) was the first to be decided by co-decision between the EP and Council. Six priority areas were identified: air, pesticides, waste prevention and recycling, natural resources, soil, marine environment, and urban environment. The Sixth EAP was informed by the looming 2004 enlargement, which raised the question of how the EU would reconcile the commitment to sustainability with the accession of 10 new member states that have undergone economic and political transformations, and within which the environment has not always been a top priority. The attitudes that these new member states will adopt – would they be leaders or laggards? – was an important question (Jordan and Fairbrass, 2001).

In relation to climate change, the Sixth EAP was overtaken by events. For example, the Stern Review (2007) for the UK government had a major effect on attitudes to climate change and helped to build the case for action. At EU level, the 2007 Climate and Energy Package set 2020 targets for reduced greenhouse gas emissions, increased use of renewable energy and energy efficiency. The EU Emissions Trading Scheme set up in 2005 put a price on carbon. There were also increased efforts in the area of adaptation policy. Overall the EU was expected to meet the Kyoto Protocol target of reducing emissions by 8 per cent by 2012 (CEC, 2011).

The result is that British environmental policy cannot be understood without reference to the EU. In the 1990s, Lowe and Ward (1998) showed how British environmental policy since the 1970s had gone from being largely driven by domestic concerns to one that was Europeanized in key respects. EU impacts on British environmental policy will be strongly influenced by national administrative traditions and structures. Knill and Lenschow (1998: 597) argued that pressure for change arising from EU action needs to be related to the national political context. In Britain, they described the context in the area of environmental policy as a preference for flexible policy instruments with a pragmatic style preferring consensual and informal relationships.

The effects on British environmental policy tend to differ by sector. Some areas (such as land use planning, housing and local government finance) remain largely untouched by the EU, while others (such as water quality) are extensively Europeanized, with prescriptive Europe-wide standards to be enforced at national level. The impact of the EU on environmental policy-making was to 'break open' the pre-existing policy community. Responsibility also shifted away from local government (which did have prime responsibility for implementation) towards other public bodies, including central government and agencies. Many of these groups then act almost as pressure groups at EU level, pursuing a 'British' agenda. The nature of the British agenda has also been challenged by devolution. DEFRA – with its combined agriculture and environment brief – has changed its modus operandi in order to ensure extensive consultation with the Scottish and Welsh governments and the Northern Ireland executive (James, 2011: 97).

An overall effect of Europeanization has seen standards rise as a result of EU obligations, although benefits in some areas are offset by costs in others, such as the detrimental effects of the CAP. The UK has moved, since the 1970s, from a defensive and sceptical posture, and the stigma of being labelled the 'dirty man of Europe', to a more pro-active and policy-shaping role.

Conclusion

This chapter has explored Britain's differential engagement with core EU policies and suggested that we need to pay attention to the features of EU policies, variation by sector, the factors that have influenced British governmental preferences and the impact on the British political system. Almost all aspects of domestic policy now possess a European dimension. We explored the capacity of UK governments to shape the EU agenda. Britain could be a 'pace-setter', 'foot-dragger' or 'fence-sitter' (Börzel, 2002: 196–208). Pace-setting involves attempts actively to shape the EU agenda, and presupposes well-established national policy preferences and the capacity to push them through. In the area of single market integration, the UK can be seen as a consistent pace-setter, although not all member states will be keen to follow the UK down the road to market liberalization. The UK has tended to be either a foot-dragger where it has resisted integration, or a fence-sitter, neither taking the lead nor actively resisting. In some areas, such as the CAP, the UK has been a thwarted advocate of reform when other member states have been foot-draggers. In addition to this, the UK has also opted out of various EU policies (the eurozone and Schengen are two prominent examples. Opt-outs accommodate UK preferences, but also the preferences of other member states that want to push ahead. These tensions have inhibited the capacity of European integration to become fully embedded as a constitutive component of the interests, preferences and identities of key political actors in Britain. This will become even more clear in Chapter 7, in which the effects of European integration on areas of 'high politics' are examined.

Chapter 7

Britain and the EU's Move into High Politics

This chapter analyses policy areas that can all be understood as 'high politics' and that relate very directly to state sovereignty. The Maastricht Treaty of 1992 pioneered this move into high politics and in Britain (as in other member states) it also led to more public debate about European integration. First, EMU and the creation of the euro are analysed. How and why was the eurozone built? Why did Britain choose not to replace sterling with the euro, and is there any chance that Britain will join the euro? What were the origins and effects of the post-2008 financial crisis and subsequent politics of austerity that have shaken the EU to its core? The chapter then assesses EU action on internal security, including migration, asylum and police cooperation. It asks why EU states have taken action in areas that relate so closely to national sovereignty? Why has Britain stood aside from the Schengen area's removal of border controls for travel within the EU? Focus then shifts to foreign, security and defence policy. We see that the EU has been able to develop common structures in areas that are closely related to state sovereignty. We also see that Britain has tried to take on a leading role within the EU, but under certain conditions. Britain and France are Europe's leading military powers. Both countries have nuclear weapons and a permanent seat on the UN Security Council. Working with France, Britain has taken initiatives to develop Europe's defence and security capacities, albeit that these are located within the US-led NATO alliance. When it came to the crunch in Afghanistan after 9/11 and, more importantly, Iraq after 2003, Britain sided with the USA.

The picture presented in this chapter is of the difficulties that Britain has had engaging with EU moves into areas of high politics. This should hardly be a surprise, given the analysis in Chapter 6 of Britain's often difficult relationship with core EU policy concerns.

The key defining issue that will shape the EU is the fate of the euro-zone, and it is to this that we turn first.

Economic and Monetary Union

The creation of an EMU and the euro has had, and will continue to have, huge implications for the British economy and political system. On 16 September 1992, sterling's ejection from the ERM shattered the reputation for economic competence of the Conservative government and ignited tumultuous conflict within the Party about the EU that toxified the Conservative brand and contributed to Conservative defeats at the 1997, 2001 and 2005 general elections (Geddes and Tonge, 1997, 2002, 2005). David Cameron was elected Party leader on a eurosceptic platform, including a pledge to leave the EPP. Cameron was also determined to re-connect with voters by 'modernizing' the Conservative Party. Tim Bale (2010: 378–9) writes that Cameron was fortunate when he became Party leader in 2005 because: 'the heat ... appears to have gone out of the [European] issue [because of] the realization that this country is unlikely to adopt the euro and the obstacles faced by the Lisbon Treaty has put Europe where it has long been for most of the electorate, if not most of the Conservative Party – namely, way down their list of priorities'.

By 2011, the heat was back on after 81 backbench Conservative MPs defied Cameron to vote in favour of a referendum on Britain's EU membership; *The Economist* characterized David Cameron as a 'Eurosceptic mugged by reality'. Cameron continued to argue in favour of EU membership, but it is abundantly clear that Britain would not replace sterling with the euro under governments led by any of the main political parties. To even suggest such a course would be to attract ridicule. By 2012, the Conservative Party was resolutely eurosceptic, while Labour had more pro-EU instincts, but also ruled out euro membership. In the House of Commons on 6 December 2011, the Shadow Chancellor, Ed Balls, was pressed by Conservative MPs to state Labour's position on the euro. He said:

> The euro is not succeeding as a single currency, which is why we were right not to join in 2003. There is no possibility of a British Government joining the euro at any time in my lifetime. (*Hansard*, 2011)

Assuming Ed Balls enjoys an average lifespan, he was apparently ruling out British membership of the eurozone until around 2045. It is unlikely that such a commitment will be binding on his successors, but the statement is remarkable in demonstrating the level of aversion to the euro.

For both advocates and opponents alike, EMU cannot be passed off as a largely technical concern. Control over the currency and economic policy go to the heart of national sovereignty. The entry into circulation of the single currency on 1 January 2002 was a visible manifestation in people's pockets and wallets of the drive to closer European integration. The eurozone crisis that began following the 'credit crunch' of 2008 raised major questions about the future of Europe. There are those who argue that EMU was always unrealistic and doomed to fail. The same points have been made about other ambitious steps in the creation of an integrated Europe. This time, the sceptics might be correct. Perhaps the euro is riddled with structural flaws and doomed to fail, but British governments over the last 50 years have doubted the intent of other European governments and watched from the sidelines while policy and institutional priorities are established in their absence. This was the lament of Deputy Prime Minister Nick Clegg, following the British attempt to veto Treaty change at the December 2011 Brussels summit (see Chapter 4 for discussion of the veto that never was). Clegg feared that the UK would be cast adrift in mid-Atlantic unable to exercise influence in areas of key strategic interest. Clegg's comments were also shaped by domestic politics. For the pro-EU Liberal Democrats within the Conservative-led coalition, the attempted veto was an uncomfortable moment, but languishing in the opinion polls, the only option for the Liberal Democrats was to grit their teeth and stay in the coalition. Meanwhile, eurosceptics on the Conservative backbenches argued that this was now the moment for Britain to push for a fundamental renegotiation of Britain's terms of membership, with the outcome then put to a referendum. As both Cameron and Clegg knew full well, any such move would shatter the coalition.

The decision of the British government to block Treaty reform was a key moment in British relations with the EU, but to understand this outcome we must first explore the origins of EMU and the plans that were put in place in the ambition to create a single European currency. We then factor into the analysis the hugely destabilizing impact of the financial crisis, and also think about the era of severe fiscal austerity that could be ushered in by what has been called the 'fiscal compact'.

The origins of Economic and Monetary Union

The over-arching questions are whether a European currency union can work; and the nature of the implications of such arrangements for democratic government. Although there is no precedent for a monetary union on such a scale, the historical omens are ambivalent because as many currency unions collapsed during the twentieth century as were created. In Europe, the Belgium–Luxembourg monetary union survived until the creation of the euro, but the Austro–Hungarian Empire, Czechoslovakia and Yugoslavia all saw political disintegration accompanied by monetary disunion.

Title II of the Treaty of Rome called for 'progressively approximating the economic policies of member states'. A Monetary Committee was established to seek monetary policy coordination, although there was no clear intention at that time to set up a currency bloc in Europe. By the late 1960s, the basic structures of the Common Market had been set in place and heads of government, meeting in The Hague in 1969, took steps to form an EMU to protect the CAP, because common agricultural prices depended on currency stability, so that instability and exchange rate fluctuation would not threaten its basis. Luxembourg's Prime Minister, Pierre Werner, was commissioned to bring forward a plan for EMU. He proposed three stages culminating in an irrevocable fixing of exchange rates and free circulation of people, goods, services and capital. However, Werner's plan was undermined by events in the 1970s, when dollar instability created by the burgeoning US budget deficit was compounded by the 1973 oil crisis and the failure of EU governments to agree a coordinated economic and political response.

The French and German governments remained convinced of the merits of further economic integration. In 1978, the Bremen summit established the European Monetary System (EMS) and its ERM, with the European Currency Unit or Ecu as a parallel unit of exchange and a forerunner of a single currency. The EMS aimed to formalize economic cooperation between the member states leading to eventual convergence. The Ecu was based on a 'basket' of member state currencies and related to their economic strength. Each national currency was valued in relation to the Ecu and, thus, to all other EU currencies with central rates of exchange.

The British joined the EMS in 1979, thus making sterling one of the component currencies of the Ecu, then joined the ERM in October 1990 and left rather unceremoniously on 16 September 1992 when sterling was placed under unsustainable pressure on 'Black Wednesday' (Stephens, 1996).

As discussed in Chapter 3, the decision to join the ERM caused severe tensions within the final Thatcher government between the Prime Minister, Chancellor Nigel Lawson and Foreign Secretary Sir Geoffrey Howe. Lawson and Howe were both pro-ERM. In her memoirs, Thatcher (1993) recounts being bounced into the ERM at the Madrid summit against her will when Lawson and Howe ganged up on her, as she saw it. They were not key members of her government for much longer, although Thatcher's own political demise was not far removed and was closely connected to these arguments about EMU.

For its advocates, ERM membership was viewed as an external constraint that would inhibit any return to the 'boom and bust' policies of the 1980s, when rapid economic growth had been followed by sharp recession. If the UK were tied to a credible external mechanism such as the ERM, then this could impose anti-inflationary discipline on the UK economy. This reasoning also informed the selection of an exchange rate with the Deutschmark when Britain eventually entered the ERM, which turned out to place unsustainable pressures on sterling. Sterling entered the ERM on 5 October 1991 at a rate of DM2.95 to the £. This was unsustainable because of the strength of the Deutschmark. 'Black Wednesday' saw the pound face frenzied selling on international currency markets, with interest rates increased to 15 per cent (with devastating effects on mortgage holders). At 7.40 p.m. on 16 September, the Chancellor of the Exchequer, Norman Lamont, announced that 'Today has been an extremely difficult and turbulent day' and that Britain's ERM membership was suspended (never to be reactivated). His special adviser, a certain David Cameron, lurked in the background while Lamont gave his press statement. The ERM experience remains a strong card for those arguing against joining the EMU. Yet, it is also worth recalling that membership of the ERM was linked to a desire to impose anti-inflationary discipline. This means that political choices made by the British government were key elements in the humiliation of Black Wednesday. Also born from these events was Treasury euroscepticism, with the belief that economic policy 'credibility begins at home' (Dyson, 2000).

Key features of Economic and Monetary Union

In the Maastricht Treaty, EMU was specified as meaning a single currency, common economic policies and mechanisms for inter-regional exchange. It was also argued that EMU required fiscal union, too, but this was not a feature of the original plan. This omission was central to the near collapse of the euro in the wake of the credit crunch, as discussed below (pp. 185–8). Two political factors have been identified as central to whether or not a currency union can work (Cohen, 1998). First, can a hegemon guarantee stability of the system? An argument advanced for EMU was that it would actually reduce the hegemonic power of Germany; or, as Chancellor Kohl put it, a European roof would be put over Germany, rather than the other way around. The lack of a hegemon was seen as a factor contributing to the post-2008 eurozone crisis. The German government was reluctant to become the guarantor of the euro because of the domestic political costs of being seen to bail out more profligate member states. Second, does a sense of community exist among participating nations? The eurozone bailout certainly tested this idea to the limit. While Gordon Brown, as Prime Minister, did seek to involve the British government in the eurozone debate, David Cameron made it clear that Britain would be an interested spectator, but that it was a matter for eurozone countries themselves.

The drive towards EMU had a strong intergovernmental basis. A core motive for EMU was French *raison d'état* centred on concerns about Germany's post-Cold War development. Following German reunification in November 1989, the French were keen to hasten movement towards EMU in order to put the German economic powerhouse within structures of collective economic management. There were some doubts in Germany, as many thought the foundations of German economic success – an independent Bundesbank committed to price stability – could be put at risk by participation in EMU. The driving forces behind the EMU proposal were Paris and the Commission, with support from Italy, Belgium and Spain. Germany's main reason for agreeing to participate was that political commitment to EMU demonstrated continued faith in European integration. Germany also attempted to ensure that the economic priorities of the EMU plan matched those that had under-pinned postwar German economic success. This included the 'Stability and Growth' pact that sought to impose limits on budget deficits.

TABLE 7.1   *General government debt, 2010, EU 27 (percentage of GDP)*

Zone	Member state	Debt level GDP (%)
Eurozone:	Austria	71.8
	Belgium	96.2
	Cyprus	61.5
	Estonia	6.7
	Denmark	43.7
	Finland	48.3
	France	82.3
	Germany	83.2
	Greece	144.9
	Ireland	92.5
	Italy	118.4
	Luxembourg	19.1
	Malta	69.0
	Netherlands	62.9
	Portugal	93.3
	Slovakia	41.0
	Slovenia	38.8
Non-Eurozone:	Bulgaria	16.3
	Czech Republic	37.6
	Denmark	43.7
	Hungary	81.3
	Latvia	44.7
	Lithuania	38.0
	Poland	54.9
	Romania	31.0
	Sweden	39.7
	UK	79.9

Source: Eurostat (2010).

Germany was actually one of the first victims, as the German economy suffered a slowdown and high levels of unemployment. The weakness of the Stability and Growth pact was highlighted by the post-2008 crisis, as member states accumulated high levels of debt. The 'fiscal compact' of 2012 was designed as a way to toughen-up EU economic governance by including fiscal rules in a way that

Maastricht had not. Table 7.1 shows levels of sovereign debt for the EU 27 (eurozone and non-eurozone) in 2010. It is useful to remember when looking at Table 7.1 that a level of 60 per cent was the 'convergence' target in the plan for EMU laid down at Maastricht.

The EMU plan

In June 1988, the European Council set up a Committee for the Study of Economic and Monetary Union, chaired by the Commission President, Delors. Its report, submitted in April 1989, put forward a three-stage plan for EMU (Committee for the Study of Economic and Monetary Union, 1989). This formed the basis of the timetable agreed at Maastricht. The three stages on the path to EMU were as follows:

- *Stage One* prescribed that all countries were to enter the ERM. Sterling finally joined on 8 October 1990, but market pressure forced it out on 16 September 1992.
- *Stage Two* set out that by 1 January 1994 all currencies were to enter the ERM's narrow band (2.25 per cent).
- *Stage Three* specified four convergence criteria (price stability, non-excessive government debt, stable currency and low interest rates) deemed necessary for countries wishing to participate in the third stage of EMU, when a single European currency would be established and an independent European Central Bank set up to run monetary policy.

At Maastricht, the British and Danes secured opt-outs from this third stage of EMU. The Maastricht timetable was cast into doubt by the ERM crises of 1992 and 1993. German reunification was hugely costly and pushed up German interest rates, which led to a stronger Deutschmark. The strong Deutschmark put pressure on other ERM currencies under pressure to maintain their ERM parities with it. This was particularly difficult for economies in recession, or struggling to emerge from it – such as the British, Spanish and French. They were all forced to maintain high interest rates in order to sustain their ERM membership, even though such policies neglected the needs of their real economies.

The events of 1992 and 1993 made it impossible to proceed to the third stage of EMU in 1997, as originally planned. The Commission was asked to bring forward further recommendations on progress towards convergence as early as possible. This it did in a report accepted by the Commission on 25 March 1998. This report was the culmination of a two-year debate about convergence. There was some creativity in interpretation of the criteria, which allowed countries making progress in the direction of attainment to be deemed to have converged. Convergence criteria were not strictly applied and fiscal rules were weak. Yet, there was a strong political momentum behind EMU and, at a meeting of heads of government in Brussels between 1 and 3 May 1998, it was agreed that 11 member states met the criteria. On 1 January 2002, euro banknotes and coins entered circulation, with a complete changeover to the euro in public administration. By July 2002, national currencies had been cancelled as legal tender. By 2011, 17 countries had replaced their currency with the euro. The 13 countries that joined the EU between 2004 and 2012 are all committed to euro membership (Cyprus, Slovakia and Slovenia had joined by 2011). Britain remains outside and has no intention of joining. Sweden is committed by its accession treaty to membership, but has not joined the ERM and thus is not 'converging' as required by the Treaty. This gives Sweden a *de facto* opt-out, with little sign that there is much support amongst Swedes for euro membership.

For and against Economic and Monetary Union

Pro-single currency advocates in Britain face an uphill task. What are the arguments in favour? Participating member states and pro-Euro advocates identify four main merits of EMU.

- the reduction of transaction costs generated by currency exchange
- the reduction of uncertainty caused by exchange rate fluctuations which undermine the ability of business to plan ahead
- the coordination of EU economies could create the world's most powerful trading bloc – the EU27 has a population of around 500 million people
- from a British point of view, scepticism about core EU objectives has, in the past, led to Britain being excluded when the 'rules of the game' are established; these rules are then not necessarily in the UK's interests and can make adaptation a more difficult process.

Opponents of the euro also have four main arguments:

- On political grounds, the creation of an EMU cedes economic authority to distant and unaccountable institutions at EU level. This could be an argument for strengthening EU institutions to make them more democratic and accountable, but opponents of EMU tend to see the nation state as the best level for decision-making.
- On economic grounds, the EMU creates one-size-fits-all economic policies that may not suit all participating states. The level of interest rates set by the European Central Bank may not fit with economic priorities in an EU that encompasses 17 eurozone countries.
- Far greater fiscal and political integration would be necessary, if an EMU were to work effectively.
- An emphasis on 'stability' and low inflation within the eurozone punishes member states within which public spending is deemed 'excessive' by EU rules. This can lead to cuts that include significant reductions in public service provision and the institutionalization of austerity.

A further economic argument from a British point of view is that Europe needed to embrace the kinds of economic reform undertaken in Britain since the 1980s, if the European economy is to be flexible enough to withstand economic shocks. There is a view within the Treasury that the eurozone needs to become more 'Anglicized' before UK membership can occur (Dyson, 2000). This view is far less popular outside the UK. With good reason, French President Sarkozy was swift to identify the excesses of the banking system and of the Anglo-American model of deregulated capitalism as causes of the credit crunch and financial crisis. Sarkozy's successor in the Elysée Palace, François Hollande, announced his intention to challenge the EU-wide politics of austerity and the tight budget rules introduced within the so-called 'fiscal compact' (see Chapter 4, for fuller discussion of the origins and effects of this agreement).

Britain and Economic and Monetary Union

The UK opt-out in the Maastricht Treaty postponed a decision on entry. The ERM disaster of 1992 had holed the Conservative government beneath the waterline. Joining the euro was inconceivable during the Major administration. New Labour in power after 1997 shifted from Major's 'wait and see' approach to what they called 'prepare and decide' – which was pretty much the same strategy, only differently worded. A national changeover plan was launched so that, if the decision were made to join, then the UK would be ready. The government claimed that any decision to join would be on an economic basis, rather than a political one. In fact, the politics cannot be easily detached from the economics, especially when the 'five economic tests' devised by Gordon Brown in order to assess British membership allowed a significant margin for interpretation.

On 27 October 1997, Chancellor Brown made a statement that professed to outline the government's policy on EMU, although Philip Stephens (2001: 73) wrote that the 'statement was not so much a policy as a conscious decision not to have a policy unless and until the Chancellor said otherwise'. Brown noted that: 'in principle, a successful single currency within a single European market would be of benefit to Europe and Britain'. He argued that there were no constitutional impediments to membership, although a referendum would be required. Brown grounded the case in pragmatic terms: 'If a single currency would be good for British jobs, British business and future prosperity, it is right in principle to join. The constitutional issue is a factor in the decision, but it is not an overriding one' (*Hansard*, 1997).

If the government were to advocate replacing sterling with the euro, then, Brown announced, five economic tests would have to be satisfied. The Treasury would be responsible for determining whether or not these had met. The tests assessed:

• sustainable convergence between Britain and the economies of a single currency
• sufficient flexibility to cope with economic change
• the effect on investment
• the impact on the UK financial services industry
• the impact on employment.

In June 2003, Chancellor Brown announced that just one of the tests (on financial services) had been met. The House of Commons Treasury Select Committee noted a lack of precision about what was required. As one expert remarked: 'The Chancellor's tests are so loosely defined that anyone will be able to say that they have either been passed or failed according to the dictates of political expediency' (House of Commons Treasury Select Committee, 1998). This may be exactly what the Chancellor had in mind, because the political controversy surrounding EMU membership made it a risky proposition to bind the government to one position or another. This was particularly the case during Labour's second and third terms. Stephens (2001: 73) notes that a more insidious effect of the five tests was that the government cast itself as a passive bystander, rather than a leader of the debate. If Britain were to join the Euro, then the case would need to be made – but no government has sought to engage with the British people on this issue. One reason for this is that a referendum would be divisive and detract from the pursuit of other objectives.

The great crash and the sovereign debt crisis

Joining the euro is effectively off the British political agenda, but the eurozone crisis had huge implications for Britain because of the close linkages between Britain and eurozone economies. This section explores the origins and effects of the crisis before we analyse Britain's stance on future European economic governance.

The origins of the crisis are complex, but a combination of reckless behaviour by financial institutions, a credit-led boom in some countries and high levels of public debt in others all came together to create a perfect storm. This occurred in the context of a highly interdependent global economy. It is often said that, if the USA sneezes, then the rest of the world catches a cold. It was far worse than this in 2008, when the US property market bubble burst and the world's biggest economy slid into deep recession. Risky mortgage lending (so-called 'sub-prime mortgages') left major US financial institutions perilously exposed. The contagion effects crossed to Europe. In Britain, the property market bubble burst, while UK banks were exposed by risky lending and aggressive growth strategies that occurred in a context of lax regulation and the equation of the interests of the City of London with the national interest (a trend continued by the Conservative–Liberal Democrat coalition). As Chancellor, Gordon Brown had often claimed to have ended 'boom and bust' economics, but the near-collapse of the banking system prompted a bailout for the banks that began in 2008 and, at its peak, reached £1.2 trillion (National Audit Office, 2011: 5). The

TABLE 7.2   *Top ten largest government deficits in the EU, 2010*

Member state	Deficit (percentage of GDP)
Ireland	–32.4
Greece	–10.5
UK	–10.4
Spain	–9.2
Poland	–7.9
Slovakia	–7.9
Latvia	–7.7
Lithuania	–7.1
France	–7.0
Romania	–6.4

Source: *Eurostat* (2012).

effect was huge increases in public debt followed by severe austerity. Outside the eurozone, the Bank of England was still able to set interest rates, which fell to record low levels, while interest rates on UK government bonds also remained relatively low. Despite a budget deficit that is behind only Ireland and Greece in its size, the UK maintained its AAA credit rating. Indeed, the credit rating agencies through their 'downgrades' or threatened 'downgrades' were to become key players in the crisis, even though they had not actually seen signs of the impending crash.

The crisis was a major test for eurozone economic governance. Eurozone countries were also exposed to the credit crunch and decline in world trade. In both Spain and Ireland, property market bubbles burst with spectacular and deeply damaging effects. In Spain, unemployment rose to around 25 per cent of the workforce. In Ireland, the money simply ran out. As Table 7.2 shows, the deficit as a proportion of Irish GDP rose to over 32 per cent. It was simply not possible for the Irish government to access the funds to sustain that level of debt. In November 2010, an EU/IMF-funded bailout package of €85 billion was agreed. The political consequences for Irish citizens were severe austerity budgets that saw public expenditure slashed. The *Irish Independent* newspaper reported that the 2012 Budget would take €3.8 billion out of the economy in cuts and taxes while, between 2013 and 2015, a further €8.6 billion would be cut. In the absence of growth, this would amount to €5443 from the disposable income of every household (*Irish Independent*, 16 December 2011).

To prop-up ailing eurozone economies, the 27 member states set up the European Financial Stability Fund in May 2010 as a 'firewall', with a €440 billion lending capacity. This was to take place in July 2012 by means of a European Stability Mechanism with €500 billion lending capacity. The Commission also managed a smaller (around €50 billion) European Financial Stabilisation Mechanism. In May 2010, a €78 billion bailout package for Portugal was also agreed. In both countries, the condition was that governments embark on severe austerity programmes to bring down debt levels. Greece was the big test for these mechanisms. High levels of Greek public debt, an under-performing economy and a political system with limited reform capacity all combined to threaten the eurozone itself. A reason for this was that much Greek debt was held by banks in other EU member states. The contagion effects of Greek default would be severe. A Greek bailout of €110 billion financed by an EU and IMF loan was agreed in May 2010. In June 2011, Greece's credit rating was downgraded by Standard & Poor's to CCC, the lowest in the world. In October 2011, Europe's leaders agreed to create a €1 trillion firewall to try to limit the spread of contagion because of concern that this could spread to bigger economies such as Italy, or even France (*The Economist*, 2011). These countries were not too big to fail, but would be too big to bail out. It was essential that EU leaders found some way to strengthen the eurozone. Its collapse would plunge EU economies (including Britain) into another recession and send shockwaves across the world. In December 2011, the ratings agency Standard & Poor's placed 15 eurozone members on 'CreditWatch'. They identified systemic stresses from five interrelated factors: tightening credit conditions across the eurozone; markedly higher risk premiums on a growing number of eurozone governments, including some that were rated 'AAA' (such as France); continuing disagreements among European policy-makers on how to tackle the immediate market confidence crisis and, longer term, how to ensure greater economic, financial, and fiscal convergence among eurozone members; high levels of government and household indebtedness across a large area of the eurozone; and, the rising risk of economic recession in the eurozone as a whole in 2012. The indecisive outcome of the May 2012 Greek elections and success for anti-austerity parties did little to ease anxiety, although opinion polls suggested that between 70 and 80 per cent of Greeks wanted to stay in the euro. A problem was that their voting behaviour did not seem consistent with this preference.

The Conservative-Liberal Democrat coalition led by David Cameron was not central to any of these debates about future eurozone governance. As shown in Chapter 4, the British government stood aside from the fiscal compact, which gave them only observer status as the French and German governments led the EU in an attempt to come up with a plan to save the euro, the eurozone and, ultimately, the EU.

Justice and home affairs

There has been rapid development of institutions and policies in the area of internal security. This includes migration, asylum, police and judicial cooperation, and anti-terrorism. Progress has not been even and there is still some variable geometry, with police and judicial cooperation remaining more intergovernmental, while migration and asylum have been made the subject of a common policy within the main Treaty structure (Geddes, 2012). This section identifies the factors that drive policy and Britain's relationship to them. Returning to a point made earlier, many effects of European integration are 'under the radar'. For example, Britain is not a member of the Schengen agreement, which was the accord initially reached by five countries (Belgium, France, Germany, Luxembourg and the Netherlands) to move more rapidly to attain free movement objectives. In effect, this meant passport-free travel within the Schengen area. Britain is formally not a Schengen member, but does cooperate on a wide range of Schengen-related issues and has opted back into some key measures, such as asylum policy.

The end of the Cold War changed thinking about internal security. A new series of challenges were identified, such as large-scale migration or international organized crime, which were seen to threaten the borders of EU member states and, thus, require some form of collective response. Two points need to be borne in mind. First, perceptions of security and insecurity are based on fears that may or may not have a basis in reality. For instance, people imagine that the scale of immigration is far greater than it actually is but, even though the general public over-exaggerate the extent of immigration, the fear of it creates perceived threats that have very real social and political effects. This means that we need to explore the ways in which issues are seen as security concerns. Second, Europe's security/insecurity agenda has changed since the end of the Cold War, with a new focus on what has been called 'societal security' which centres on the control of population, rather than the control of borders. New forms and types of security control and new types of monitoring, surveillance and observation have developed.

There was informal cooperation on internal security dating back to the creation of the Trevi Group of interior ministers in the 1970s. Throughout the 1970s and 1980s, British governments participated in these intergovernmental structures. Maastricht's JHA pillar formalized this cooperation and brought it within the EU. It recognized immigration, asylum, policing and judicial cooperation as matters of common concern, and put in place structures for intergovernmental cooperation from which the Commission, CJEU and EP were largely excluded. Cooperation was to occur in nine areas: asylum; external frontier controls; immigration; combating drug addiction; combating international fraud; judicial cooperation in civil matters; judicial cooperation in criminal matters; customs cooperation; and police cooperation. The existing informal structures were included in a complex five-tier structure: specific working parties, steering committees, a Coordinating Committee set up under Article K.4 of the Union Treaty, the Committee of Permanent Representatives and the Council of Ministers for JHA. An additional complication was the Schengen provisions, which became a laboratory of the kinds of measure that the EU would need to introduce, if the single market were to be accompanied by internal security measures. The problem was that not all EU member states were Schengen states (the UK has not joined).

The JHA pillar contained provisions for decision-taking mechanisms, but these were based on intergovernmentalism and required unanimity, which was difficult to achieve and very rarely forthcoming. This meant that provisions for 'joint positions', 'joint actions' and conventions in international law were difficult to realize. This also led to pressure for change, because the measures were not only inefficient, but were also criticized for being undemocratic and unaccountable.

Amsterdam defined the EU as an Area of Freedom, Security and Justice and, thus, gave a major impetus to internal security policy. Migration and asylum moved into the main Treaty structure and the Commission began to make proposals for the development of a common migration and asylum policy. It is important to note that some, but not all, areas of policy were included. EU action has been much more focused on preventing entry by asylum-seekers and irregular migrants. The EU is specifically excluded from any role in policies determining the numbers of non-EU nationals to be admitted. The Lisbon Treaty marked another major step to a common migration and asylum policy by making most of Title IV subject to the OLP and with scope for lower courts in member states to seek preliminary rulings on migration and asylum issues from the CJEU. It now makes sense to talk about a common migration and asylum policy, albeit one that applies to some areas (asylum, irregular migration) and not others (admissions) (Geddes, 2008; Boswell and Geddes, 2011).

Britain and justice and home affairs

Cooperation on JHA is a tricky issue for the British government. There has been reluctance to cede the ability to control the UK's external frontiers as would be required by full accession to Schengenland. The reason for this is that Britain, as an island, can exert strong controls at the external frontiers, and has traditionally placed less reliance on internal security mechanisms such as identity cards. Indeed, New Labour proposals to introduce identity cards were unpopular and were subsequently ditched by the coalition. Full adherence to Schengen would change security mechanisms and jeopardize the historically preferred response in UK to the regulation of international migration.

That having been said, there has been integration beneath the radar. Since the enactment of the Amsterdam Treaty, the UK has opted into a range of migration and asylum measures, including steps towards the development of a common EU asylum system. This has been done because the UK saw common EU action as way of resolving what was, for New Labour, a difficult domestic issue in the early 2000s; namely, increased numbers of asylum-seekers. Tony Blair argued that the general EU opt-out provisions, coupled with opt-ins on issues such as asylum, allowed Britain 'to get the best of both worlds' (Geddes, 2005). To a certain extent, subterfuge can be a path to compliance with EU norms and institutions, and also demonstrates that the effects of European integration can be shielded from the general public. This is facilitated in an area such as JHA, where there is already a tendency to secrecy.

There have been EU-level developments in other areas linked to internal security. It would be easy to link these to a post-9/11 focus on 'homeland security' but, while it is the case that 9/11 did have important effects, it is also true that the groundwork was laid for EU action long before the attacks on the USA. A European Police Office (Europol) based in The Hague now has more than 600 staff. From its creation in the 1970s, Europol has seen its role develop in relation to the perceived internal security challenges raised by the single market and free movement and, subsequently, to the end of the Cold War and terrorist attacks, such as those on the USA, London and Madrid. The Europol Convention agreed in Rome in July 1995 provides the base for cooperation, while around 130 liaison officers from national police forces work with Europol on common investigations. The European Arrest Warrant (EAW) applies the principle of mutual recognition to internal security. The EAW was agreed in 2004 and allows a warrant for arrest to be valid throughout the EU. One of the persons responsible for the failed London bombings at the end of July 2004 was arrested in Italy and returned to the UK under an EAW. More controversially, a British citizen, Andrew Symeou, was arrested in Greece following a nightclub death in 2007. Symeou was charged with manslaughter and spent 11 months in a Greek prison. He denied the charge, while there were also allegations of mistreatment of witnesses. Symeou was cleared of all charges in June 2011, but after four years of uncertainty, including imprisonment.

We have seen that Britain formally opts out of much EU action on internal security, but has chosen to opt in where it feels that its strategic interests are better suited by common EU action. The main effect of the opt-out has been to place limits on the jurisdiction of EU institutions, such as the CJEU, and reaffirm a preference for intergovernmentalism.

The common foreign and security policy

When push comes to shove, does Britain look to Europe or the USA? The war in Iraq exposed huge divisions within the EU as the UK sided with the USA (along with the governments of Spain, Italy, Denmark, the Netherlands and most of the accession states). The conflict also raised some rather fundamental issues about the nature of European power. The EU, as an organization, has been deeply committed to multilateralism – not least because it is a notion central to the EU's self-identity – and to respect for international law. The eight-year war in Iraq that ended with the withdrawal of

US troops at the end of 2011 was a direct challenge to these precepts, and deeply disturbing to many EU governments and their citizens for precisely these reasons.

The EU CFSP also raises the issue of EU power. A prevailing view has been that the EU was a civilian or 'soft' power centred on economic concerns, as opposed to a military power: an economic giant but a political dwarf, as one observer put it (Buchan, 1993). Hedley Bull (1979: 151) wrote that: 'Europe is not an actor in international affairs ... and does not seem likely to become one.' Since then, there have been moves to consolidate a stronger EU presence in international affairs through formal cooperation on CFSP and the creation at the Cologne summit meeting of EU heads of government in June 1999 of a European Security and Defence Policy (ESDP).

The ways in which the EU and the member states deal with CFSP issues was clearly affected by the post-Cold War context, which changed previous understandings of threats. During the Cold War period, west European security was guaranteed by the USA through NATO. Since the end of the Cold War, British governments have remained strong supporters of an Atlantic framework within NATO for European security, and see any EU responses as nested within it.

Common Foreign and Security Policy development

In 1970, the six EC member states instigated foreign policy cooperation known as European Political Cooperation (EPC). EPC attempted to establish an external political profile to match the EC's burgeoning economic power and ensure, where possible, coordination. In 1987, the SEA strengthened EPC by establishing a secretariat to support its operations. The Maastricht Treaty boldly declared in Article J that: 'a common foreign and security policy is hereby established'. In reality, the CFSP pillar was a formalization of existing EPC procedures, rather than a radical new venture; however, it did contain some innovations with potential for future development. Within the pillar arrangements, foreign and security policy was to be decided by a system of 'joint action' with unanimity as the decisional modus operandi. However, once 'joint action' had been agreed in principle, majority voting could be used for measures of detail. Any decision (say) to send election monitors must be made unanimously, but subsequent decisions about numbers involved, and so on, could be decided by qualified majority. These provisions also allowed for the discussion of defence issues previously confined to NATO, EUROGROUP (of European defence ministers) and, from 1984, the revived West European Union (WEU), the European constituent of NATO. In the 1980s, the French and Germans were keen to establish a stronger European defence profile. They intensified their own cooperation by setting up the 4,000-strong Franco–German brigade, based in Bavaria. Other nations remained wary. The Maastricht CFSP 'pillar' sought to strengthen the WEU by moving the latter's secretariat to Brussels, setting up a planning unit and inviting all non-WEU members of the European Community (Denmark, Greece and Ireland) to join. The European Council and Council of Ministers, acting unanimously, were to be central decision-making authorities for both foreign and defence policy. Although the differential memberships of the EU and WEU (five of the EU states were only observers in the WEU) make this difficult, NATO is still supreme on the defence side.

War in the former Yugoslavia was a severe test for EU foreign policy. The carnage and chaos in Bosnia indicated that the EU failed the test. The USA at first urged Europeans to take the lead in mediating a peaceful solution to a European problem. Yet, by 1993, the war's scope and intensity appeared to be beyond the ability of the Community to resolve. 'This is the hour of Europe', Luxembourg's foreign minister, Jacques Poos, had proclaimed in June 1991 after brokering another short-lived ceasefire. The Union's failure to resolve a bitter dispute on its doorstep proved a chastening experience. The economic strength of the Union served as a useful asset in peacetime, but offered little in the face of bitter ethnic and religious dispute.

The Amsterdam Treaty added some new provisions to the foreign and security policy pillar. A new post of High Representative was established. This was seen as a way of answering the criticism attributed to Henry Kissinger that Europe did not have a phone number. To Kissinger's point, the Council appointed a High Representative with his very own phone number. The Council was also given power to adopt by unanimity a 'common strategy' to be implemented by joint actions and common positions adopted by QMV, although decisions having military or defence implications would still rely on unanimity. The Amsterdam Treaty also strengthened the 'soft security', peacekeeping and humanitarian intervention role of the EU by adding the WEU's 'Petersberg tasks' (humanitarian and rescue tasks, peace-keeping and combat-force in crisis management, including peace-making) to the issues for which the CFSP would be responsible.

The Treaty of Nice contained new CFSP provisions relating to a European defence and security policy that covered all matters relating to EU security, including the gradual formulation of a common defence policy. The EDSP was, thus, to be part of the CFSP. Arrangements have also been made for regular EU–NATO consultation.

The CFSP was decidedly intergovernmental. The member states in the Council and European Council held the upper hand, while the Commission was weak. The Commission was 'fully associated' with the CFSP, but did not have the exclusive right to submit initiatives. Instead, these came mainly from the Presidency, a member state or the High Representative. The EP was only consulted and briefed on developments.

The basic instruments of CFSP differ from the 'directives' and 'regulations' of other more supranationalized policy areas. Instead, CFSP instruments are common strategies, common positions, joint actions, decisions and the conclusion of international agreements.

Britain and the Common Foreign and Security Policy

By 2003, it was absolutely clear that Tony Blair's prime allegiance was to the USA. Since 2010, David Cameron has done little to shift this alignment. A key question is whether the USA remains as focused on Europe as once it was. The balance of global power is shifting towards the BRICs (Brazil, Russia, India and China). The USA seems more likely to look east to Asia and the Pacific than to look west to Europe.

As prime minister, Blair's apparent enthusiasm for common EU measures in areas such as foreign and defence policy was framed by a belief that these needed to be linked to strong transatlantic ties. Very early in his first term in office, Blair took a step that was wrongly seen by some of his opponents as questioning Britain's commitment to NATO and the USA. In a March 1998 speech to the French National Assembly, he identified defence and security policies as areas in which France and the UK were well-equipped to cooperate. In December 1998 in St Malo, this declaration was given more substance when Blair and President Chirac called for full and rapid implementation of the Treaty of Amsterdam's CFSP provisions. Where would these kinds of steps leave the British? The CFSP

presents some difficulties. There is Britain's long-standing preference for intergovernmental cooperation, which could be accommodated within existing structures, but which is challenged by more
ambitious ideas about closer European integration. Britain's so-
called 'special relationship' with the USA is still referred to, but may
better be seen as showing that Britain's foreign policy interests seem
not to be particularly Europeanized. Whether Britain's 'national
interest' can be accommodated within European defence and security structures remains an open question, but one that is clearly open
to serious doubt (Howorth, 2000).

These were put to the test by Afghanistan and Iraq. In the immediate aftermath of the 9/11 attacks, there had been attempts to
resuscitate the European Rapid Reaction Force and use it in anti-
terror operations, but Blair opposed this and argued that any
response needed to be through NATO. Relations with France dete-
riorated in the build-up to and aftermath of the invasion of Iraq.
That having been said, all was not lost for European cooperation,
with signs that Britain still remained committed to operations in the
context of the ESDP where these complemented NATO. In March
2003, EU forces replaced NATO forces in Macedonia. In summer
2003, the EU intervened to restore order in the Democratic Republic
of Congo. In December, EU forces replaced NATO's stabilization
forces in Bosnia (Allen and Smith, 2004: 97). In 2006, EU forces
were deployed once again in Congo while, in 2008, a joint EU–UN
force protected refugee camps on the border of Chad and the
Central African Republic. By 2011, a total of 11 ESDP missions had
been completed, while a further 13 were ongoing.

A key institutional change was brought about by the Lisbon
treaty and the creation of the High Representative of the EU for
Foreign Affairs and Security Policy and Vice President of the
Commission. The Labour politician and former Trade
Commissioner Baroness Ashton was appointed to this role in
November 2009. She chairs the Foreign Affairs Council and is also
head of the European External Action Service, which is supposedly
designed to evolve into the EU's diplomatic corps. One effect of this
is that what were called EU 'Representations' now become EU
embassies. The first to change title was in Washington, where there
is now an EU embassy speaking for the Commission, Council and
the member states. That having been said, Britain and other member
states do maintain their own representation in the USA.

Conclusion

This chapter has shown that the EU now acts much more directly and with a much stronger treaty basis in areas that impinge far more directly upon state sovereignty. We have seen an ambivalent relationship on the part of British governments to EMU; internal security; and foreign, security and defence policy. Britain did not join the Euro and will not do so any time soon. It has, however, been deeply exposed to the effects of the credit crunch and the simultaneous sovereign debt and eurozone governance crises. Prime Minister Cameron did, however, make it clear that Britain would not agree to strengthened European economic governance without assurances about what were seen as vital national interests – mainly relating to the City of London. When these were not forthcoming, Britain stood aside. Agreement will now occur outside of the formal Treaty framework, but could lead to a significant strengthening of eurozone economic governance. We saw variable patterns of interaction in other areas of high politics. Internal security demonstrates the ways in which integration can occur under the radar. An example of this is the formal opt-out from Schengen and the various opt-ins that have then occurred on issues such as asylum policy. We saw, too, the rifts within the EU cases by the US-led invasion of Iraq. Under the radar, though, has been extensive UK involvement in ESDP operations all over the world.

If we were to reflect on these developments in terms of the 'Britain in Europe' and 'Europe in Britain' themes, then we could conclude that Britain has often been a front-runner in areas of high politics, so long as the cooperation is on an intergovernmental basis. The closer that the cooperation moves to the Treaty and to supranational decision-making, then the more reluctant have become British governments. The solution found has been the employment of 'variable geometry' in the form of Britain's opt-out from the euro and Schengen. These need to be understood as political solutions to preference divergence on the shape and future of European integration. So far, the EU has been able to accommodate British divergence, but the big question for the future is whether this will remain the case. One plausible vision of the future is of a more closely integrated inner core. The creation of stronger eurozone governance is a step in that direction.

Chapter 8

The British State and European Integration

This chapter examines the ways in which the British state has organized for Europe and the impacts of European competencies on the organization of the British state. It does so against a backdrop of significant change in the organization of the British political system, particularly the movement of power 'up' to the EU and 'down' to sub-state nations in Scotland, Wales and Northern Ireland. These moves challenge the 'power hoarding' assumptions of the Westminster model, and an approach to the analysis of British politics that is focused only on Whitehall and Westminster (Matthews, 2011). That having been said, Britain's EU policy is a power that continues to reside with the Westminster government within a tightly coordinated policy network, although devolution has changed the ways in which Britain interacts with the EU, and also with how the EU affects Britain.

The chapter shows that a 'Whitehall ethos' and the impact of devolution since 1997 are to the fore as processes that filter and refract the influence of Europeanization. The story is not one of straightforward adaptation; particularly in central government, there were well-established 'British ways of doing things' before accession occurred. Since 1973, the level of engagement with the EU has had important effects on both the functional (responsibilities exercised by the British state) and territorial (locations at which this power and authority is exercised) dimensions of British politics. At the same time, these effects are not uniform and it would be a mistake to adopt too sweeping an approach to the analysis of 'Europeanization' and assume that the EU alone has transformed British politics. As was suggested in this book's Introduction, European integration will be filtered through domestic logics of politics and policy-making, and there are grounds for expecting core elements of established national 'ways of doing things' to endure. In

British central government, for instance, the persistence of a 'Whitehall ethos' can be detected while other changes may have domestic, rather than supranational logics, such as the important implications of devolved government in Scotland, Wales and Northern Ireland that were driven more squarely by domestic political factors, but within which the EU has played a role.

Contextual factors

Underlying this chapter's analysis are some contextual factors, on which it is important at this initial stage to elaborate. Above all, there has been a marked change in the framework that underpins analysis of the British state with a move away from concern with 'government' as formal structure towards the analysis of 'governance' as an activity that goes beyond the boundaries of the state to include a range of public, private and voluntary actors (Rhodes, 1997; Marsh *et al.*, 2001). This points towards the changed location of some political processes away from the traditional focus of Parliament and Whitehall, although there is an active debate about whether the state is being hollowed out, or has actually grown more powerful and intrusive (Moran, 2007). This reflects a debate within EU studies about whether European integration between those who argue that European integration can strengthen the state (Moravcsik, 1994) and those who see new multi-level dynamics that do not render states redundant but do mean that they operate in different ways and increasingly share power (Marks *et al.*, 1996).

European integration does challenge traditional constitutional relationships, but there are other changes, too, and we must locate European integration alongside factors such as the deregulation and privatization of state activities, the profusion of agencies fulfilling state tasks, the growing influence of international organizations such as the International Monetary Fund and World Trade Organization, and the power of neo-liberalism as an organizing principle for the international economy. These have all had powerful effects on the sovereign authority and capacity of the British state. The emergence of new patterns of governance is one to which eurosceptic rhetoric in Britain has been slow to adapt because of its strong focus on the classic locations of power, authority and accountability; namely, Parliament and the principle of legislative supremacy.

Europeanization is seen as one element of this 'hollowing out' of the British state, with movement towards a differentiated polity 'characterized by functional and institutional specialization and the fragmentation of policies and politics' (Rhodes, 1997: 3). Holliday (2000) contests this 'hollowing out' thesis, and argues that the core of British central government is now more substantial and integrated than ever before. The survey of the Europeanization of central government in this chapter demonstrates the maintenance of a core EU policy grouping that centred on the FCO, Treasury and the Cabinet Office. For example, on the issue of the euro during the New Labour government, this network became even more intensively focused on the Treasury and Downing Street, with some marginalization of the FCO (Bulmer and Burch, 2009; James, 2011). In other areas, however, the increased demands of the EU, as well as the technical nature of many EU issues, has required specialist involvement by government departments and associated networks of expertise.

Europeanization, according to Bulmer and Burch (1998: 603), has both inter-state and intra-state dimensions. This chapter is particularly concerned with the intra-state dimensions understood as: 'the impact of EU policies, rules, practices, and values upon member state activities in respect of both the making and implementation of policy'. It is this 'intra-ness' of European integration that is a particularly important dynamic. We see in this chapter the need to look at changes within the UK state. In Chapter 9 we shall see that Europe has been an issue that has had strong intra-party effects. This implies that, while power moves 'up' to Brussels, these EU competencies feed into national processes of policy-making and implementation, as well as 'down' to sub-national levels of government. Bulmer and Burch (2005) elaborated a framework for analysis of institutional change arising from European integration that distinguishes between what they describe as 'projection' and 'reception'. These are similar to the notions of uploading and downloading that were discussed earlier, but the difference is that they relate to institutional processes, rather than the content of policy. Projection looks at the way institutions such as government departments interact with the EU. Reception, in contrast, is much more diffuse because it looks at the ways that European integration affects institutions within the British political system. In their application of these ideas, Bulmer and Burch argue that before 1997 there was a strong organizational basis for reception, and that after 1997 Blair tried to improve Britain's capacity to project its interest and policy preferences. They saw this as an attempt to move away from a 'passive and reactive approach to the EU' (Bulmer and Burch, 2005: 43; see also James, 2011, ch.3).

The impacts of membership on central government were noted just prior to accession in 1972 by the British Ambassador to Paris at that time, Nicholas Soames (1972, cited in Jordan, 2000: 2) when he observed that 'each department will be responsible for its own European thinking, for knowing the European rules and for having a feel for [the EC's] aspirations ... [W]hole departments must now be learning to "think European" and to take account at all times of the obligations imposed by membership.' Europeanization is an important part of a wider process of both the internationalization and sub-nationalization of the British state that 'appears to be fundamentally altering structures and processes of British government' (Page, 1998: 803) as the UK becomes 'caught up in a multi-level framework of rules and negotiations' with national governments 'holding the gate between domestic and international politics for a shrinking number of policy areas' (H. Wallace, 1997: 452). The impact is generally regarded as significant but, as Bulmer and Burch (1998: 603) note, the precise effects are often rather fuzzy and a simple stronger versus weaker dichotomy may well not capture the more complex dynamics of state adaptation and change.

Central government

When asked to judge the EU's impact on British institutions, Tony Blair's Europe adviser and Head of the European Secretariat in the Cabinet Office, Sir Stephen Wall (2002: 16), said that he thought European integration had had a 'fairly radical impact' and that this was particularly evident since the 1980s:

> When I was dealing with European issues in the early 1980s, you had two or three departments that really knew about Europe: the Foreign Office (because the Foreign Office was responsible for dealing with foreigners), the Ministry of Agriculture (because the CAP was an important part of life) and the DTI [Department of Trade and Industry] (because an important part of trade and industry had aspects of the single market). The Home Office, for example, had no experience of the EU. Basically, negotiations within Whitehall were infinitely more difficult than negotiations in Brussels because people tended to come with absolutely firm departmental positions: that was the British position that had to

prevail in Brussels. But then, of course, over the years, more and more people have had experience of serving in the UK Representation. Now when you have discussions in Whitehall, clearly we have British positions, but we also (and majority voting has been a factor) have learnt that you can't just say 'well this is the British position'. You have to say 'who are our allies?' 'How do we make alliances?' 'What is the endgame going to look like?'

All Whitehall departments now find that some of their competencies have an EU dimension. Some departments have stronger European links than others: agriculture and fisheries, for instance, are areas where there is a common European policy, rather than national policies. For many years, the old MAFF (now part of the Department of Environment, Food and Rural Affairs, or DEFRA) had close and intensive ties with EU institutions and other member states, which meant that a small part of British foreign policy was exercised by MAFF ministers and officials. This gave MAFF a *raison d'être* that allowed a relatively small department to survive even when its core functions centred on subsidies and market intervention had become deeply outmoded ideas in Whitehall. The FCO and the Department of Business, Innovation and Skills (the old DTI) are also departments with close EU links. Other departments, such as the former Department of the Environment (now within DEFRA), have developed EU ties relatively recently, but have acquired extensive EU know-how. The development of EU internal security responsibilities (crime, border controls, asylum) impinges on the work of the Home Office, which has led this quintessentially *domestic* department concerned with the core sovereign concerns of the British state to become, to some extent, Europeanized.

The picture is therefore one of growing intensity of British relations with the EU, with an intensification of effects on the British polity. Following the creation of the EC in 1958, the key players were the Treasury, the Board of Trade, the Foreign Office, MAFF, the Commonwealth Relations Office and the Colonial Office. The Foreign Office played a key role, particularly when UK attentions turned to membership in the 1960s. Indeed, Marsh *et al.* (2001: 215) argue that the EC gave the Foreign Office a new lease of life following the trauma of the end of empire. Accession negotiations were led by the Foreign Office, while relations with the EEC within Whitehall were coordinated by the Treasury with three tiers of committees at various official levels. At the top level was the Economic Association Committee (EQ) chaired by the Prime Minister. It was within EQ that the agenda shifted from association to membership (Bulmer and Burch, 1998: 608). When membership was decided upon in 1961, then the Common Market Negotiations Committee replaced EQ. Following General de Gaulle's '*Non*' in 1963, a European Unit was established within the Cabinet Office, which was renamed during the 1970s as the European Secretariat, and which coordinated negotiations and discussions across Whitehall.

Upon accession in 1973, it was agreed that there would not be a separate Ministry for Europe because this would cut across the traditional functional and territorial distributions of responsibility within Whitehall, with their emphasis on coordination and collective responsibility. Heath also wanted to encourage national ministers to see Europe as integrally connected to domestic politics and not as a foreign policy issue. In this response can be detected the way in which central government responded to European integration in a way that made sense in relation to established organizational practices and can, thus, be initially viewed as a 'thin' institutional constraint, although over time, as EU competencies have grown, this constraint has become much 'thicker' and become much more deeply embedded as a part of Whitehall's standard operating practices. Wallace and Wallace (1973: 261) predicted 'gradual adaptation rather than ... radical change'. EC accession in 1973 did not induce a collective attitude shift across Whitehall; rather, 'opinions were divided and "neutralism" towards the Community was sometimes the most positive of attitudes in some departments' (Willis, 1982: 25).

Upon accession, Britain organized for Europe in the following way: it was decided that the Foreign Secretary would represent the UK on the General Affairs Council and would chair a cabinet committee on EC matters – the Overseas and Defence Policy Committee, or ODP (E) – that would report to the cabinet. The European Unit in the Cabinet Office would seek to coordinate across Whitehall. The Foreign Office would play the leading role in negotiations with other member states and with the EC institutions through UKRep as an 'all of Government' operation and deal directly with the Head of what is now known as the European and Global Issues Secretariat in the Cabinet Office, who is also the Prime Minister's adviser on EU affairs (House of Commons, 2011).

This was still the basic structure that was in place when New Labour came to office in 1997. At the core of Britain's relations with the EU were the Cabinet Office, the FCO, the Treasury and UKRep (James, 2011: 55). Meetings were held every Friday, chaired by the head of the Cabinet Office European Secretariat (COES) and attended by UKRep, as well as departmental leads on EU affairs. These meetings were to coordinate EU business within UK central government (Bulmer and Burch, 2009). A key change under New Labour was an increase in EU capacity within 10 Downing Street. One of Blair's first actions as Prime Minister was to devote more resources to the COES in order to increase the 'in-house' foreign policy expertise (James, 2011: 62–3). By the time Blair left office in 2007, there were 34 full-time staff in the COES (James, 2011: 82).

Blair also broke down the foreign policy adviser role into two jobs: One was Adviser on EU Affairs and Head of the Cabinet Office European Secretariat; the other was Adviser on Foreign Affairs and Head of the Overseas and Defence Secretariat. Both of these roles were at the rank of Permanent Secretary. In 2011, under David Cameron, the re-titled European and Global Issues Secretariat within the Cabinet Office was led by Sir Jon Cunliffe who, in January 2012, replaced Sir Kim Darroch as the head of UKRep in Brussels.

In terms of coordination across government, James (2011: 108) writes that 'Labour greatly accelerated the longer-term trends across the UK policy-making process towards the use of more informal and ad hoc processes of consultation and communication'. The key committee after 1998 was the Joint Ministerial Committee (Europe) (JMC(E)) chaired by the Foreign Secretary. As Keating (2010: 155) notes 'JMC(E) was 'the only JMC that actually worked between 2002 and 2008'. JMC(E) included government ministers, the head of the Labour EP delegation and representatives from the devolved administrations.

The tension between Blair and Brown at the heart of the New Labour government was also evident in EU policy. The Treasury extracted EMU from more general cabinet discussion and made it a matter for bilateral discussions between the Chancellor and Prime Minister (Dyson, 2000). In the context of the 'prepare and decide' policy on the euro, a European Strategy Committee was also created, chaired by the Prime Minister and with the Chancellor among its members, but it met only three times (James, 2011: 111).

The COES has sought coordination across Whitehall and the diffusion of information. Yet, as EU competencies have grown, it has become more difficult for this central coordinating machinery to keep a tight grip on all aspects of policy. Moreover, departments of state have become much more proficient and experienced in their dealings with the EU because of the increasing number of policy issues that now possess a European dimension.

The UK has managed to develop a strong and effective coordinating mechanism for the development and pursuit of British interests that has been admired in other member states. The FCO continues to play a key role. In the early days of British membership, the FCO's main responsibility was to coordinate Britain's relations with the EC. This changed as more sectoral, specialist and technical Councils developed competencies that required input from national ministries with appropriate expertise. At the same time, as the EU moved into areas of high politics such as CFSP post-Maastricht, the FCO became more involved in this area of EU activity. The Foreign Secretary continues to play a key role: 'In nine cases out of ten, it is he who concludes ministerial correspondence and ministerial discussions on any particular issue' (Wall, 2002: 17).

As prime minister, Blair sought to play a greater role in the projection of British interests. The step change initiative launched by Blair in 1998 sought a significant shift in the UK's ability to make its case in Europe. The key relationship within the EU is between France and Germany. The Elysée Treaty of 1963 formalized this cooperation, and it has been deeply institutionalized ever since. One aspect of Blair's plan for a step-change in British relations with the EU was the attempt to build coalitions and alliances with other member states. For example, the UK aligned itself with Italy and Spain over market liberalization, while there was also optimism that new member states who joined after 2004 would be UK allies, given the strong pro-US stance of the governments of many accession states. However, as noted in Chapter 7, their stances on the budget, regional development and agriculture do not make them natural UK allies on these issues.

The main emphasis within Whitehall is on securing cross-departmental agreement on major issues. Britain used to stand apart from other EU member states because of single-party government, which was seen as making consensus-building a more straightforward task. We look at the impact of coalition government later in this chapter. Bulmer and Burch (1998: 607) argue that Whitehall has

made a much smoother transition to EU membership than
Parliament (as will become clearer when the Parliamentary arena is
analysed in Chapter 9). The important thing, however, is that both
Whitehall and Parliament must work together, because it is no good
having a smoothly working and well-oiled central government
machine if there is a lack of political leadership. Administrative and
technical expertise cannot fill a political vacuum such as that which
existed during much of the 1990s or, more recently, on the single
currency. Or, as one official more bluntly puts it: 'there's no point
having a Rolls Royce machinery if the driver's a lunatic' (cited in
Bulmer and Burch, 1998: 607). During John Major's premiership,
for instance, the paralysis caused by deep divisions within the
Conservative Party precluded the longer-term planning of EU
policy. Blair's EU adviser, Sir Stephen Wall (2002: 16), made it clear
that:

> What civil servants like is strong leadership. If you have a situa-
> tion where people feel that that doesn't exist, and with regards to
> Europe in the last year or so before 1997 that was the perception,
> then you will find that they are unhappy and seek to follow what
> they believe to be the consensus line in the national interest.

There were no serious divisions within the Labour Party in
Parliament during Blair's three terms in office, although his record
on the EU was mixed. As seen in Chapters 6 and 7, Britain did push
for deepening of single market integration and was a leading player
in the development of EDSP. In other areas, such as the CAP, it was
more difficult to secure objectives while Britain was outside the
eurozone and Schengen. Britain's reception capacity remained
strong, but the development of greater projection through the step-
change initiative was seen as uneven in its effects (Bulmer and Burch,
2005). Most notably, the Treasury was reluctant to embrace EU-
level networking and alliance-building.

Impacts on the core executive

Bulmer and Burch (1998) identified four measures of the ways in
which the EU could lead to institutional change. Effects could be
evident on: formal institutional structures; procedures and
processes; codes and guidelines; and in terms of cultural/normative
change. In each of these areas, their conclusion is that central

government's adaptation to the EU has been in accordance with established patterns of domestic government. The main changes that they found related to adaptation to specific requirements of EC law and to the demands of negotiation and bargaining at EU level. In other respects, they argue that the main aspects of the Whitehall process have remained intact, with continued emphasis on the search for a 'line', and emphasis once this line has been agreed, on collective responsibility and the sharing of information across Whitehall and with devolved governments. This has led to a growing institutionalization of the EU, but in accordance with a traditional Whitehall approach. This echoes the finding of Burch and Holliday (1996: 606) that points to the ways in which 'a pervasive Europeanization of British central government was consistent with the "Whitehall model" of government ... European integration has been absorbed into the "logic" of the Whitehall machinery'. This finding also meshes with a key strand of work on Europeanization more generally which argues that adaptation to the EU often occurs with 'national colours' (Green Cowles *et al.*, 2001).

The Whitehall machinery favours 'unity, loyalty and consensus seeking', with an emphasis on prior cross-departmental agreement and information sharing (Dyson, 2000: 903). An additional norm has also been transplanted into the Whitehall machinery: effective transposition of EU legislation into national law. The UK has not been a particularly 'awkward state' when it comes to the implementation of EU decisions, which reinforces the point made by Wilks (1996) that it is useful to distinguish between the UK as a sometimes 'awkward partner' but, often, a less awkward state in terms of the capacity to adapt to EU requirements.

The case of the old Department of the Environment (DoE, now part of DEFRA) is interesting in this respect, as the DoE shifted from an initially sceptical and defensive reaction to a more proactive role within the EU. Moreover, the structure of environmental policy-making was extensively Europeanized. Jordan (2000) studied the DoE's relations with the EU between 1970 and 1997, and the ways in which the Department's organization structured the scope and depth of Europeanization. This emphasizes the shaping effects of a Whitehall ethos and established standard operating procedures on adaptation by the British state to European integration's effects.

The leadership provided by secretaries of state can also be an important factor. For most of John Major's 1992–97 premiership, the DoE was run by John Gummer, one of the stronger pro-Europeans in the cabinet. Gummer moved to the DoE from MAFF, which he saw as more tuned in to the EU than the DoE, which he thought tended to see the EU 'as something over there ... The Department hadn't quite learnt that they had to take responsibility for what they had agreed. It was a question entirely of coming to terms with reality' (Gummer, cited in Jordan, 2000: 24). Jordan shows that the DoE had engaged more positively with the Commission's Directorate General, dealing with environmental policy and with the EP. The DoE also made more effort to get its officials to work in Brussels and gain experience there. Jordan (2000: 26) concludes that 'Europeanisation has significantly reduced the DoE's ability to make domestic policy independent of other actors, but it has provided new points of leverage over more powerful domestic departments, allowing the DoE to project its influence onto a broader European plane.'

The relationship between Whitehall and Westminster is also of fundamental importance. Mechanisms for parliamentary scrutiny of EU legislation have been established, with the Select Committee for European legislation in the House of Commons and the EU Select Committee of the House of Lords. The Commons tends to sift proposed legislation, while the House of Lords undertakes more detailed inquiries into particular issues. Since 1980, it has been established practice that no minister will enter into an agreement in the Council of Ministers if the proposed measure has not been scrutinized in the House of Commons. EU documents are sent to the relevant committee within 48 hours of receipt, and within 10 days a document outlining the government's position is sent by the relevant minister to the committee. In addition, debates will be held on the floor of the House and MPs can ask ministers oral or written questions. Patterns of scrutiny and accountability have been criticized because the volume of EU legislation makes it difficult to keep a close check on developments. The EU's move into matters of 'high politics', such as CFSP and JHA – which are prone to secrecy at national level anyway – has been seen as exacerbating problems of oversight and control.

Closer analysis of the Treasury's role provides affirmation of the ways in which understandings of the EU can differ across Whitehall in line with departmental histories and interests. Dyson (2000) identifies the 'limited Europeanisation' of the Treasury and suggests a number of reasons for this. First, EMU and the process of economic convergence was not an external source of policy change for the UK, as it was for countries such as France and Italy. The UK has under-gone economic changes since the 1980s that did not require the external discipline of EMU. Second, Dyson identifies both a linger-ing euroscepticism among Treasury mandarins, plus the powerful role of economic beliefs within the Treasury that have tended to have a strong Atlantic, rather than European, component. Third, scepticism about EMU was reinforced by the ERM ejection in September 1992, which consolidated the view that 'credibility is made at home' (Dyson, 2000: 902). Finally, the position of the City of London as a global financial centre has been central to the UK's position on EMU, as reaffirmed by David Cameron in 2011. The result was that EMU was viewed as a set of external constraints on the UK economy, while Treasury officials had not routinely been exposed to EU socialization effects and had not 'internalized' EU norms. The result of these two factors is that the 'five tests' revealed 'a conditional and instrumental view of participation ... linked to a Treasury agenda of exporting British ideas about structural economic reform to goods, labour and capital markets. The Euro-zone was to be "Anglicized" rather than Britain "Europeanized"' (Dyson, 2000: 899). The case of the Treasury illustrates once again how European integration has had important effects on central government, but that these effects have been consistent with the formal, informal and cultural logics of Whitehall.

Over time, institutional knowledge and know-how within Whitehall has steadily developed. Officials have access to guidance notes that detail the proper manner for dealing with EU business. In addition, departments issue their own notes which supplement these. These notes are not codified in any official statute or directive, but it is well-established that matters such as correspondence with the European Commission that have implications for other depart-ments will also be copied to that department and to devolved governments.

The coalition and the European issue

Coalition government presents many challenges to existing under-standings of British government and politics but, in this section, we see that the work of the coalition is set against longer-term changes in patterns of domestic and EU politics. There has not been a radical overhaul of Britain's approach to the EU under the coalition, but we do see some evidence of a change from the days of New Labour of the manner in which coordination occurs within central government.

At the heart of the coalition government is the relationship between David Cameron as prime minister and Nick Clegg as his deputy. Evidence from the first two years of coalition government suggests that, despite coming from different parties, there is a more stable and harmonious relationship than there was between Blair and Brown. Overall, if we think about the respective powerbases of Cameron and Clegg, then the former possesses greater institutional and personal resources. The Conservatives are the stronger party within the coalition and, on the EU issue specifically, ensured that the coalition agreement broadly reflected the Conservative position. The main problem for Cameron is backbench Conservative dissent over the EU issue because of perceived concessions to the Liberal Democrats. Bennister and Heffernan (2011) argue that Cameron is no more constrained by Clegg than he would be by a rival within his own party.

Within central government, coalition government has meant emphasis on coordination. This is to be expected, given the need to 'balance' within the coalition government with ministers from both of its component parties. After 2010, there were five Liberal Democrat cabinet ministers, including policy areas with significant EU dimensions, such as BIS and DECC. There were also 24 other Liberal Democrats in government in more junior ministerial positions. This has meant some weakening of the Prime Minister's power of patronage because of the need to ensure Liberal Democrat representation. For example, when Chris Huhne resigned in December 2011 from his role as Secretary of State for DECC, he was replaced by another Liberal Democrat, Ed Davey. However, the three most important offices of state – the Treasury, FCO and Home Office – are all assigned to Conservative secretaries of state. An emphasis on coordination is now new, but has been reinforced by the exigencies of coalition. The result, as Bennister and Heffernan (2011: 27) put it, is that 'coalition government means government by committee, but cabinet committee meetings on important matters have usually been preceded by meetings of the key principals led by Cameron and Clegg or their surrogates'.

In their analysis of the role of UKRep in the area of policing, de Maillard and Smith (2012) do find some impact of coalition government on the role of UKRep and the projection of British interest at EU level. One of their interviewees commented that: 'We do speak with one voice mostly ... . The fact that we now have a coalition government does however slow things down. We have to be extra careful now about consulting all the departments.'

As noted earlier in this chapter, under Blair and Brown the key roles in EU policy were played by the Treasury and Cabinet Office. The FCO was still an important actor, but became more marginal to the formulation of British EU policy. This reflected both the increased role of the European Council, but also the increased technical know-how about the EU issue within Whitehall that meant less reliance on the FCO. The coalition government changed this dynamic. A House of Commons committee enquiry into the FCO role found a re-establishment of its role in setting EU policy and a less interventionist prime minister. The key relationship in British EU policy under the coalition is between the FCO and the Cabinet Office. The Foreign Secretary chairs 'a revitalized ... European Affairs Committee', with the Secretary of State for DECC (Huhne, and then Davey) as Deputy Chair. A key issue is that the Foreign Office is a 'line ministry', which means that the Cabinet Office still plays a key role in coordinating the organization of the European issue within British central government (House of Commons, 2011).

New territorial politics within the UK

Devolution since 1997 has altered the political equation. Even before devolution, Scotland had been more purposeful in its dealings with the EU. Since devolution, there has been more scope for 'territorial tensions' within the British polity. The EU is, as Keating (2010: 154) notes: 'fundamentally an organisation of states'. EU policy is a matter reserved for the Westminster government. The devolved governments in Scotland, Wales and Northern Ireland can, and do, seek to influence UK policy, and also seek to mobilize at EU level to lobby on behalf of their people and key sectoral interests.

As we noted at the beginning of this chapter, there is debate between those who see European integration as strengthening states and those who think that MLG within the EU can weaken states, in the sense of taking some powers away from them and leading to the sharing of other powers. A key component of this multi-level thesis is the development of sub-national levels of governance. Any discussion of government in the UK must take account of the fact that the United Kingdom of Great Britain and Northern Ireland is a multi-national state and that 'British' national identity is a problematic concept. England, Scotland, Wales and Northern Ireland are more than 'regions', but less than independent states.

The rise and fall of the English regions

New Labour carved England into nine regions with Regional Development Agencies, Regional Assemblies and Regional Government Offices. In their analysis of developments in England, Burch and Gomez (2002) identified an elite-driven 'new regionalism' that reflected a strategic readjustment on the part of regional tiers of government to new opportunity structures provided by the EU. They saw this as particularly driven by the EU's structural funds targeted at regional economic development and, in the case of England, as not being reflective of deep-seated regional identities. Access to resources played an important part in English regionalism. In particular, the growth and development of the EU's structural funds for regional economic development were highly influential in the development of the 'third level' of European governance and the inculcation of what Jeffrey (2000) calls 'sub-national mobilization'. Sub-national mobilization has three main elements. First, there is direct regional involvement in EU decision-making through the Committee of the Regions and other mechanisms for consultation and dialogue. Federal states such as Austria, Belgium and Germany also send representatives of their regions to the Council for matters that affect their competencies. Second, there has been increased EU-level activity by sub-national government which can, for instance, take the form of the creation of European committees, or the appointment of European officers. 'Europe' has become institutionalized as a responsibility at sub-national level with greater attention paid to the opportunities on offer. Third, the development of cooperation between EU regions can either be within national units or between them. Perhaps because of their relatively isolated geographical position, regions within the UK have been slower to respond to the opportunities for cross-regional link-ups than other parts of Europe, where land borders lead to more obvious links between regions. One result of sub-national mobilization was the creation of a culture of 'mutual dependence', in the sense that the EU needs the regions for the disbursement of funds and the development of regional regeneration strategies, while regions need Europe because it provides a new 'opportunity space' for them to build policy responsibilities (Burch and Gomez, 2002: 768).

As shown in Chapter 6, the EU's structural funds have grown to around 40 per cent of the total EU budget. The pursuit of funding and the need to build capacity to manage EU schemes was a key driver of the push to English regionalism. Burch and Gomez (2002) saw this and a range of other factors as being relevant. They saw a changed mentality at regional level which has seen less moaning about central government and a greater determination to promote the interests of sub-national government. The immediate aims of this mobilization were economic and linked to economic regeneration. They were, thus, inspired by the single market programme and by the development of the structural funds. This mobilization developed within the regions, rather than being inculcated from London. In this sense, it was an authentic, albeit elite-driven, expression of regional interests, rather than top-down Whitehall paternalism, and was directed towards Brussels as much as it was towards London. It was also based on partnership between the private and public sectors. In terms of its legitimacy base, there was little evidence of popular demand for regional government. Overall, English regionalism can best be understood as a pragmatic response to changed opportunities, rather than as deeper-seated expressions of identity.

The creation of the Greater London Assembly (GLA) and elected mayor have been relative successes and refocused London politics on its elected local leadership. Elected mayors have also been introduced in a number of other English towns and cities with more variable effects. However, plans for elected regional assemblies outside London never got off the ground and were ditched in 2007 in the government's 'Single Regional Strategy', which gave increased powers to Regional Development Agencies (RDAs) in England. The Conservative–Liberal Democratic coalition scrapped the RDAs in its June 2010 Localism Bill and has no interest in pursuing Labour's plans for regional government in England. Cameron's Conservatives have little enthusiasm for regional government. Instead, ideas about the 'big society' place more emphasis on voluntary associations, rather than elected politicians.

Devolution

The UK is a multi-national state with significant devolved power. This adds a further dimension to the discussion of sovereignty and is suggestive of a movement towards federalization within the UK, or even its break-up. The shape and form of devolution has differed.

Scotland has a Parliament with primary legislative and tax-varying powers, while the Welsh Assembly initially had neither of these powers. The new devolved government in Wales did not get off to a good start with the European Commission when, in November 2004, a map of the new enlarged EU was produced that omitted Wales. Limited law-making powers were introduced for the Welsh Assembly in 2006, and then expanded after a 2011 referendum (Wyn Jones and Scully, 2012). After the May 2011 elections, the Welsh Assembly Government (WAG) renamed itself the Welsh Government.

There is evidence that people in Wales and Scotland are less eurosceptic than those in England, but this is relative, in the sense that euroscepticism is prevalent across the UK. For example, the Scottish Social Attitudes Survey of 2009 did find a 'pervasive Euroscepticism' although it was 'slightly, but consistently, less pronounced in Scotland than in England' (Keating, 2011: 15). There is also evidence that national identity can influence views on the EU as much as, if not more than, utilitarian cost–benefit factors (Carey, 2002). Evidence from Wales shows that people who hold a Welsh identity are more likely to hold positive attitudes to European integration (Clements, 2011). In contrast, people in England who identify as English are more likely to be hostile to European integration (Keating, 2011).

European integration has played a role in the shaping of political identities in both Scotland and Wales. For example, in Scotland, the decision taken in 1988 to pursue 'independence in Europe' was a way to make the Scottish National Party (SNP) appear 'more cosmopolitan and outward-looking than many of their unionist opponents' (Keating, 2011: 5).Claims for devolved power in Scotland and Wales were quite strongly domestic and rooted in resentment at Thatcherism's English characteristics, but the new opportunities offered by Europe also played a part in arguments for devolved power. This was because a united Europe and the development of a 'Europe of the regions' offered a sustainable future to smaller nations and regions that would exert more influence within a united Europe than they could if they sought independence. The situation in Northern Ireland has been rather different and complex because of the deep social divide and post-conflict situation. Northern Ireland was in receipt of Objective One funding for the EU's least economically developed regions. The EU also launched a Programme for Peace and Reconciliation in Northern Ireland and the Border Region of Ireland known as the PEACE I (1995–99) and PEACE II (2000–06) Programmes. Murphy (2011) argues that the formalization of devolved power has actually increased the central coordinating role played by Whitehall and UKRep and, thus, limited the autonomy of sub-national governments to pursue their interests at EU level.

Cole and Palmer argue that European integration has led to the development of enhanced capacity within the Welsh government and increased know-how, while they also identify the 'constructive' potential of engagement with the EU for sub-state nations. They see three components of this potential. First, there is scope for cultural affirmation, with regions such as Brittany and Catalonia within the EU and Quebec in Canada as examples. Second, there can be 'comparing up', where smaller nations or more powerful regions are used as an example of the constructive potential of further devolution of power. Examples here include smaller member states such as Ireland and Latvia, as well as the Baden-Wurttemberg region in Germany and Catalonia. Finally, there is potential for resource-based alliance-building, with Ireland and Brittany used as examples. Wales has sought to increase its engagement with other regions within what is known as the Atlantic Arch, running from Ireland to Wales, down to Cornwall along the Atlantic coast of France and down to the Basque country and Portugal and also, more surprisingly, with Sicily (Cole and Palmer, 2011).

Devolved government operates in the context of a UK system within which central government maintains a tight grip on EU policy, with a particular concern to monitor the EU budget and financing system. Whitehall's gate-keeper role is redolent of its role in a unitary state, rather than the more complex intergovernmental relations within a federal system. The Scottish and Welsh governments need to identify their key interests and then seek to use the UK network in their pursuit. While the sub-national and regional tier of government has developed quite rapidly, there was much work to be done to define the role that these tiers would play in the formulation of EU policy and to build capacity within devolved government for the implementation of EU schemes, such as funding programmes. Between 2000 and 2006, for example, Wales was in receipt of Objective 1 funding for West Wales and the Valleys. The WAG would be responsible for administering these funds, which would be a test for nascent devolved institutions. Indeed, Cole and Palmer (2011: 381) cite an official in the Welsh government who summed up very neatly the challenge faced by the WAG: 'managing the structural funds was a nightmare for which the young institution was unprepared and under-staffed. It is to our credit that we pulled through'.

For the devolved administrations, there are three main ways to seek to influence the UK's EU policy. First, Welsh and Scottish ministers do not have the right to participate in Council meetings, but can be invited to do so by the UK government ministers. Welsh government ministers have, for example, participated in Council meetings on issues such as agriculture, education and minority languages. The most important route to influence for the devolved administrations is to seek to influence UK government policy. The JMC(E) cabinet committee provided a forum for representation of the interests of the devolved administrations. This was more straightforward when the political majority in the Wales and Scotland has coincided with that in Westminster. Since 2007, Scotland has been governed by the SNP (between 2007–11, in a minority administration and, since its landslide victory in 2011, with a large majority).

Second, the devolved administrations can also pursue their own strategies to exercise influence at EU level through, for example, their own representation. Scotland, Wales and Northern Ireland all have their own offices in Brussels, but work within what is called 'the UKRep family'. As noted in the previous section, UKRep sees part of its role as being to ensure the representation of the UK's territorial interests.

Third, another route to influence is through EU regional structures. The most obvious route is the Committee of the Regions (CoR) created by the Maastricht Treaty. The creation of the CoR marked the enthusiasm for regionalism during the 1980s and 1990s. This enthusiasm has diminished, not least because of the diversity of regional tiers within the EU (some seeking independence, while others seek a greater role in national systems) and the very different ways in which they are incorporated into national government. Both the Scottish and Welsh governments have been keen to participate in alternative networks, such as the group of Regions with Legislative Powers (REGLEG). The Scottish first minister, Jack McConnell, was President of REGLEG in 2004, while his Welsh counterpart, Rhodri Morgan, held the role in 2006.

In terms of the interests that are to be represented, there has been little evidence of divergence between sub-state nations within the UK, albeit with some divergence on agricultural policy and fisheries.

Scotland and Wales have different kinds of agricultural sector to that in England. For example, the interests of Scottish hill farmers are different from those of large-scale agri-businesses in England while, in both countries, the fishing industry is relatively larger.

Devolution left a number of unanswered questions because of the incremental development of the devolution programme and the territorial tensions that can arise. The big question, as Mitchell (2002) saw it, is whether devolution has helped resolve some of the problems of territorial politics in Britain, or whether it has undermined coherent government through further territorialization. In Mitchell's view (2002: 762), 'asymmetrical devolution created asymmetrical problems with asymmetrical preparation'. Moreover, while the transition to European integration by central government was fairly smooth and closely coordinated, transformation to a Europe within which sub-national and regional tiers of government play a more prominent role raises all kinds of boundary, responsibility and coordination problems. This is because the 'ongoing Whitehall process' has the durability to remain an ongoing Whitehall process, while the 'ongoing devolution process' is more of a venture into the constitutional unknown.

Conclusion

This chapter explored the effects of European integration on the British polity and showed that there remains a strong emphasis on the tight coordination of UK policy by the Westminster government. Outside London, attempts to develop a stronger tier of regional government in England have not been successful. In contrast, devolved power to Scotland and Wales has reshaped British politics, although EU relations are still dominated by the centre. Over time, the EU has become a 'thicker' institutional constraint on the British core executive with effects that are noticeable across central government and that also stretch out to sub-national level, too. Over time, these competencies and intensive interactions with the EU institutions and other member states have meant that 'Europe' has become more deeply constitutive of the identities and interests of domestic political actors. At the same time, these effects are not uniform. Thus, as has been shown throughout this book, the lens provided by the domestic political and institutional context has filtered the effects of European integration. For instance, adaptation by central government has been strongly influenced by existing and well-established patterns within Whitehall, and by different departmental histories and interests. While European integration has clearly had important effects on central government, the coordination of responses to these effects has tended to be in line with the established Whitehall ethos. This can lead to varying patterns of adaptation across Whitehall, with some policy areas such as agriculture and trade extensively Europeanized, while others (such as the Home Office) have less direct contact with the EU, although this is changing as the EU deals with crime, policing and border controls. The key role of the Treasury in the debate about EMU and the euro was also highlighted.

In contrast, the development of sub-national government in the UK has been a process for which there are no well-established historical precedents and templates from which responses can be drawn; but here, too, we see adaptation in line with established ways of doing things. Britain has undergone significant changes because of the devolution of power introduced by the Labour government after 1997. European integration has also played a part in the development of sub-national government. The expansion in structural funding offered new opportunities for the regions. European integration also strengthened claims from Britain's sub-state nations for greater autonomy because they could point to other small-sized units that were viable actors in a united Europe. Devolution has, however, created uncertainties, blurred responsibilities and led to some territorial tensions. While the EU has created new 'opportunity spaces' for sub-national mobilization, the more precise institutional parameters of these 'spaces' remain to be clearly specified, because the devolution process in the UK is still unfolding.

Chapter 9

British Party Politics and the Rise of Euroscepticism

European integration has been both a divisive and, at times, explosive issue in British party politics. This chapter explains why, since the 1950s, neither of the two main national parties has adopted a consistent stance on European integration, and also why European integration still has such explosive potential, particularly for the Conservative Party. Divisions on Europe tend to be within, rather than between, parties and are crucially affected by the size of the governing party, party majorities or the effects of coalition government. Party leaders have been understood as seeking to balance between pro- and anti-EU wings of their parties, but with varying degrees of success. Balancing within and between parties has become more difficult in the context of coalition since the 2010 election. We also look at the rise of eurosceptic parties, particularly UKIP, as a distinct force in British politics, albeit without having yet made a breakthrough in 'first order' national elections to Parliament. The growth of euroscepticism is indicative of the 'uncorking of the bottle' of popular dissent about the European project and the move from a 'permissive consensus' to a 'constraining dissensus', as Hooghe and Marks (2008) put it. The implication of a permissive consensus was that people would take their cues on Europe from political parties. A constraining dissensus implies that parties may take their cues from a sceptical electorate. Cause and effect are difficult to disentangle, but, at the very least, the relationship between voters and parties on European integration has become far more complex.

For and against Europe in the 1960s and 1970s

Euroscepticism has been seen to include a range of positions that share a common opposition to European integration. These positions can be critical of European integration, or be outright opposition (Taggart and Szczerbiak, 2004). The term 'eurosceptic' was first used in the early 1990s (in 1992 in *The Economist*, according to the *Oxford English Dictionary*), but there were already dissenting voices in the main political parties. There was a tendency to view perceived economic costs and benefits as the drivers of public support or opposition to European integration. Analysts of euroscepticism have focused on two other powerful driving factors. The first of these is group membership and national identity, and whether there is space within an individual's conceptualization of their national identity for Europe. Another draws from public loss of confidence in politics and politicians, which would imply not just a specific opposition to the EU, but also a more general loss of confidence in the political system (Hooghe and Marks, 2007: 121–2). This move from a focus on a cost–benefit basis for attitudes to a focus on the effects of national identity and trust in politics has been linked to the EU's move from 'market-making' to 'polity-building' (Eichenberg and Dalton, 2007). Franklin *et al.* (1994) saw the Maastricht treaty as particularly significant in this respect because it moved the EU into areas of high politics such as economic and monetary policy, foreign and security policy, and immigration and asylum.

Conservative opponents of European integration were largely excluded from the party mainstream in the 1960s, 1970s and much of the 1980s. Conservative 'anti-marketeers' in the 1970s, such as Teddy Taylor MP, gave up ministerial careers to pursue from the backbenches their dislike for European economic and political integration. Only after Thatcher's 1988 Bruges speech (more on which later) and the Maastricht Treaty ratification saga was 'euroscepticism' legitimated as a mainstream school of thought within the Party.

Labour has followed a different trajectory. Divisions over Europe were evident at the highest levels of the Party through the 1960s and 1970s. Only after Labour's crushing 1983 election defeat were anti-EC/EU views pushed to the Party's margins as it undertook root and branch 'modernization'.

Between the election of Edward Heath's Conservative government in 1970 and the referendum on the Labour government's renegotiated membership terms in June 1975, a debate about Britain's place in the EC spilled over from Parliament into wider public debate, culminating in Britain's first-ever national referendum. The

June 1975 referendum on the membership terms renegotiated by the Labour government after their 1974 return to power resulted in a resounding victory for the 'yes' campaign, but the issue was far from resolved. The legacy of the 1975 referendum was an intensification of anti-EC sentiment within the governing Labour Party which aided the Party's descent into warring factions after its 1979 election defeat.

EC membership was largely an elite concern in the 1960s and 1970s. The general public was not enthusiastic about joining the Common Market, but these opinions were neither strongly held nor deeply felt. In Parliament, however, the staking out of battle lines between pro-and anti-accession forces can be detected since the early 1960s, with strong feelings on both sides.

The size of the governing party's majority has important effects on the potential for anti-EC opposition to make an impact. In the late 1960s and early 1970s, Labour and the Conservatives were closely matched and majorities in the House of Commons were narrow. For instance, when Edward Heath proposed to take Britain into the EC, his Commons majority was a mere 30, while a leading Conservative opponent of EC membership, Neil Marten, estimated that there were between 70 and 80 opponents on the Conservative benches (Forster, 2002b: 33). It was cross-party support from 69 Labour backbenchers (including Roy Jenkins, Roy Hattersley and the future Party leader John Smith) that secured Britain's EC membership.

Although there were anti-EC groups in both the main parties, they found it difficult to coalesce into a credible and cohesive force. Instead, there tended to be groupings within the parties that did not readily form alliances across the party divide. The organizations within the Conservative Party which expressed this anti-EC sentiment were the Anti-Common Market League, founded in 1961, and the 1970 Group, founded as a right-wing dining club that had close links to Enoch Powell (Forster, 2002a: 35). Enoch Powell was a key figure in the development of Conservative euroscepticism and to him can be attributed a right-wing, free market and nationalist critique of European integration (Gamble, 1998: 18). Powell had been sacked from the Shadow Cabinet in April 1968 following inflammatory comments about immigration and immigrants. Labour MPs were unlikely to have much sympathy for Powell's right-wing brand of anti-EC thought. Powell's influence rapidly diminished when he left the Conservative Party and called for a

Labour vote in the February and October 1974 general election because Labour offered a referendum on accession. Powell's philosophical legacy (without the anti-Americanism) had more profound effects on the Conservative Party.

In 1972, the support of 69 Labour MPs for EC accession reflected divisions within the Labour Party. Although there were prominent pro-EC voices, the majority of the Party opposed EC membership. This opposition was evident at all levels of the Party: the cabinet, the parliamentary party, the rank and file membership, and the trade union movement. The main anti-EC grouping within the Labour Party was the Labour Safeguards Committee, founded in 1967, which became the Labour Committee for Safeguards on the Common Market (Forster, 2002a: 35). Prominent left-wing groups such as Tribune were also hostile to EC membership. Anti-EC sentiment encompassed most strands of thought within the party from the left to the right. Leading figures of the day, such as Tony Benn, Barbara Castle, Douglas Jay and Peter Shore, were advocates of staying out. The scope for division is illustrated by the fact that other senior figures, such as Roy Jenkins and Shirley Williams, argued for membership. As Forster (2002a: 35) notes: 'The Labour Party was therefore more anti-market than the Conservative Party, but it was also more divided at every level of the parliamentary party, on the frontbench as well as the backbenches.' The leading trade unions also opposed EC membership, which meant that the powerful trade union block vote within the Labour Party was firmly aligned with the anti-EC camp (Robins, 1979).

The question for opponents of the Common Market was whether organizations could be established that tapped into anti-EC sentiment in both the Conservative and Labour parties, and could form the basis for a strong cross-party anti-EC coalition. This was likely to be difficult, given party loyalties and the major political differences between right- and left-wing opponents of European integration, such as Enoch Powell and Tony Benn. There were some attempts to establish broader anti-EC coalitions through the two main anti-accession organizations: the Keep Britain Out (KBO) movement established in 1962, and the Common Market Safeguards Campaign (CMSC), created in 1970. The KBO campaign sought a broad anti-EC movement beyond the parliamentary arena, but was hindered by the diversity of its membership, which included right-wing Conservative MPs and left-wing Labour MPs who found it difficult to work together. The CMSC was divided because some of its members wanted to open negotiations and then judge the terms available, while others were opposed outright to membership.

On the pro-EC side, the British Council of the European Movement (BCEM) experienced no such divisions because it was unequivocally pro-membership (Butler and Kitzinger, 1976; King, 1977; Forster, 2002a: 37). There are some parallels here with the contemporary anti-Euro campaign which suggest some potential for stresses and strains during any future referendum campaign.

As Prime Minister between 1974 and 1976, Harold Wilson's main concern was Party management. The background conditions were not good. A weak economy and poor industrial relations blighted his government. Wilson also appreciated the simmering opposition to European integration within his Party. Although Wilson had made an application for membership in 1967, he was more than happy when Labour returned to opposition to use the EC as a stick with which he could beat Heath's Conservative government. Wilson claimed not to be opposed to membership *per se*, but to oppose the terms of entry as negotiated by Heath. Wilson then called for a renegotiation and a referendum on the renegotiated terms. This referendum pledge moved Enoch Powell to desert the Conservative Party and call for a Labour vote in the 1974 general elections.

Short-term advantages for Wilson were outweighed by longer-term losses. An early indication of the European issue's potential to fracture the Labour Party was provided following Shadow Cabinet agreement in 1972 that a referendum would be held on Britain's EC membership. This prompted the resignation of the Deputy Leader, Roy Jenkins, who was not prepared to stand this affront to his pro-European sensibilities, particularly as its motives seemed grounded in the low politics of party advantage. Wilson was keen to ensure that, when a referendum campaign was held, it did not lead to further outbreaks of feuding within his government. The potential for it to do so was clear. Within the Cabinet, the renegotiated terms were agreed by 16 votes to 7 in March 1975. The opponents were Tony Benn, Barbara Castle, Michael Foot, William Ross, Peter Shore, John Silkin and Eric Varley (Forster, 2002b: 56). Divisions were even more pronounced within the Parliamentary Labour Party, with 145 voting against the terms, 137 voting in favour and 33 abstaining. A Labour Party special conference in March 1975 saw 3.9 million votes cast against membership compared with 1.7

million in favour. There was parliamentary as well as rank and file hostility to the EC. The support of Conservative MPs saw the renegotiated terms through the Commons. Wilson permitted an 'agreement to disagree' during the referendum campaign. This allowed cabinet ministers to follow their consciences during the referendum campaign, so long as they did not appear on platforms in opposition to each other. There was, though, serious trouble in store for Labour. Wilson could attempt to 'manage' these issues, but could not suppress them. As economic and political problems piled up from the mid-1970s onwards, the Labour Party became increasingly anti-EC.

The 1975 referendum was the first time that the issue of Britain's place in Europe was opened to a broader public debate. This was something of a novelty because debates about European integration had tended to be framed in technical language that did little to enthuse the electorate. During the 1975 referendum campaign, a successful pro EC campaign managed to harness a cross-party group of leading centrist politicians with broad public appeal. Their argument was that the EC offered practical economic and political advantages to Britain which far outweighed any loss of sovereignty. The anti-EC campaign had significantly less funding, lacked media support and was led by a motley collection of politicians from the left- and right-wing fringes. They argued that the terms of membership were disadvantageous and would lead to higher prices, and that EC membership was a threat to self-government.

The referendum campaign was organized by two umbrella organizations. The Britain in Europe (BIE) campaign mobilized on the pro-EC side, while the National Referendum Campaign (NRC) led the anti-EC movement. The BIE campaign had a number of advantages: it was composed of leading centrist politicians such as Edward Heath and Roy Jenkins, while the NRC was composed of politicians such as Tony Benn and Enoch Powell, who came from opposite ends of the political spectrum. The BIE campaign also enjoyed considerable financial advantages and strong support from the main national newspapers. The BIE campaign managed to raise around £1.5 million while the NRC mustered around £250,000 (King, 1977) and earned the ringing endorsement of Fleet Street. The BIE campaign also possessed a clear and unambiguous argument: membership was in Britain's interests. The NRC campaign was less focused on a single coherent theme. Some of its campaigners opposed the membership terms but did not rule out membership, while others were deeply opposed to European integration. Those who opposed the terms quickly got submerged in mind-numbing detail, while those who were outright opponents of membership were portrayed as extremists (Forster, 2002a).

Even though enthusiasm for EC membership did not run deep, these views were not strongly held and shifted during the course of a campaign as pro-EC arguments were made by relatively popular politicians expounding a simple, clear message (Butler and Kitzinger, 1976; King, 1977). With their financial advantages, media backing and government support, the result was a not wholly unsurprising victory for the 'yes' campaign, with a 67.2 per cent 'yes' vote on a 64.5 per cent turnout.

The referendum did not put the issue to rest. In fact, the campaign provided some opening shots in what was to become a damaging and divisive period in Labour's history, marked by a growing distance between the party leadership and the rank and file. There was disappointment that manifesto commitments had not been pursued in government between 1974 and 1979. This prompted calls for internal party democratization which would give activists more control over Labour MPs. A left-wing critique of Labour in power began to emerge. This involved a radical reappraisal of economic and social policies and the development, by 1983, of Labour's Alternative Economic Strategy, which contained a full-blooded commitment to Socialism. Labour's move to the left also led to a hardening of opposition to European integration. The Treaty of Rome and the constraints that it would impose on member state governments were incompatible with the kind of programme that Labour proposed to develop. Withdrawal from the EC became official party policy and was endorsed by 5 million votes to 2 million votes at a special Party conference convened in October 1980. This prompted the 'gang of four' ex-ministers (Roy Jenkins, David Owen, Bill Rodgers and Shirley Williams) and a gaggle of MPs to leave the party and found the Social Democratic Party, which soon struck up an alliance with the Liberals.

Following Labour's calamitous electoral defeat in 1983, the question was not so much whether Labour could win power, but whether it could survive. This problem faced the party leader elected in the wake of the 1983 debacle, Neil Kinnock. Kinnock had been a staunch and eloquent left-wing opponent of the EC throughout the 1970s. He was now to begin a personal and political odyssey that would see him advocate the 'modernization' of the Labour Party, endorse positive engagement with the EC, and conclude with him moving to Brussels to become a European Commissioner (Westlake, 2001).

Almost as soon as Kinnock became party leader, the commitment to outright withdrawal was watered down to a commitment to withdraw, if satisfactory renegotiated terms could not be secured. By the 1989 EP elections, Labour was advocating active engagement with the EC at a time when Conservative euroscepticism was beginning to take root in the wake of Margaret Thatcher's seminal Bruges speech. Labour would, however, need to climb an electoral mountain if they were to regain power. They were considerably aided in this task by the euro-war that broke out in the Conservative Party during the 1990s, and that helped shatter the party's electoral credibility.

Conservative euroscepticism

In the 1970s, Conservative support for the EC was based on a pragmatic and instrumental acceptance of the potential benefits that EC membership could bring. Enthusiasm for European integration did not run deep. Support could dry up if these benefits were seen to cease. Conservative support for European integration was thus based on a rather narrow trade-based idea of European integration that was unlikely to be adaptable to the ambitious programmes for deeper economic and political integration which were launched in the 1980s.

At the root of these difficulties has been a tension within the Conservative Party about Britain's place in the international economy. Baker *et al.* (1994) liken Conservative splits during the 1990s to two other deeply divisive events in the Party's history: the repeal of the Corn Laws in the 1840s and tariff reform in the first years of the twentieth century. Both consigned the Party to long periods in opposition. Thatcher's successor, John Major, was unable to navigate these serious challenges both to his Party and his leadership, with the result that Maastricht was 'the most serious parliamentary defeat suffered by a Conservative government in the twentieth century' (Baker *et al.*, 1994: 57; see also Baker *et al.*, 1993a; 1993b).

The motives of eurosceptic Conservative opponents of Maastricht were various. However, it has been argued that during the 1990s a new strain of Conservative eurosceptic thought emerged. This new strand of thought was labelled as 'hyperglobalist' by Baker *et al.*

(2002), in the sense that it sought to square the Thatcherite circle through the pursuit of neo-liberal objectives of openness, deregulation and privatization in a global economy, but with nation states remaining the pre-eminent units of international politics. This marks an attempt to evince an alternative political economy that involves a particular understanding of 'globalization' and of Britain's place in the world economy. This theme in eurosceptic thinking will be explored more fully when the main strands of eurosceptic thought within the Conservative Party are explored.

In case the impression be given that euroscepticism was rife within the Conservative Party during the 1980s, it is useful to provide a little context. Between 1979 and 1984, relations between Margaret Thatcher's governments and the EC were overshadowed by the dispute over the Britain's budget contributions. Once this had been resolved in 1984, the single market project elicited far greater enthusiasm from Conservatives about forms of European economic integration that mirrored domestic economic policies. The Thatcher decade saw the pursuit at national level of the neo-liberal doctrine encompassing deregulation, privatization and competitiveness with attempts also made to translate these ideological preferences into EC policy-making (Baker *et al.*, 2002: 400). Buller (2000) argues that Conservatives saw the single market programme as possessing the potential to embed at EC level a programme of economic changes similar in content to those introduced in Britain. Liberalization and deregulation would be elevated to a European level and a return to government interventionism would become well-nigh impossible. Thatcherism could be 'exported' to Europe and entrenched as a dominant ideology. The growth, development and virulence of Conservative eurosceptic opposition can, then, be related to the steady realization that this Thatcherite vision was not widely accepted by other EC member states.

European integration after the SEA fundamentally exposed the limitations of this minimalistic Conservative view of European integration. The SEA of 1986 heralded both a major transfer of sovereignty to the EC with single market integration and significant institutional reforms (such as increased use of QMV in the Council of Ministers). The Conservative governments of the 1980s were prepared to accept economic integration, but were unprepared to countenance the much deeper economic and political integration that the SEA was seen as presaging. As Forster (2002a: 66) puts it: 'The SEA therefore raised the stakes and changed the nature of the game'. For Thatcher's Conservative governments, the single market was an end in itself. For other member states and the Delors-led European Commission, it was a means to an end. This unhappy state of affairs was to be the source of Conservative euro-wars as Thatcherites railed against what they saw as the unwelcome spillover effects of the SEA. The practical benefits of a free-trade Europe were threatened by deeper economic and political integration which challenged the core Conservative idea that 'democracy and legitimacy are located in the nation state, which is the basic unit of all legitimate democratic politics' (Baker *et al.*, 2002: 402).

Despite its important implications, there was curtailed parliamentary debate about the SEA and a small number of opponents. Thatcher's party managers 'whipped' the legislation through Parliament. There were 43 votes against ratification at the bill's third reading, but the Conservatives enjoyed a large majority plus the support of the Liberals and Social Democrats. There was no cross-party anti-European integration organization that would bring anti-EC campaigners together across the Party divide.

The 1980s have been characterized by Anthony Forster (2002a: 66) as a period during which there were few opportunities for debates about European integration. For instance, the 1984 and 1989 EP elections were dominated by domestic concerns, although Margaret Thatcher's highly negative 1989 campaign (based on the slogan 'Don't live on a diet of Brussels') led to Labour becoming the largest British party in the EP and prompted some Conservative MPs to question her leadership. There were also some important developments beneath the surface; as Forster observes, the 1980s was a period during which eurosceptic tactics began to evolve with close scrutiny of EC measures, a developing technical expertise and a committed readiness to fight a war of attrition.

Who were these eurosceptics and in what did they believe? Hugo Young (1999) identified five strands of eurosceptic thought during the 1980s that were to meld in the crucible of opposition to Maastricht and EMU in the 1990s:

- *Irreconcilables*, such as John Biffen MP and Teddy Taylor MP, were long-standing opponents of European integration and its entire doings. Taylor's opposition was voiced from the back-benches; Biffen's was licensed within government during the 1980s, although Thatcher's press secretary was moved to describe him as a 'semi-detached' member of her government.

- *Constitutionalists*, such as Bill Cash, James Cran and Richard Shepherd, were particularly concerned about parliamentary sovereignty.
- *Free marketers*, such as Michael Spicer and Nicholas Budgen, were ardent Thatcherites but became disillusioned by what they saw as an interventionist EC that threatened Thatcherite policies. A cadre of young Thatcherites – including Michael Forsyth, Neil Hamilton, Peter Lilley, Michael Portillo, Edward Leigh, Francis Maude and John Redwood – entered the House of Commons after 1979 and were to organize within the No Turning Back Group. All were to become government ministers.
- *Nationalists*, such as John Carlisle, Tony Marlow and Nicholas Winterton.
- '*Wets*' (a term used in Thatcherite parlance to refer to those on the left of the party), such as Peter Tapsell, opposed what they saw as EC protectionism.

Baker *et al.*, (2002) supplement these classifications with what they labelled as 'hyperglobalist Conservative euroscepticism' that developed during the 1990s and constituted an attempt to envisage an alternative political economy for the UK outside the EU (see also Gamble, 1998). In its extreme form, hyperglobalization would be difficult for any national political party to accept because it would imply the redundancy of the nation state in the face of capital mobility in a global economy. Could the Conservatives reconcile their vision of politics within which the nation state is central with 'globalization'? Baker *et al.* (2002) argue that a particular notion of globalization has been articulated within Conservative euroscepticism. This posits a vision of Britain as a sovereign state with a low tax, low-spending, deregulated and privatized economy. The result is that 'The national policy-making constraints of globalization are welcomed because they rule out the kind of social democratic and socialist measures which are viewed as incompatible with British national identity, forcing the government to set the people free whatever its ideological predilections' (Baker *et al.*, 2002: 409). The language of 'no alternative' and 'no turning back' that was central to Thatcherite thinking in the 1980s ascends to a global level. In this context, the EU and its member states are portrayed as high-spending, high tax, over-regulated and uncompetitive encumbrances on the UK's ability to compete in a global economy. As we shall see, this kind of thinking was also to influence Labour's stance on EU 'modernization'. If the EU continues to pursue this path, then Conservative 'hyperglobalists' would either call for a renegotiation of Britain's terms of membership (the party's 2001 election stance), or may even head towards the exit. This is precisely the position the Conservatives find themselves in after the 2010 general election. In no other EU member state is this strand of eurosceptic thinking evident. The affinity of such thinkers is most clearly with the USA. As Baker *et al.* (2002: 423) put it: 'No other political elite or party elite has the same kind of material links, or the same kind of ideological attachment to the United States as do the British Conservatives, and New Labour would arguably come second in such a comparison'.

The Maastricht rebellion

These strands of eurosceptic thought were to coalesce into the most sustained parliamentary rebellion of the twentieth century. When tracing the historical lineage of modern euroscepticism, then pride of place needs to be given to Margaret Thatcher's Bruges speech of September 1988. This speech legitimized euroscepticism, provoked a debate within the Conservative Party about Britain's place in the global and international economy, provided an intellectual justification for euroscepticism, and impelled the organization of anti-EC groups both within and outside the Conservative Party.

The Bruges Speech understood the EC in Gaullist terms as an association of states whose core purpose was to strengthen the sovereignty of the member states. Thatcher opposed what she saw as integration by stealth driven by the Commission, rather than integration that was the conscious choice of the member states. She was also suspicious of the ability of other member states to dress up the pursuit of their national interest as being in the European interest. As she put in her memoirs, 'I had by now heard about as much of the European ideal as I could take' (Thatcher, 1993: 473). Thatcher sought to deflect criticism that she was anti-European by arguing that she was actually pro-European, but that she favoured a different vision of Europe based on looser intergovernmental ties. She alluded to a wider Europe that included Budapest and Warsaw as well as London, Paris and Bonn. At the core of her speech was a statement of her mounting objection to an emergent EC socio-economic model in which she famously stated that she had not 'rolled back' the frontiers of the state in the UK only to see new controls imposed from the EC.

Box 9.1   Extract from Margaret Thatcher's speech at the College of Europe, Bruges, 20 September 1988

My first guiding principle is this: willing and active cooperation between independent sovereign states is the best way to
build a successful European Community. To try to suppress
nationhood and concentrate power at the centre of a
European conglomerate would be highly damaging and
would jeopardise the objectives we seek to achieve. Europe
will be stronger precisely because it has France as France,
Spain as Spain, Britain as Britain, each with its own customs,
traditions and identity. It would be folly to try to fit them into
some sort of identikit European personality.

Founding fathers: Some of the founding fathers of the
Community thought that the United States of America might
be its model. But the whole history of America is quite different from Europe. People went there to get away from the intol-
erance and constraints of life in Europe. They sought liberty
and opportunity; and their strong sense of purpose has, over
two centuries, helped create a new unity and pride in being
American – just as our pride lies in being British or Belgian or
Dutch or German. I am the first to say that on many great
issues the countries of Europe should try to speak with a single
voice. I want to see us work more closely on the things we can
do better together than alone. Europe is stronger when we do
so, whether it be in trade, in defence, or in our relations with
the rest of the world.

→

The Rubicon had been crossed. Following Thatcher's Bruges
speech, a loose organization was formed centred on the Bruges
Group, which had strong financial support from Sir James
Goldsmith; the former British Airways boss, Lord King; and the
hotel magnate, Lord Forte. Eurosceptic arguments also began to
find a home in right-wing newspapers, particularly *The Daily
Telegraph* and *The Times*. The strands of the argument were as
follows (H. Young, 1999; Forster, 2002a):

→

A European super-state: But working more closely together does not require power to be centralised in Brussels or decisions to be taken by an appointed bureaucracy. We have not successfully rolled back the frontiers of the state in Britain, only to see them reimposed at a European level, with a European superstate exercising a new dominance from Brussels. Certainly we want to see Europe more united and with a greater sense of common purpose. But it must be in a way which preserves the different traditions, parliamentary powers and sense of national pride in one's own country; for these have been the source of Europe's vitality through the centuries.

Utopia never comes: If we cannot reform those Community policies which are patently wrong or ineffective and which are rightly causing public disquiet, then we shall not get the public's support for the Community's future development. What we need now is to take decisions on the next steps forward rather than let ourselves be distracted by Utopian goals. Utopia never comes, because we know we should not like it if it did. Let Europe be a family of nations, understanding each other, better appreciating each other more, doing more together but relishing our national identity no less than our common European endeavour. Let us have a Europe which plays its full part in the wider world, which looks outward not inward, and which preserves that Atlantic Community – that Europe on both sides of the Atlantic – which is our noblest inheritance and our greatest strength.

- The alleged insincerity of other member states that expressed commitment to single market integration but reneged on core free market principles.
- Basic institutional incompatibilities between British legal, political, social and economic institutions and those of other member states.
- That the EU was seen as moving in the direction of over-regulation and social democratic interventionism – the UK, in contrast, could position itself as a low tax, low regulated economy on the edge of Europe.

- That the spillover effects of the SEA were unacceptable, particularly the plans for social policy integration and EMU, as well as the role of supranational institutions in driving this process which grossly infringed on the authority and autonomy of the British executive to pursue British national interests.

- That the autonomy of supranational institutions such as the European Commission and the CJEU posed a real threat to British national sovereignty (Interestingly, despite the fact that neo-functionalist theorizing with its idea that the Commission could be a driving force had fallen into abeyance in the 1970s, it was resuscitated in grand style by the British eurosceptic press, who lambasted Delors and his sinister plots. The apotheosis was *The Sun*'s 'Up Yours Delors' front page headline of 1 November 1990 that urged its readers to tell the 'filthy French' to 'frog off'.)

- Nationalism, xenophobia and an obsession with World War II (For instance, Thatcher's notorious seminar on Germany and the Germans (Urban, 1996). Nicholas Ridley was sacked from the cabinet following an interview with *The Spectator* magazine in which he described European integration as 'a German racket designed to take over the whole of Europe'. *The Spectator* used the opportunity of Ridley's interview to portray Chancellor Kohl with a Hitler-style moustache on its front page. The Euro "96 football tournament prompted similar nationalist and xenophobic eruptions targeted at Spain and Germany.)

The significance of Thatcher's downfall and Major's Maastricht negotiations were fivefold. First, a lingering resentment simmered within the Party caused by the manner of Thatcher's departure (a 'Conservative coup' as Alan Watkins (1991) put it). Second, euroscepticism had been given an intellectual justification, the origins of which lay with core Thatcherite tenets which the EU in its post-Maastricht guise was deemed to threaten. Third, the intellectual justification for euroscepticism brought together previously disparate groups within the Party, impelled the formation of extra-parliamentary anti-EU groups, drew funding from leading business people, and found an echo in the opinion columns of right-wing newspapers. Fourth, John Major may have been the designated heir, but was an unknown quantity as prime minister. He had risen without trace, in the sense that he had quickly become a government whip and then government minister following his election to

Parliament in 1979. If he had views on Europe, then these were unclear. He was, though, happy to give the impression during the 1990 leadership contest that he was the carrier of the Thatcherite flame (and Thatcher to give the impression that she would be 'a good back seat driver', as she put it). If anything, Major's track record indicated pragmatism rather than the sort of hardline opposition to European integration that was beginning to acquire a foothold within his Party. Eurosceptic disappointment with Major was then to fuel notions of 'sell out' and 'betrayal'. Finally, and crucially, Major possessed a parliamentary majority of only 21 after his 1992 election victory. This diminished as the government lurched from crisis to crisis, from by-election defeat to by-election defeat, and from defection to defection (the pro-EU Liberal Democrats were the principal beneficiaries of these, by the way).

The anti-Maastricht rebellion was an intra-Conservative conflict. Labour eurosceptics did not make common cause with Conservative eurosceptics, although the Labour whips were happy to plot defeats for Major's government with hard-line anti-Maastricht opponents. There were generational differences at work here, too. The Conservative eurosceptics were Thatcher's children. The future belonged to them, or so they thought. Labour eurosceptics were older, nearing the end of their political careers, and easily picked off by the modernizers. If Labour and Conservative eurosceptics had been able to find common cause then, given Major's small majority, it would have been difficult to ratify the Treaty. It was, however, hard for Labour's eurosceptics (many of whom saw themselves as being on the left of the Party) to make common cause with the Conservative brand of right-wing, Thatcherite euroscepticism.

The Maastricht ratification saga

While basking in election victory in the spring of 1992, the Major government could not possibly have foreseen the scale and extent of the difficulties that would be experienced during the Maastricht ratification that would lead to the collapse of the Conservative party as an electoral force. Clearly, there was opposition to Maastricht, but party management and party loyalty should prevail, or so party managers thought. Major had also been able to declare 'game, set and match for Britain' after the Maastricht negotiations on the basis of the opt-outs from the third stage of EMU (creation of the euro) and from the Social Chapter. This confidence was dramatically, calamitously and ruinously wrong. One reason why it proved wrong was the series of blows that struck the EU and British government in 1992. These delayed the Treaty and emboldened the eurosceptics.

The first blow occurred on 2 June 1992, when the Danes rejected the Maastricht Treaty by a narrow margin of 51 per cent to 49 per cent. Despite the narrow margin, rejection was rejection and the Treaty required ratification in all member states. The ratification process was suspended. Perhaps if Major had pushed ahead at this time, then many of the later difficulties could have been avoided. The delay gave the eurosceptics a vital ingredient in any war of attrition: time. In the wake of the Danish 'No', Michael Spicer established the Fresh Start Group (FSG). The FSG collected 84 signatures for an Early Day Motion calling for the Maastricht Treaty to fall and for the negotiations to be re-opened. Even though this was an unlikely scenario, there was now some belief among the eurosceptics that the tide of European integration could be halted, perhaps even turned back. Many Tory MPs strode Canute-like to the water's edge.

September 1992 was to be another month of woe for Major's government, with serious long-term implications for Conservative credibility. In France, the '*petit oui*' (another 51 per cent–49 per cent narrow squeak, albeit this time in favour of the Treaty) in Mitterrand's referendum indicated the lack of public enthusiasm for the Treaty (as well as the declining popularity of the Mitterrand government: referendums are imperfect devices, it should be recalled). Worse was to come. On 16 September 1992, sterling was ejected from the ERM. During a day of frantic market activity and government chaos (during which interest rates were increased to 15 per cent at one point) the Conservatives' reputation for economic competence was shattered (Stephens, 1996: ch. 10). They may not have been the 'nice' party, but the public saw them as the party that knew how to manage the finances. Now, with the threat of repossession looming over mortgage-holders, this reputation for economic competence was lost. As billions of pounds were drained from the nation's reserves, Conservative claims to be effective stewards of the national economy became fanciful (Wickham Jones, 1997).

Despite being a bleak day for the country, the ERM crisis was another boon for the eurosceptics. Following his May 1993 departure from the government, the Chancellor of the Exchequer who presided over the ERM ejection, Norman Lamont, went so far as to claim that 'golden Wednesday' might be a better term, because the British economy was freed from the unwelcome shackles of EU economic rules. In fact, the golden opportunities were those provided to the Conservatives' opponents who fed off the Tories' fratricidal euro-war and the economic crisis management that saw the supposedly tax-cutting Conservative Party preside over tax hikes. Yet, in the peculiarly insular world of Conservative Party politics in the early 1990s, there were those who believed – wrongly on all counts, as it turned out – that the European issue mattered deeply to British people, that opposition to European integration could reconnect the Conservative Party with the electorate, and that the tide of events was flowing in their direction with the effect that the Maastricht Treaty could be stopped. But, put simply, the issue mattered to too few people. Those to whom it mattered were probably Conservatives anyway. The word 'Maastricht' became a synonym for tedium, while rebellions, in-fighting and sleaze were the public representation of the Conservative Party.

This relative lack of public interest mattered little to the growing number of eurosceptics within the ranks of Conservative MPs. They enjoyed financial support from wealthy patrons. They were militant in their opposition to Maastricht, and this militancy could override their Party loyalty. They had a formidable modus operandi based on a command of detail that bordered on the obsessive and far exceeded that of their opponents. Eurosceptics who had absorbed every paragraph and sub-clause took as a shocking indictment Kenneth Clarke's admission that he had not even read the Maastricht Treaty, while doubtless a copy nestled on the bedside table of every good eurosceptic.

The FSG developed a new form of opposition to European integration, with its members harbouring deep dislike of the EU and their own Party leadership, while also being prepared to liaise with Labour whips to defeat the Maastricht bill. FSG members tabled more than 500 amendments to the ratification bill, proposed 100 new clauses and abstained on 1515 occasions (Forster, 2002a: 87). The belief that the Maastricht Treaty could be stopped in its tracks set the 'unwhippable in pursuit of the unratifiable' (Baker *et al.*, 1994: 38). An attempt to transnationalize this anti-Maastricht protest occurred when Tory eurosceptics sought common cause with their colleagues in Denmark, but they had little in common and anti-Maastricht opposition remained grounded in national politics.

While ostensibly about Britain's place in Europe, the Maastricht ratification process was also a Conservative Party identity crisis. European issues were refracted through the lens of national politics and national institutions, and can tell us as much (if not more) about this politics and these institutions than they do about the EU. Political life within the Conservative Party became tumultuous and chaotic as the 1990s progressed (see, for instance, Gorman, 1993; Williams, 1998; Gardiner, 1999; Walters, 2001, for some insight into the poisonous world of Conservative Party politics in the 1990s). The Party's conferences became redolent of Labour's hate-fests of the 1980s. They were great entertainment for the viewing public but disastrous for a Party that aspired to re-election. At the 1992 Party conference, Norman Tebbit led the opposition to Maastricht and elicited huge support from the party faithful in a speech that alluded to the treachery of the Party leadership. The ranks of the eurosceptics had also been replenished by the 1992 general election, which brought hard-line Maastricht rebels such as Iain Duncan Smith and Bernard Jenkin into Parliament.

Major had a slim parliamentary majority and a divided and fractious parliamentary party, the eurosceptic wing of which was well-organized, committed and determined to do all it could to ditch the Treaty. The opt-outs from the Social Chapter and the third stage of EMU that Major had negotiated at Maastricht did little to help his position in the Commons. In fact, the opt-outs were used by Labour to oppose the ratification bill on the grounds that they should be re-inserted. Yet, the opt-outs also did little to appease Conservative eurosceptic ultras that wanted to see the whole Treaty defeated irrespective of opt-out clauses, which they saw as largely meaningless. Consequently, the government's small majority ensured repeated embarrassment due to the persistent strength of the rebellion and the willingness of the two main opposition parties to support amendments that were pro-Maastricht (including the Social Chapter) but destroyed the government's semi-detached position (Baker *et al.*, 1994: 38). The ratification process was an unmitigated nightmare for Major's Conservative government. The government slumped to by-election defeats in Christchurch and Newbury, and lost 500 seats in the May 1993 local council elections.

Meanwhile, the ratification bill limped through Parliament for over a year. There were 70 parliamentary votes and 61 debates. By the third reading in May 1993, there were 41 Conservative rebels and five abstentions (Baker *et al.*, 1994). The bill was only passed in

July 1993, when the government chose the 'nuclear option' and made the issue a matter of confidence in the government. All but one Tory MP (the absentee being Rupert Allason, the member for Torbay) supported the government. The bill was carried, but the blood spilt within the Conservative Party during the ratification process had inflicted terminal damage. It was impossible to pretend that euroscepticism was the preserve of a few backbench fanatics. There were eurosceptics at all levels of the government. Even so, europhile cabinet ministers such as Kenneth Clarke and Michael Heseltine were a small but powerful minority. Within the cabinet were those such as John Redwood, Michael Portillo and Peter Lilley, who had been members of the No Turning Back Group. Their views were probably more reflective of Party sentiment, but they were seen as troublemakers by Major and his pro-European colleagues.

In the 1970s, Edward Heath had kept the harder-line opponents of British membership of the EC out of his cabinet. By the 1990s, the presence of prominent eurosceptics within Major's cabinet prompted one of the most famous off-guard moments in British politics. At the end of a television interview on 23 July 1993, the day on which his government had just secured a vote of confidence, Major thought that the microphone had been switched off. It had not. What he had to say illustrated the scale of his problems and his inability to deal with them:

> The real problem is only a tiny majority. Don't overlook that I could do all these clever decisive things which people wanted me to do – but I would have split the Conservative Party into smithereens. And you would have said I acted like a ham-fisted leader. Just think it through from my perspective. You are the Prime Minister with a majority of 18, a party that is harking back to a golden age that never was, and is now invented. You have three right-wing members of the cabinet who actually resign. What happens in the parliamentary party? ... I could bring in other people. But where do you think most of the poison is coming from? From the dispossessed and the never possessed. You think of ex-ministers who are going round causing all sorts of trouble. We don't want another three more of the bastards out there. (Cited in Baker *et al.*, 1994: 37)

The aspersions on legitimacy were directed at Lilley, Portillo and Redwood, although the more fanatical and determined

Conservative eurosceptics adopted the term as a badge of honour for the irreconcilable 'bastards' (Gorman, 1993). Maastricht did not end the in-fighting. Instead, attention turned to EMU and other instances of the Major government's 'betrayal, complacency, lack of attention to detail and complicity' (Forster, 2002a: 93).

There were to be two more set-piece confrontations that were landmarks on the Party's path to opposition. The first occurred in November 1994, when eight Conservative MPs (Nicholas Budgen, Michael Cartiss, Christopher Gill, Teresa Gorman, Tony Marlow, Richard Shepherd, Sir Teddy Taylor and John Wilkinson) defied a three-line whip to oppose the European Community (Finance) Bill. The whip-less eight were then joined by Sir Richard Body, who combined euroscepticism with opposition to what he saw as draconian tactics by the party whips. For a few brief months the rebels became important, if never quite serious, political figures who revelled in 'the adrenalin of the camera and the allure of the lens' (Williams, 1998: 72). Scarcely a television debate could be held without these champions of euroscepticism advertising the deep divisions within the Conservative Party. Even when the rebels were readmitted to the Party fold in April 1995, they were able to boast that they had not been forced to repudiate their views (Williams, 1998: 77).

The second landmark was John Major's resignation on 22 June 1995 from the Party leadership. In a bid to test the eurosceptics' mettle, Major invited a challenge to his leadership. The more obvious eurosceptic challenger, Michael Portillo, wavered while the Secretary of State for Wales, John Redwood, decided to stand. Redwood's campaign did not get off to the best of starts when the brightly garbed whip-less rebels provided the backdrop to the press conference launching his campaign. As Redwood's own special adviser noted: 'The impression was that of a coup launched by a group of dissident Latin-American colonels who had just taken over the local airport and cancelled all flights' (Williams, 1998: 105). Apparent eccentricity belied the seriousness of Redwood's challenge, the threat it posed to Major's leadership, and the dedicated group of eurosceptics (such as future Party leader, Iain Duncan Smith) who supported it. Major needed to secure a simple majority of the 329 MPs eligible to vote, and he also needed to be 15 per cent ahead of his challenger. However, simply to win was not enough; Major needed a convincing margin of victory. By the time of the election, it had been established – following furious briefings and counter-briefings from each side – that a vote against Major by 100 MPs would seriously undermine his leadership. On Tuesday, 4 July 1995, 218 MPs voted for Major, 89 for Redwood, and 22 either abstained or spoilt their ballot papers. Fewer than 100 MPs had voted for Major's challenger, but 111 – one-third of the parliamentary party – had failed to endorse his leadership. As soon as the results were announced and in a well-planned media-management operation, Major loyalists appeared on television screens and radio stations to pronounce upon the Prime Minister's resounding triumph. But the victory was pyrrhic because 'Major's summer contest had institutionalized conflict within the Party' (Williams, 1998: 121).

What did the eurosceptics achieve? Above all, it could be argued that the divisions that were exposed were central to the Conservative's 1997 and 2001 election defeats. There were other consequences. First, persistent anti-EU campaigning forced Major to convince his Chancellor, Kenneth Clarke, that British euro membership would need to be conditional on a referendum. Labour, too, made a commitment to a referendum in the run-up to the 1997 general election in order to avoid being outflanked on this issue. Second, constraints were imposed on Major's government because the scale of rebellion made it clear that no further measures could be brought before Parliament that would increase the EU's role. Third, Major's government ceded to the eurosceptics a greater voice in policy-making, although Major continued to bounce between the pro-European and eurosceptic wings of the Party. Fourth, the election in 2001 as party leader of one of the most inveterate Maastricht rebels, Iain Duncan Smith, showed how the eurosceptic wing had captured what remained of the Party. Fifth, Conservative eurosceptics linked their campaigning to like-minded and often wealthy extra-parliamentary organizations. Eurosceptic think-tanks were created, such as the European Foundation run by Bill Cash and the European Reform Group run by Michael Spicer. In the aftermath of his defeat in the leadership election, John Redwood established Conservative 2000 to advance his particular brand of Conservatism. In addition to this, there were campaigning organizations within the Conservative Party and beyond, such as the Campaign for UK Conservatism, the League of Concerned Conservatives, and Conservatives Against a Federal Europe.

There were also groups pushing for a referendum on Maastricht. The Maastricht Referendum Campaign organized a phone-in in which it managed to elicit 94 per cent support from respondents for their demand for a referendum. The multi-millionaire financier, Sir James Goldsmith, who used his personal fortune to advance his own views on European integration, took up this challenge. Goldsmith's Referendum Party ran candidates in the 1997 general election against any MPs that refused to pledge their support for a referendum, which would not be on EMU but on the question of whether Britain should stay in the EU. The Referendum Party contested 547 seats and garnered 810,778 votes, which, when the £20 million spent by Goldsmith on the Party is taken into account, works out at £24.67 a vote (Geddes, 1997). UKIP was initially overshadowed by Goldsmith's dramatic entry onto the British political scene. Goldsmith's party failed to win a single seat, but did contribute to the removal of some Conservative MPs – most famously in Putney, where Goldsmith himself stood against cabinet minister David Mellor and contributed to Labour's victory.

The Referendum Party soon faded. But UKIP began to gather more support. It capitalized on the shift in the basis of eurosceptic thinking that was identified at the start of this chapter. Its opposition to European integration was expressed in terms of its threat to national identity (particularly English national identity) and also through a more general attack on the political system and political class. Revealing in this respect is that UKIP has two main areas of focus; its opposition to the EU and to immigration. Both are represented as a threat to national identity and as indicative of the ways in which the political class has 'sold out' the British people. UKIP has been seen as a threat to the Conservative vote. This led David Cameron, in 2006, to describe UKIP as 'fruitcakes, loonies and closet racists, mostly'. Evidence from the 2010 general election shows that UKIP has actually taken votes from Labour (as, too, has the BNP), particularly from working-class voters feeling abandoned by New labour's obsession with maintaining its support in middle England. UKIP's ideology and its relatively strong performance in second-order elections conforms with Ray's (2007) analysis that sees eurosceptics as on the political fringes and associated with the populist right. In Britain, the radical right critique of the EU as a threat to national identity has been massively more evident in public debate than a radical left critique of the EU as a capitalist club serving the interests of business.

Europe in the 1997 General Election

The European issue was not a salient concern at the 1997 general election. Even the very limited scope for 'clear blue water' to be opened between Labour and the Conservatives was swiftly neutralized by Labour, which was eager to adopt a similar unyielding stance on core sovereign concerns. As noted in Chapter 4, Blair even felt moved (or, at least, Alastair Campbell, his press officer, did) to pen an article for *The Sun* in which he proclaimed his 'love for the £'.

At the 1997 general election, one of the main party's manifestos called for 'an alliance of independent nations choosing to cooperate to achieve the goals they cannot achieve alone. We oppose a federal European superstate.' The fact that this is from the Labour Party's manifesto demonstrates that Labour's position did not differ markedly from that expressed in the Conservative manifesto. On the issue of EMU, both Labour and the Conservatives pledged to hold a referendum. Labour also promised to uphold the national veto on taxation, defence and security, immigration, the budget and changes to the Treaty. The main difference between the two parties was on their stance on the Social Chapter. Labour said that they would sign up. During the campaign, and to counter accusations of being insufficiently patriotic, Labour used a British bulldog – often an emblem of the far right – in one of their Party election broadcasts. The Conservatives retaliated with an election poster showing a miniature Tony Blair sitting on Chancellor Kohl's knee, with the implication that senior EU statesmen would bamboozle the naive Blair.

The salient concerns in 1997 were, however, not the EU; instead, they were the divisions, incompetence and sleaze that were seen to characterize the Conservative Party. The electorate appeared to make no judgement about the stances of MPs as they voted both eurosceptics (such as Michael Portillo) and pro-EU Conservative MPs (such as Edwina Currie) out of the House of Commons. The result was the election of a New Labour government with a cautiously expressed, but generally more positive, approach to the EU, albeit with reservations about the euro.

The fading significance of the European issue in the 2000s

The 2001 general election was noticeable for William Hague's unsuccessful attempt to make European integration a key issue and to festoon his campaign with the motif 'save the pound'. Never before had a national campaign by an aspiring party of government veered so close to single-issue politics. The Conservatives had effectively managed to turn a potential asset (their euroscepticism chimed with the public mood) into an electoral liability (Evans, 1998). In 2001, Hague sought to open 'clear blue water' between the Conservatives and Labour. European integration was one of the few issues on which voters seemed to prefer the more sceptical stance of the Conservatives to that of Labour. There was an element of contradiction here, because Blair was vastly more popular as a potential prime minister – and, thus, Britain's representative in Europe – than Hague, whose personal ratings in the polls were resolutely negative.

Four reasons have been identified for the Conservatives' 2001 embrace of euroscepticism as a key campaign theme (Geddes, 2002: 145). First, since 1997 pro-EU voices such as Michael Heseltine and Kenneth Clarke had been marginalized. Second, Hague and his advisers – after an early flirtation with a more inclusive version of Conservatism that notoriously saw him bedecked in a 'Hague' baseball cap at the Notting Hill carnival – saw a series of core issues on which they might stand some chance of eroding Labour's dominant position (Europe was one, asylum and tax cuts were the others). Third, there was a lingering bitterness within the Party surrounding Thatcher's removal from office in 1990. The disputes in the 1990s were in many ways a battle for the Party's soul. Fourth, eurosceptics dominated the Parliamentary Conservative Party.

Clear blue water was, indeed, opened in 2001. The Conservatives advanced a vision of a 'network Europe' with states coming together in areas of mutual benefit. States could opt into or out of those parts of the *acquis* that they favoured. The euro was ruled out for the lifetime of two Parliaments, while any further extension of competencies to the EU would be opposed. 'In Europe, not run by Europe' was Hague's campaign theme. This minimal vision of the EU would be reinforced by the creation of powers reserved for the British state and, therefore, forbidden from becoming EU competencies. Such a policy would raise serious questions about Britain's continued membership of the EU because the UK government would be placed in a position of almost perpetual opposition to other member states. In a speech made on 4 March 2001, Hague alluded to Britain as a 'foreign land' with a second-term Labour government and called for cross-party support in what he portrayed as a last-ditch defence of the British nation state (Hague, 2001).

Labour's stance at the 2001 general election reflected some core underlying themes that have informed elite attitudes to European integration: a preference for intergovernmentalism, rejection of federalism and the maintenance of strong ties with the USA. Labour's support for the euro would also depend on the five economic tests being met. This was highly unlikely, given that the tests were vague and, essentially, designed to maintain the dominant position of the sceptical Treasury on this issue.

The Liberal Democrats had profited from Conservative divisions through both the defection of some disaffected Conservative MPs to their ranks and of previous Conservative voters. The Liberal Democrats supported transfers of sovereignty to the EU when in the national interest, and were more positive about the euro (although with a referendum as the basis for entry). Yet, their manifesto also revealed an underlying conceptualization of the EU as an association of sovereign states that is distinct from the kind of unionist style federalism that informs the thinking of their sister parties in other member states. The Liberal Democrats tend to see a 'lower-case' federalism focused on the local level, rather than connected to any grand plan for an upper-case Federal Europe. Moreover, Liberal Democrat support for European integration is tempered by some on-the-ground realities with a Party membership with strong eurosceptic inclinations. This has been seen as a central aspect of the Liberal Democrats' 'dual identity', with some distance between the Party in Westminster and the Party membership, and a 'flexible' approach to local politics that saw them being neither left nor right, as it has been put (Russell and Fieldhouse, 2005). A study of Liberal Democrat members found them to be 'scarcely more pro-European than the electorate as a whole' (Bennie *et al.*, 1995: 141; see also Russell and Fieldhouse, 2005). Furthermore, Liberal Democrat support is at its strongest in the south-west of England and parts of rural Wales and Scotland, where agriculture and fishing interests are strong and which, as a result, do not tend to be hotbeds of pro-EU sentiment.

The result in 2001 was another landslide victory for New Labour. The Conservative campaign failed because Hague was not popular and because his core themes, such as European integration, mattered to too few people, and those to whom it mattered would probably vote Conservative (or UKIP) any way. The key election issue was the state of Britain's public services. The Conservatives had almost nothing to say on this issue.

New Labour's engagement with the EU after 2001 can be explained in both conceptual and strategic components, although much also hinged on the dysfunctional relationship at the heart of New Labour between Tony Blair and Gordon Brown. In conceptual terms, the majority of Labour MPs have moved, since the 1980s, to a position that is supportive of economic and political integration. The great fissure over Europe that existed in the late 1970s and early 1980s has dissipated, to be replaced in the aftermath of the second Iraq war with divisions over Blair's alignment with the USA (particularly when led by neo-Conservative President George W. Bush). Even if there were much eurosceptic opposition to the EU within the Labour Party, then it would be difficult for it to make its voice heard, given the Party's crushing parliamentary majorities after the 1997 and 2001 general elections. Most Labour MPs seem to have embraced what Baker *et al.* (2002: 413–15) characterize as 'open regionalism'. This involved acceptance of major changes in the global economy that diminished the sovereign authority of states and which meant that 'traditional goals of national economic management are now best pursued at the collective level of the EU, rather than left to the nation state alone'.

To this conceptual re-orientation can be added strategic calculation. This introduces a complication into the analysis because of the necessary interaction between this support for 'pooling' sovereignty and the core concerns of the new Labour government. New Labour were elected in 1997, and re-elected in 2001 and 2005, to make good their promises to deliver high-quality public services. Delivery became a key theme with, as Hood (2006) put it, its own science (deliverology) and pathology (deliveritis). At the 2001 and 2005 elections, the economy and welfare services were key campaign themes, while European integration was a marginal concern.

It is, however, worth noting that, while New Labour appeared to be in a dominant position following two crushing landslide victories, their share of the vote was a little over 40 per cent, while turnout slipped to a mere 59 per cent at the 2001 general election (Fielding, 2002a; 2002b). New Labour's coalition was fragile, based as it was on an appeal to 'middle England'. It was unlikely that any journey to 'the heart of Europe' would be made if 'middle England' were not felt to be ready to accompany New Labour on this expedition, or if it were to jeopardize the attainment of public service objectives that were central to the success or failure of New Labour. New Labour managed to lose 5 million votes between 1997 and 2010, with much of this loss of support actually coming from core working-class voters that felt taken for granted by New Labour's pursuit of the votes of 'middle England' (Geddes and Tonge, 2010).

The third factor in addition to conceptual and strategic concerns was the relationship between Blair and Brown and their coteries of advisers (see Rawnsley (2010), for the definitive account). New Labour in power with their crushing majority exposed the myth of parliamentary sovereignty, demonstrated the weakness of cabinet government and showed the potential for concentrated power around key governmental figures. Scarcely a day went by without stories emerging of divisions between Tony Blair and Gordon Brown. The debate about the EU was subsumed to the issue of the succession. Brown was obsessed by the prospect of replacing Blair as prime minister. Brown sought to dominate the domestic agenda, including the issue of whether or not to join the euro. As we have already noted, Brown was not an instinctive European and disliked EU meetings. Brown's time at Number 10 was dominated after 2008 by the effects of the credit crunch and near collapse of the banking system. Brown showed far more willingness than Cameron to work with other EU leaders in developing a common response, but his domestic support base was weak and his attempts to save the world economy garnered little domestic credit.

The EU was scarcely an issue during the 2010 campaign. The Conservatives had resolved to focus on other issues that they saw as more likely to broaden their appeal to the political centre ground. There was little incentive for Labour to focus on Europe, as this was an issue on which they were not strong. A similar argument applied to the Liberal Democrats. No party was really interested in talking about Europe. The Conservatives stance on Europe was closer to the broadly eurosceptic position of the electorate but the issue was not salient, so there was little electoral benefit to be extracted from a strong focus on Europe. In mid-March 2010, voters were asked to identify the issues that would be very important in helping them decide for which party to vote. Not surprisingly, in light of the near meltdown of the global financial system, the key issue was the economy, followed by health and education. Europe barely figured. Between 2005 and 2010, opinion poll data suggests that the proportion of the electorate who saw the EU as the most important issue facing the country was only rarely above 5 per cent. In contrast, at the time of the 2010 general election, 70 per cent of respondents saw the economy as the most important issue (Carey and Geddes, 2010: 269).

At the 2010 election, all three of the main national parties reaffirmed the importance of EU membership. The key innovation of the Conservatives was the European Union Bill (see Chapter 4). The Conservative manifesto also proposed to seek a 'mandate to negotiate' repatriated powers in areas such as social and employment legislation. Labour's campaign and manifesto also downplayed the EU issue. Labour attempted to trigger lingering memories of Conservative euroscepticism with a reference to 'sullen resistance' to EU cooperation on key challenges, such as climate change. In contrast to the Conservatives, Labour also engaged with day-to-day issues, such as budget reform and the CAP. Labour thus showed that they were dealing with the EU as an issue that was integrated into the standard operating practices of British politics. The Conservatives represented Europe as a foreign policy issue with the emphasis on negotiation with other governments. The Liberal Democrats faced the usual tension of a pro-EU leadership and tendencies towards scepticism in its electoral base. The result was that Europe was neither a key campaign, nor manifesto theme for the Liberal Democrats.

UKIP saw the 2010 as their chance to make a breakthrough at a national level. They had enjoyed a very strong performance at the 2009 EP elections, securing 16.5 per cent of the votes and pushing Labour into an ignominious third place. In the same EP elections, the extreme-right BNP got just over 6 per cent of the vote and sent two MEPs to Strasbourg. UKIP's main target at the 2010 general election was the Buckingham seat held by the Speaker of the House of Commons, John Bercow. By tradition, the speaker's seat is not contested by the main parties, but UKIP grabbed the chance to pursue a high-profile campaign, and also sought to capitalize on the anti-political mood gripping the country in the wake of the MPs' expenses scandal that had badly damaged public confidence in politics. The media-savvy UKIP leader and MEP, Nigel Farage, was the Party's candidate. His and UKIP's campaign focused on two themes: Europe and immigration. UKIP pledged to leave the EU and to end what it called 'uncontrolled immigration' with an immediate five-year freeze on immigration for permanent settlement and tough border controls. Farage also dealt with local issues in the Buckingham constituency, which led to him to make some startling claims. For example, when discussing a gypsy encampment with a local resident in the village of Nash, he was reported to say: 'We have an open door to 10 million Romany gypsies in Eastern Europe. To be honest with you, sir, they all have total free access to come in. To my mind, it's mad. What's happening in Nash could be a microcosm of what's to come' (*Daily Telegraph*, 6 May 2011). Ten million people arriving in a small village in Buckinghamshire would doubtless be a challenge. More significantly, Farage's language is a familiar theme of right-wing claims about potential mass migration, and plays into both public fears and the idea that the ordinary man or woman in the street is being sold-out by out-of-touch elite.

Another novelty of the 2010 campaign was the introduction of debates between the main national party leaders, plus separate debates between the party leaders in Scotland, Wales and Northern Ireland. In the first of the three UK-wide debates, Clegg attacked Cameron's decision to leave the EPP and associate, instead, with 'a bunch of nutters, anti-Semites, people who deny climate change exists, homophobes'. Cameron used the debates to make it clear that, under his leadership, the Conservatives would not join the euro. In each of the debates, questions were asked about immigration, but in a way that connected them to a discussion of European integration. In particular, Cameron and Clegg got into a testy exchange when Clegg asked Cameron how he could impose a cap on immigration when 80 per cent of migrants came from other EU member states and, thus, had a right to move to the UK that was protected by EU law.

Both UKIP (and the extreme right BNP) saw an increase in their vote share, but they failed to make a breakthrough in terms of representation. UKIP saw a 50 per cent increase in its vote to 3.2 per cent, but this left them far short of securing a seat at Westminster. Farage campaigned hard in Buckingham, including a pledge to drink a pint in every pub in the constituency, but was to suffer the injuries caused by being involved in a plane crash on the day of the election and the indignity of being shunted into third place, securing 14,000 fewer votes than Bercow.

Did this increase in UKIP support hit the Conservative vote and stop it from securing a majority? At first glance, there does seem to be evidence that it did. In 21 constituencies in 2010, the combined Conservative and UKIP vote was greater than the Labour or Liberal Democrat majority. However, in his analysis of the election results, Denver (2010: 14) found no significant relationship between

Conservative support and UKIP performance. In fact, he shows that it is more likely that UKIP cost Labour votes because the more UKIP improved, then the worse Labour did. The same flow of the vote argument also applied to the BNP. Denver attributes this to alienated working-class voters abandoning New Labour and moving to the populist- (UKIP) or extreme- (BNP) right.

The European issue within the coalition

Chapter 4 showed that the coalition agreement reflected the fact that Europe was a red line issue for the Conservatives. We can now assess the European issue post-2010 during the early years of the Conservative–Liberal Democrat coalition. Despite the mood of optimism that accompanied Cameron and Clegg's first joint press conference in the Downing Street garden, there were those on the Conservative backbenches and in the media who thought that Cameron had got the campaign wrong and had not won the election because he had failed to campaign hard enough on core Conservative themes such as Europe and immigration. There is little to suggest – and, actually, plenty of evidence to the contrary – that such a campaign would have successfully resonated with people's concerns about the economy and public services (Evans, 1998; Bale, 2010). There were also Conservative backbench MPs who resented the alliance with the Liberal Democrats and who had hoped that Cameron would form a minority Conservative government followed by a swift general election in an attempt to secure a larger majority, along the lines of the 1974 general elections called by Labour's Harold Wilson. Here, too, the Conservatives would have been running a risk. Even with a deeply unpopular Labour government and prime minister, and one of the worst economic crises in the country's history, Cameron could still not secure a majority. It would have been a considerable gamble to stake the Party's future on another general election, given the effects of the British electoral system, and underlying shifts in the geography and social base of British electoral politics that have led some to ask whether single-party government is any longer the likely outcome of British general elections (Curtice, 2010).

An obvious point of contrast is between the Conservative government of John Major, elected in 1992, and the coalition government led by David Cameron. In 1992, the Conservative Party was riven by divisions over Europe and was on the verge of civil war. In 2010, the Conservatives were a eurosceptic party. The issue bubbling beneath the surface was the existence of a more hard-core eurosceptic grouping on the Party's backbenches who see the coalition agreement as conceding too much to the Liberal Democrats. This group would far rather see a referendum on the question of UK membership than guarantees through the European Union Act (2011) (see Chapter 4) of referenda on further extension of powers. There was also a new generation of Conservative MPs elected to the House of Commons in 2010 who were overwhelmingly eurosceptic. Within one year of the election, there were reports of rumblings from the Conservative backbenches about a lack of involvement regarding policy-making. This included strong expressions of eurosceptic sentiment. The Secretary of the influential 1922 Committee of Conservative MPs, Mark Pritchard, called for a referendum and wrote that Britain had become 'become enslaved to Europe – servitude that intrudes and impinges on millions of British lives every day. Brussels has become a burdensome yoke, disfiguring Britain's independence and diluting her sovereignty' (*Daily Telegraph*, 2011a). On October 24 2011 a debate was called by Conservative MP David Nuttall on the issue of a referendum on Britain's EU membership. Nuttall argued that Parliament was becoming 'ever more impotent' as the EU's 'tentacles ...intruded into more and more areas of national life'. Another Conservative MP, Anne Main, argued that the public had been 'fobbed off' by the political elite on the subject of Europe. Douglas Carswell was damning in his assessment of the EU's impact on Britain: 'We have a fisheries policy with no fish; red tape strangling small businesses; financial regulation that suffocates the City; and now we are being asked to spend billions of pounds bailing out a currency that we never even joined' (House of Commons, 2012)

Other backbench MPs saw the need to stake out a Conservative agenda for a 2015 general election that would be fought separately by the two coalition partners. One contribution to this debate came from five of the 2010 intake who published *After the Coalition: A Conservative Agenda for Britain* (Kwarteng *et al.*, 2011). The chapter on Europe in this book developed a vision that was consistent with the Party as it had developed under Cameron's leadership, arguing for a two-speed EU (with the UK in the slow lane) that would have the single market as its core, but within which Britain could opt out from social policy, JHA and foreign policy.

The Foreign Secretary William Hague rejected the idea of a referendum, emphasized the European Union Act and its 'referendum lock' as a brake on further extension of EU powers and held open the possibility of future re-negotiation of British relations with the EU (*Daily Telegraph*, 2011b). In July 2012, Hague also announced a government review of all aspects of British relations with the EU to report in 2014. Others on the Conservative backbenches were more hard-line in their position. This included veteran eurosceptic MPs such as Bill Cash and Patrick Jenkin, as well as relative newcomers such as Pritchard and Douglas Carswell. The Conservative position within the coalition government leaves open the possibility of a referendum on the EU being included within the Conservative manifesto for the next general election (planned for 2015). In an interview on the Andrew Marr show in BBC1 on 1 July 2012, Hague suggested that closer economic and political integration could require a referendum in Britain. If the Conservatives were to favour a referendum, then the Labour Party would need to consider whether it could risk being out-flanked on the EU issue by the Conservatives and whether it too should pledge to hold a referendum. The leaders of the two main parties do not favour exit but are moving towards a position where such a possibility becomes a very real option that could be presented to the British people. If a vote were to be held then snapshots of public opinion suggest support for exit. In opinion polls conducted between May 2011 and June 2012, YouGov, consistently found a majority in favour of exit. Interestingly, when Cameron wielded 'the veto that never was' in an attempt to block the fiscal compact at the Brussels summit in December 2011 there was also a reflection in opinion polls that saw pro- and anti- opinion move to level pegging (House of Commons, 2012: 11). This led Peter Kellner from YouGov to suggest that this showed that British people were more likely to accept the EU if they thought that 'vital financial powers' could be protected (cited in House of Commons 2012: 11). As it became clear that Britain had not blocked further extensions of powers to the EU there was an increase in the number of people supporting exit from the EU.

By 2011, the context at EU level had changed, too, in rather dramatic ways when compared with 1992. Most notably, the eurozone had been plunged into a crisis that threatened the future of the Union itself. Cameron's attempt to block the incorporation of the 'fiscal compact' into the main Treaty was discussed in Chapter 4. His backtracking at a February 2012 summit meeting of EU leaders and his agreement that the fiscal compact could be included within the Treaty – and, thus, subject to institutional jurisdiction and decision-making rules – raised hackles on the Conservative backbenches and in the eurosceptic press. In the space of just under five months, between October 2011 and February 2012, Cameron went from being a euro-pragmatist in the face of backbench calls for a referendum on EU membership to a self-declared sturdy defender of the national interest at the December 2011 summit, and back again to a euro-pragmatist by February 2012, when he agreed to the incorporation into the Treaty of the fiscal compact.

Conclusion

This chapter has shown that divisions about Europe have tended to be within, rather than between, the main parties; but it has been difficult for eurosceptic forces to unite across the party divide and to coalesce into powerful anti-integration groups. Labour's 'modernization' involved renouncing opposition to the EC/EU and adopting a far more positive stance towards European integration, but in ways that involved a 'third way' reappraisal of both Britain's place in the global economy and the main strands of European social democratic thought. Conservative debates about European integration acquired a more ideological character in the 1990s and created space on the right for eurosceptic parties such as UKIP. The size of the majority of the governing party has been a key variable. For example, the knife-edge majority of John Major's government between 1992 and 1997 provided ample scope for exploitation by eurosceptic Conservative MPs. During New Labour's time in office between 1997 and 2010, there was minimal backbench dissent on the European issue, while key questions, such as the euro, were effectively kicked into the long grass. The European issue still possesses significant disruptive potential within the Conservative Party and this tension is compounded by the coalition agreement with the ostensibly pro-EU Liberal Democrats.

Chapter 10

Conclusions: Britain and the European Union Assessed

No account of political change in Britain can ignore the ways in which European integration works its way into the nooks and crannies of British political life. For more than 40 years, 'Europe' has become institutionalized as a core concern of the British state, with important effects on political actors, the strategic environment within which they operate, and the various elements that need to be accounted for when political change in Britain is assessed. This book has sought to account for these effects, for the changes that European integration has brought about in British politics, and has endeavoured to weigh these developments alongside other causes of change. The analysis has addressed the ways in which current engagement has been shaped by the past, but has also asked whether the past is a reliable guide to the future in light of both the increased politicization of the European issue and the wider debate about the EU's future.

The analysis centred on Britain's *conditional* and *differential* engagement with European integration. The roots of this conditional and differential engagement were traced to decisions made about Britain's place in Europe and the world after World War II. Decisions made at this time have had important structuring effects on political outcomes ever since because they ordered the strategic environment within which politicians have operated. To return to the historical institutional analogy used in Chapter 1, choices made after World War II can be likened to a tree from which have grown, over the last 50 years, three strong branches of Britain's European policy. Even though the EU has developed considerably since the 1950s while the British state has undergone major changes, they still remain identifiable aspects of the contemporary British approach. The first branch is a preference for intergovernmentalism, rather than supranationalism, combined with a dislike of federal solutions

252

and a self-consciously pragmatic distrust of grand designs aimed at Europe's *finalité*. The second branch is in the realm of the international political economy and marked by a preference for global free trade, which has brought with it, since the 1980s, a consistent support for market liberalization that has united Conservative, Labour and coalition governments. The third branch is the continued emphasis placed on the Atlantic alliance as a core British interest. These three branches have been consistent elements of Britain's European policy. Not only do they form a fairly stable set of preferences at the core of Britain's EU policy, but they also encapsulate a normative vision of Britain in the world that is aligned with the USA and promotes globalization as a vehicle for liberalization.

The book then developed its analysis of Britain's conditional and differential engagement by distinguishing between two analytical themes that each explored the ways in which Britain has participated in the EU and the ways in which the EU has then impacted on British politics. First, a 'Britain in Europe' theme assessed Britain's role in European integration through analysis of relationships with developing processes of integration since the 1950s with other member states and with EU institutions. This involved thinking about the ways in which national policy preferences in the UK have been pursued at European level since the 1940s. Second, a 'Europe in Britain' theme allowed examination of the 'Europeanization' of British politics and the ways in which European integration has been absorbed as a concern in domestic politics and the effects on laws, institutions, policies and collective identities. A number of questions were raised in Chapter 1, to which we now return.

What factors have motivated British policy towards the European Union?

The underlying issues here are the continuities and changes in British relations with Europe during more than 40 years of membership. Have there been major variations in British relations with the EU, or can strong continuities be detected? It has been argued that there are strong core elements – the three branches referred to in the previous section – that continue to have important structuring effects on British relations with the EU. Preferences for intergovernmentalism, market liberalization and Atlanticism mean that judging British governments by their ability to locate themselves at the heart of Europe is a flawed exercise. It could be argued that there has never been a British government with this intention.

New Labour in power provided a good test of the continued resonance of these branches of Britain's European policy. It also demonstrated the constraining effects of eurosceptic public opinion. Beneath Blair's genuine pro-EU beliefs and his call for 'constructive engagement' was a series of well-engrained national preferences that are not so readily moulded into a policy stance that facilitates any move to the heart of Europe. Present, too, were electoral calculations linked to the broader objectives of the Labour government. Europe was not a strong issue for the party and evidence suggests that political parties have lost their capacity to provide the cues to public opinion that helped to generate the permissive consensus. Blair's government was an excellent and vivid example of the constraining effects of dissensus (Hooghe and Marks, 2008).

Have British governments possessed the capacity to turn preferences into European Union priorities?

The first point here is whether or not British governments have had a consistent set of preferences. This book has shown that, since the 1980s, there has been a consistent focus on single market integration as a core British priority and that this has been shared by Labour, Conservative and coalition governments. If we look at the scope, direction, form and content of European integration since the mid-1980s, then the development of forms of deeper integration and a shift into areas of high politics can be seen. This did not coincide with British interests expressed in the run-up to these negotiations, but that require some form of British accommodation with their central objectives once they are adopted and implemented. Moreover, there has also been an integrative dynamic led by other member states and supported by key EU institutions (such as the Commission and CJEU) that has sometimes aroused suspicion in the UK, particularly in the eurosceptic right, who fear a creeping federalist agenda and are willing to proclaim the bad faith of EU partners. Britain has constructively pursued single market integration. This has been consistently evident since the 1980s. Ways have also been found to manage British awkwardness. The most notable of these is the scope for flexibility first seen in the opt-out provisions on social policy and the third stage of EMU. This was accompanied by non-participation in the Schengen free movement system. Britain did opt back in to the social chapter when New Labour came to power in 1997, but Blair and Brown's government maintained the opt-out from the border control aspects of the Schengen system and dodged the euro issue through the five tests, through fear of the effects on both the finely-balanced internal politics of the New Labour government and also the strength of eurosceptic opinion that made it unlikely that a majority in a referendum could be secured. In 2012, Britain's flexible engagement with the EU was affirmed when the fiscal compact proceeded as an agreement of 25, with Britain and the Czech Republic as observers. In summary, Britain has struggled to deal with the implications of the shift, since the 1990s, from market-making to polity-building. Its preferences have been quite narrowly focused, which has led to some scope for positive engagement, primarily on market issues, but more defensive engagement on a wider range of concerns.

Have British governments been particularly effective players of the European Union game?

The evidence accumulated over more than 40 years of British membership is that Britain has not always been a particularly effective player of the EU game. At the most basic level, the UK has spent a good part of its time as an EU member in dispute with other member states (renegotiation in the 1970s, the budget in the early 1980s, the Maastricht saga and Conservative euroscepticism in the 1990s). One reason for this is that membership in the 1970s was not based on wholehearted conversion to the merits of supranational European integration. Another is that the 'EU game' requires rather different skills from those required in the winner-takes-all UK system. The EU centres on coalition building, compromise, deal-making and the search for consensus. Not surprisingly, these were anathema to Margaret Thatcher, the arch conviction politician. As it became ever more clear that other EU leaders did not share her convictions (and neither, it must be said, did key members of her own government), her distaste for the EC grew concomitantly. The capacity to win arguments at EU level can depend on the maintenance of a stable domestic coalition. Between 1988 and 1997, UK governments were wracked by divisions over Europe, which made the development of a consistent EU policy well-nigh impossible. The Major government was predictably unpredictable to its EU partners, while peering anxiously over its shoulder at the turmoil within the Conservative parliamentary party. This was not the strongest position to be in while engaged in complex intergovernmental negotiations. Blair was able to heal some of these fractured relations, not least because his crushing parliamentary majority marginalized the small number of eurosceptic voices in his parliamentary party. Yet, Blair's legacy was that, while he was able to make the case for Britain in Europe (although the war in Iraq badly fractured some relationships), he was not able to make the case for Europe in Britain. The coalition government's EU policy was driven by Conservative party preferences. This has led to a 'this far and no further' approach, as exemplified by the European Union Act of 2011 with its referendum lock. There does, however, remain a consistent emphasis on the pursuit of single market integration reflective of the strong neo-liberal turn in British politics since the 1980s. Cameron enthused his eurosceptic backbenchers with his 'veto' (although, in reality, it was no such thing) at the December 2011 Brussels summit, but soon displayed a more pragmatic approach to the fiscal compact and to working with other EU leaders on single market integration. The coalition seems likely to maintain Britain's place in the 'slow lane' or 'outer circle' of the EU. Few, if any, other member states would see this as a desirable place to be.

It is here that the book's analysis switched to the 'Europe in Britain' theme and assessed the ways in which European integration has been incorporated as a core concern in British politics.

What impact has European integration had on the organization of the British political system?

The intra-state dimension of Europeanization is the issue at stake when exploring the effects of European integration on the organization of the British political system. It was noted that those who identify the EU as a threat to parliamentary sovereignty need also to take account of other important changes in the British political system – particularly, the devolution of power to sub-national governance, and also other ways in which power is dispersed within the British political system, such as through the increased role of private companies and the market.

Rather than simply absorbing European integration's effects and prompting uni-directional change driven by European integration, it was shown that the British political system (similar to those in other member states) will refract these effects in accordance with the standard operating practices and animating ideas of the domestic process. It is necessary to distinguish Europe's effects on the British political system from other sources of political change. The EU's impact on Whitehall, Westminster and devolved government were all explored, and various explanations for change assessed. It was shown that a well-established Whitehall ethos was the template on which the adaptation of British central government to European integration was based and that, despite the substantial changes which European integration has brought with it, this Whitehall ethos based on coordination, collective responsibility and informa-tion-sharing remains strong, supplemented by an emphasis on effective transposition into UK law of agreed policies. Europe's impact on devolved government since 1997 was set against the impetus from a domestic constitutional reform agenda driven in the main by domestic politics. The EU's structural funds also created new politi-cal opportunities for regional and sub-national government, and contributed to their post-1997 growth, particularly in Scotland and Wales. There was no enthusiasm for regional government in England; the idea withered and died.

There has been no well-established template from which regional and sub-national governmental responses to European integration could draw because these were new issues for the British state. EU policy is a matter for central government but, as the powers of devolved governments increase and the UK moves towards either a more federal system, or even break-up, then questions will remain about the role and function of sub-national tiers of government in Britain's EU policy. In Scotland, for example, the SNP proclaimed 'independence in Europe' – but would an independent Scotland join the euro? In the wake of the financial crisis, Scotland's First Minister, Alex Salmond, noted that an independent Scotland would not join the euro and would prefer an EMU with England and Wales, rather than one with the rest of the EU.

We also saw that some of the most tumultuous EU-related events have occurred in the legislative arena. The main divisions over Europe have occurred within, rather than between, the main parties. Anti-European integration sentiment has evolved from the anti-marketeers of the 1960s and 1970s into a distinct brand of (mainly) right-wing and Conservative euroscepticism since the 1990s. This has been within the Conservative Party and also in the form of the populist, right-wing eurosceptic UKIP. Although the issues of Maastricht, the euro and Lisbon have tended to engage the political class rather more than they did the general public, arguments about Europe were flushed out into the open and eurosceptics (supported by key sections of the press) developed a powerful critique of the EU. The key drivers of this euroscepticism were the EU's move into areas of high politics (EMU and the Maastricht Treaty, in particular) in the late 1980s and early 1990s. Eurosceptic rebellion was assisted by the small parliamentary majority of John Major's Conservative government between 1992 and 1997.

The more general point is that the politicization genie is now out of the bottle and will not be put back in. The permissive consensus has been replaced by the more constraining effects of dissensus. As we saw, this helps explain what Bulmer (2008) called 'utilitarian supranationalism', where even governments that advocate integration will face significant domestic constraints.

To what extent do British policy priorities and the organization of the British economy and welfare state 'fit' with those in other member states and with an emerging European Union model?

The question of the Europeanization of British politics does, of course, extend beyond the arena of Whitehall and Westminster. It also touches upon core socio-economic priorities. A series of core EU policy issues were explored, and a varied pattern of adaptation and change was found, although it was also seen that Britain's late membership meant that key policy priorities were established in the UK's absence and were not necessarily to the UK's advantage. This was, then, the basis for wrangling as the UK sought a better deal from other member states (with their own interests tied up with these policy choices) which were not always disposed to accommodate UK demands. Underlying these policy debates has been a branch of UK European policy that prefers free trade and market liberalization. The UK economy has become more closely linked with the EU since accession, although this has not necessarily generated demands for 'more Europe' in the way that transactional approaches might suggest. Rather, there remains a perception that the UK socio-economic approach is different, even in the face of greater concentration of economic activity within the EU. These developments motivated the desire of the Thatcher governments to raise economic liberalization to a European level through the single market programme, and New Labour's links between British participation in the euro and economic reform mirroring UK emphasis on liberalization and labour market flexibility. The 'Anglo-Saxon' approach seems as likely to engender suspicion as it does support in other member states.

In search of a critical juncture?

The arguments developed in this book have explored the ways in which there has been a historical institutional patterning of Britain's relations with the EU. Reluctance, awkwardness and semi-detachment have been based on the three well-established branches of policy. The effects of historical choices on the interests and identities of political actors are fairly well-entrenched components of the strategic environment within which they operate. In such circumstances, it can be easier to explain institutional persistence than it is to account for political change. But is the past a reliable guide to the future? The world in the 2010s is far different from that in the 1950s. The EU faces the challenge of responding to the economic crisis that brought it to its knees after 2008, and managing the effects of austerity and the search for economic growth. While the economic crisis wrought by the irresponsibility of banks and the huge exposure to debt in EU states has had calamitous and damaging effects on the lives of millions of EU citizens, it has also opened a genuinely pan-European debate about the future of the European economy. The key questions are whether the EU possesses the capacity to lead this debate, and in which direction it will choose to go. Both questions go right to the heart of the debate about the EU's future. Not only does the EU face this 'internal' challenge to its economic governance, it also faces an external challenge in the form of major shifts in the global economy, such as the rise of the BRICs (Brazil, Russia, India and China). Power relations in the global economy are changing. Will Europe's slow-growing economies, ageing populations and creaking welfare systems be able to respond to these challenges? They will also have to do so where traditional alignments are also shifting. Most notably, the USA is now far more likely to look east to Asia and the Pacific than it is to Europe. What future is there for the old continent?

There are also changed political dynamics in the EU that mean that the past might not be a reliable guide to the future. Since the 1990s and the EU's move from market-making to polity-building, there has been a growth in euroscepticism driven by perceived threats to national identity and fuelled by a wider public dissatisfaction with politics. Populist, right-wing euroscepticism has become far more prominent within the UK, with the strong performance of UKIP in second-order elections. Eurosceptics have tended to be on the margins but, in an age of austerity, there is scope for it to move closer to the mainstream either through co-option by mainstream parties, or through success of populist parties. Perhaps more significant in the British context is the creation of a coalition government that sees a eurosceptic Conservative Party in alliance with the Europhile Liberal Democrats. Cameron is a eurosceptic, but has also shown himself to be a pragmatist. He has argued strongly in favour of EU membership, although consistent with the 'slow lane' or 'outer circle' of a two-speed Europe. There remains scope for Europe to divide the Conservative party and this scope is increased by the complex requirements for Cameron to balance within the coalition and within his party; then, as the 2015 election approaches, to seek to differentiate the Conservatives from their Liberal Democrat partners. The Conservative stance on European integration is closer to that of the electorate than either of the other two main parties, but Cameron is well aware that a strategy that sees a strong focus on core issues such as Europe and immigration may not be the best way to build a winning electoral majority.

In the light of these circumstances, what predictions can be made about future engagement with the EU and its core projects? The first of these could be seen as relatively bold. It is that Britain will likely remain an EU member state, but that it will find itself (through choice) in a 'slow lane' or 'outer circle'. The 'this far and no further' approach of the coalition agreement will condition policy with tensions and grumblings within the Conservative Party. It is unlikely that Cameron will be able to renegotiate substantially other aspects of Britain's relations with the EU. Experience from the 1970s suggests that renegotiation engenders ill will and delivers little. It is hard to see why other EU member states would agree, at a time of crisis, to a debate about aspects of Britain's relationship with the EU. Britain seems very likely to remain outside the euro, outside of the Schengen system and outside of the fiscal compact. Britain seems likely to remain 'with but not of Europe', as Churchill put it in the 1950s, although other member states may now have more grounds to doubt the extent to which Britain is still even 'with' Europe.

Bibliography

Allen, D. and Smith, M. (2004) 'External Developments', *Journal of Common Market Studies*, 42 (s1): 95–112.

Anderson, B. (1991) *Imagined Communities: Reflections on the Origin and Spread of Nationalism* (London: Verso).

Anderson, P. and Weymouth, A. (1998) *Insulting the Public? The British Press and the European Union* (London: Longman).

Aspinwall, M. (2000) 'Structuring Europe: Power-sharing Institutions and British Preferences on European Integration', *Political Studies*, 48 (3): 415–42.

Aspinwall, M. (2003) 'Britain and Europe: Some Alternative Economic Tests', *Political Quarterly*, 74 (2): 146–57.

Bache, I. (1998) *The Politics of European Union Regional Policy: Multi-level Governance or Flexible Gate-keeping* (Sheffield: Sheffield Academic Press).

Bache, I. and Nugent, N. (2007) 'Europe', in A. Seldon (ed.), *Blair's Britain* (Cambridge: Cambridge University Press): 529–50.

Baker, D., Gamble, A. and Ludlam, S. (1993a) '1846...1906...1996? Conservative Splits and European Integration', *Political Quarterly*, 64 (2): 420–35.

Baker, D., Gamble, A. and Ludlam, S. (1993b) 'Whips or Scorpions? The Maastricht Vote and the Conservative Party', *Parliamentary Affairs*, 46 (2): 151–66.

Baker, D., Gamble, A. and Ludlam, S. (1994) 'The Parliamentary Siege of Maastricht 1993: Conservative Divisions and British Ratification', *Parliamentary Affairs*, 47 (1): 37–59.

Baker, D., Gamble, A. and Ludlam, S. (2002) 'Sovereign Nations and Global Markets: Modern British Conservatism and Hyperglobalism', *British Journal of Politics and International Relations*, 4 (3): 399–428.

Bale, T. (20101) *The Conservative Party from Thatcher to Cameron* (Cambridge: Polity).

Balls, E. (2002) 'Why the Five Economic Tests', Cairncross Lecture, St Peters College, Oxford, 4 December 2002.

Bauman, Z. (2002) *Society Under Siege* (Cambridge: Polity).

Beloff, M. (1970) *The Intellectual in Politics and Other Essays* (London: Weidenfeld & Nicolson).

Bennie, L., Curtice, J. and Rudig, W. (1995) 'Liberal, Social Democrat or Liberal Democrat? Political Identity and British Centre Party Politics', in D. Broughton *et al.* (eds), *British Elections and Parties Yearbook 1994* (London: Frank Cass).

Bennister, M. and Heffernan, R. (2011) 'Cameron as Prime Minister: The Executive Politics of Britain's Coalition Government', *Parliamentary Affairs*, advance access, doi: 10.1093/pa/gsr061.

Billig, M. (1995) *Banal Nationalism* (London: Sage).

Blair, T. (1994) Speech to the Annual Conference of the Labour Party, Blackpool, September 1994, available on-line at: http://www.britishpoliticalspeech.org/speech-archive.htm?speech=200.

Blair, T. (2003) 'Speech at the Foreign Office Conference', 7 January 2003, http://www.number10.gov.uk/output/Page1765.asp.

Börzel, T. (2002) 'Member State Reponses to Europeanization', *Journal of Common Market Studies*, 40 (2): 193–214.

Börzel, T. and Risse, T. (2009) 'Revisiting the Nature of the Beast: Politicization, European Identity, and Postfunctionalism: A Comment on Hooghe and Marks', *British Journal of Political Science*, 39(1): 217–20.

Boswell, C. and Geddes, A. (2011) *Migration and Mobility in the European Union* (London: Palgrave Macmillan).

Brookes, M. (1999) 'Newspapers and National Identity: The BSE/CJD Crisis and the British Press', *Media, Culture and Society*, 21 (2): 247–63.

Buchan, D. (1993) *Europe: The Strange Superpower* (Aldershot: Dartmouth).

Bull, H. (1979) *The Anarchical Society: A Study of Order in World Politics* (London: Macmillan).

Buller, J. (2000) *National Statecraft and European Integration: The Conservative Government and the European Union 1979–97* (London: Pinter).

Bulmer, S. (2008) 'New Labour, New European Policy? Blair, Brown and Utilitarian Supranationalism, *Parliamentary Affairs*, 61(4): 597–620.

Bulmer, S. and Burch, M. (1998) 'Organizing for Europe: The British State and the European Union', *Public Administration*, 76 (4): 601–28.

Bulmer, S. and Burch, M. (2005) 'The Europeanisation of UK Government: From Quiet Revolution to Explicit Step-change?', *Public Administration* 83(4): 861–90.

Bulmer, S. and Burch, M. (2009) *The Europeanisation of Whitehall: UK Central Government and the European Union* (Manchester: Manchester University Press).

Bulmer, S., Burch, M., Hogwood, P., and Scott, A. (2006) 'UK Devolution and the European Union: A Case of Cooperative Asymmetry', *Publius*, 36 (1): 75–93.

Bulmer, S. and Wessels, W. (1987) *The European Council: Decision-making in European Politics* (London: Macmillan).

Burch, M. and Gomez, R. (2002) 'The English Regions and the European Union', *Regional Studies*, 36 (7): 767–78.

Burch, M. and Holliday, I. (1996) *The British Cabinet System* (London: Prentice Hall).

Burgess, M. (1986) *Federalism and Federation in Western Europe* (London: Croon Helm).

Butler, D. and Kitzinger, U. (1976) *The 1975 Referendum* (London: Macmillan).

Camps, M. (1964) *Britain and the European Community 1955–63* (London: Oxford University Press).

Caporaso, J. (1996) 'The EU and Forms of State: Westphalian, Regulatory or Post-modern?, *Journal of Common Market Studies*, 34 (1): 29–52.

Capotori, F. (1983) 'Supranational Organizations', in R. Bernhardt (ed.), *Encyclopaedia of Public International Law* (Elsevier: Amsterdam).

Carey, S. (2002) 'Undivided Loyalties: Is National Identity an Obstacle to European Integration?, *European Union Politics*, 3 (4): 387–413.

Carey, S. and Geddes, A. (2010) 'Less is More: Immigration and European Integration at the 2010 General Election', *Parliamentary Affairs*, 63 (4): 849–65.

CEC (2002) *Mid-Term Review of the Common Agricultural Policy*, COM(2002) 394 final.

CEC (2011) *The Sixth Community Environment Action Programme: Final Assessment*, COM(2011) 531 final.

CIE (1999a) *First Report on Allegations Regarding Fraud, Mismanagement and Nepotism in the European Commission*, http://www.europarl.eu.int/experts/default_en.htm.

CIE (1999b) *Second Report on Reform of the Commission: Analysis of Current Practice and Proposals for Tackling Mismanagement, Irregularities and Fraud,* __http://www.europarl.eu.int/experts/default_en.htm.

Clegg, N. (2004) 'Europe: A Liberal future', in D. Laws and P. Marshall, *The Orange Book: Reclaiming Liberalism* (London: Profile).

Clements, B. (2011) 'Understanding "Utilitarian" Support for European Integration in Scotland and Wales: The Role of Economic Interests, National Identity and Party Support', *Regional and Federal Studies*, 21 (1): 1–21.

Clift, B. (2001) 'New Labour's Third Way and European Social Democracy', in M. Smith and S. Ludlam, *New Labour in Power* (London: Macmillan, now Palgrave Macmillan).

Coen, D. (1997) 'The Evolution of the Large Firm as a Political Actor in the European Union', *Journal of European Public Policy*, 4 (1): 91–108.

Coen, D. (2007) 'Empirical and Theoretical Studies in EU Lobbying', *Journal of European Public Policy*, 14 (3): 333–45.

Cohen, B. (1998) *The Geography of Money* (Ithaca, NY: Cornell University Press).

Cole, A. and Palmer, R. (2011) 'Europeanising Devolution: Wales and the European Union', *British Politics*, 6 (3): 379–96.

Colley, L. (1992) *Britons: Forging the Nation* (New Haven, CT: Yale University Press).

Committee for the Study of Economic and Monetary Union (1989) *Report on Economic and Monetary Union in the European Community* (Luxembourg: Office for the Official Publication of the European Community).

Conservative Party (2010) *Invitation to Join the Government of Britain. The Conservative Manifesto 2010* (London: Conservative Party).

Cram, L. (1994) 'The European Commission as a Multi-organisation: Social Policy and IT Policy in the EU', *Journal of European Public Policy*, 1 (2): 195–217.

Curry, D. (2002) *Farming and Food: A Sustainable Future* (London: Cabinet Office).

Curtice, J. (2010) 'So What Went Wrong with the Electoral System? The 2010 Election Result and the Debate about Electoral Reform', *Parliamentary Affairs*, 63 (4): 623–38.

Daddow, O. (2011) *New Labour and the European Union: Blair and Brown's Logic of History* (Manchester; Manchester University Press).

Daily Telegraph (2011a) 19 September.

Daily Telegraph (2011b) 5 October.

Daly, M. (2006) 'EU Social Policy after Lisbon', *Journal of Common Market Studies*, 44 (3): 461–81.

De Maillard, J. and Smith, A. (2012) 'Projecting National Preferences: Police Co-operation, Organizations and Polities', *Journal of European Public Policy*, 19 (2): 257–74.

Denver, D. (2010) 'The Results: How Britain Voted'. *Parliamentary Affairs*, 63 (4): 588–606.

Dicey, A. V. (1885) *Introduction to the Law of the Constitution* (London: Macmillan & Co).

Dyson, K. (2000) 'Europeanization, Whitehall Culture and the Treasury as Institutional Veto Player: A Constructivist Approach to Economic and Monetary Union', *Public Administration*, 78 (4): 897–914.

Easton, D. (1965) *A Framework for Political Analysis* (Englewood Cliffs, NJ: Prentice Hall).

Economist, The (2011) 29 October.

Edwards, G. (1993) 'Britain and Europe', in J. Story (ed.), *The New Europe: Politics, Economy and Government Since 1945* (Oxford: Basil Blackwell).

Eichenberg, R. and Dalton, R. (2007) 'Post-Maastricht Blues: The Transformation of Citizen Support for European Integration', *Acta Politica*, 42 (2–3): 128–52.

Ellison, J. (2000) *Threatening Europe: Britain and the Creation of the European Community 1955–58* (London: Macmillan).

Eurobarometer (2011a) *Standard Eurobarometer 76*. Brussels: CEC.

Eurobarometer (2011b) *Attitudes towards the EU in the United Kingdom*, Flash Barometer 318. Brussels: European Commission.

Evans, G. (1998) 'Euroscepticism and Conservative Party Support: How an Asset Became a Liability', *British Journal of Political Science*, 28 (4): 573–90.

Evans, G. and Butt, S. (2007) 'Explaining Change in British Public Opinion on the European Union: Top Down or Bottom Up?', *Acta Politica*, 24 (2): 173–90.

Fairbrass, J. and Jordan, A. (2001) 'European Union Environmental policy and the UK Government: A Passive Observer or a Strategic Manager?', *Environmental Politics*, 10 (2): 1–21.

Farrell, D. and Scully, R. (2003) 'MEPs as Representatives: Individual and Institutional Roles', *Journal of Common Market Studies*, 41 (2): 269 88.

Farrell, D. and Scully, R. (2010) 'The European Parliament: One Parliament, Several Modes of Political Representation on the Ground?', *Journal of European Public Policy*, 17 (1): 36–54.

Fella, S. (2002) *New Labour and the European Union: Political Strategy, Policy Transition and the Amsterdam Treaty Negotiations* (Aldershot: Ashgate).

Fielding, S. (2002a) *The Labour Party: Continuity and Change in the Making of New Labour* (Basingstoke: Palgrave Macmillan).

Fielding, S. (2002b) 'No-one Else to Vote For? Labour's Campaign', in A. Geddes and J. Tonge (eds), *Labour's Second Landslide: The 2002 British General Election* (Manchester: Manchester University Press).

Follesdal, A. and Hix, S. (2006) 'Why There is a Democratic Deficit in the EU: A Response to Majone and Moravcsik', *Journal of Common Market Studies*, 44 (3) 533–62.

Forster, A. (2002a) *Euroscepticism in Contemporary British Politics: Opposition to Europe in the British Conservative and Labour Parties since 1945* (London: Routledge).

Forster, A. (2002b) 'Anti-Europeans, Anti-marketeers and Eurosceptics: The Evolution and Influence of Labour and Conservative Opposition to Europe', *Political Quarterly*, 73 (3) 299–308.

Fox, R. (2010) 'Five Days in May: A New Political Order Emerges', *Parliamentary Affairs*, 63(4) 607–22.

Franklin, B. (1994) *Packaging Politics: Political Communication in Britain's Media Democracy* (London: Edward Arnold).

Franklin, M., Marsh, M. and McLaren, L. (1994) 'Uncorking the Bottle: Popular Opposition to European Unification in the Wake of Maastricht', *Journal of Common Market Studies*, 32 (4) 455–72.

Gabel, M. (1998) *Interests and Integration: Market Liberalization, Public Opinion and European Integration* (Ann Arbor, MI: University of Michigan Press).

Gamble, A. (1988) *The Free Economy and the Strong State: The Politics of Thatcherism* (London: Macmillan).

Gamble, A. (1998) 'The European Issue in British Politics', in D. Baker and D. Seawright (eds), *Britain For and Against Europe. British Politics and the Question of European Integration* (Oxford: Clarendon Press).

Gamble, A. (2003) *Between Europe and America: The Future of British Politics* (Basingstoke: Palgrave Macmillan).

Gamble, A. and Kelly, G. (2000) 'The British Labour Party and Monetary Union', *West European Politics*, 23 (1): 1–25.

Gardiner, G. (1999) *A Bastard's Tale: The Political Memoirs of George Gardiner* (London: Aurum).

Garton Ash, T. (2001) 'Is Britain European?', *International Affairs*, 77 (1): 1–14.

Gavin, N. (2000) 'Imagining Europe: Political Identity and British Television Coverage of the European Economy', *British Journal of Politics and International Relations*, 2 (3): 352–73.

Geddes, A. (1997) 'Europe: Major's Nemesis', in A. Geddes and J. Tonge (eds), *Labour's Landslide: The 1997 British General Election* (Manchester: Manchester University Press).

Geddes, A. (2002) 'In Europe, Not Interested in Europe', in A. Geddes and J. Tonge (eds), *Labour's Second Landslide: The British General Election 2001* (Manchester: Manchester University Press).

Geddes, A. (2005) 'Getting the Best of Both Worlds? Britain, the EU and Migration Policy', *International Affairs*, 81 (4): 723–40.

Geddes, A. (2006) 'Political Parties and Party Politics', in I. Bache and A. Jordan (eds) *The Europeanization of British Politics* (Basingstoke: Palgrave Macmillan): 119–34.

Geddes, A. (2008) *Immigration and European Integration: Beyond Fortress Europe?* (Manchester: Manchester University Press).

Geddes, A. (2012) 'Security Interests: Police and Judicial Co-operation', in J. Peterson and M. Shackleton, *The Institutions of the European Union*, 3rd edn (Oxford: Oxford University Press).

Geddes, A. and Guiraudon, V. (2004) 'The Emergence of an EU Policy Paradigm Amidst Competing National Models: Britain, France and EU Anti-discrimination Policy', *West European Politics*, 26 (4).

Geddes, A. and Tonge, J. (1997) *Labour's Landslide: The 1997 British General Election* (Manchester: Manchester University Press).

Geddes, A. and Tonge, J. (2002) *Labour's Second Landslide: The 2002 British General Election* (Manchester: Manchester University Press).

Geddes, A. and Tonge, J. (2005) *Britain Decides: The UK General Election 2005* (London: Palgrave Macmillan).

Geddes, A. and Tonge, J. (2010) *Britain Votes 2010* (Oxford: Oxford University Press).

George, S. (1998) *An Awkward Partner. Britain in the European Union* (Oxford: Oxford University Press).

Golub, J. (1996) 'British Sovereignty and the Development of EC Environmental Policy', *Environmental Politics*, 5 (4): 700–28.

Gorman, T. (1993) *The Bastards: Dirty Tricks and the Challenge to Europe* (London: Pan Books).

Grant, W. (1997) *The Common Agricultural Policy* (London: Macmillan).

Green Cowles, M., Caporaso, J. and Risse, T. (eds) (20010) *Transforming Europe: Europeanization and Domestic Change* (Ithaca, NY: Cornell University Press).

Greenwood, J. (2003) *Interest Representation in the European Union* (London: Palgrave Macmillan).

Haas, E. (1971) 'The Study of Regional Integration: Reflections on the Joy and Anguish of Pre-theorizing', in L. Lindberg and S. Scheingold (eds), *European Integration: Theory and Research* (Englewood Cliffs, NJ: Prentice Hall).

Hague, W. (2001) 'Speech to the Conservative Party Spring Forum', Harrogate, 4 March 2001.

Hansard (1990) Vol. 178, col. 869, 30 October.

Hansard (1997) Vol. 299, col. 583–4, 27 October.

Hansard (2011) Column 190, 6 December.

Hansard (2012) Column 484-i, 3 July.

Harris, R. (ed.) (1997) *The Collected Speeches of Margaret Thatcher* (London: Harper Collins).

Hay, C. and Rosamond, B. (2002) 'Globalization, European Integration and the Discursive Construction of Economic Imperatives', *Journal of European Public Policy*, 9 (2): 147–67.

Hayes-Renshaw, F. (1999) 'The European Council and the Council of Ministers', in L. Cram, D. Dinan and N. Nugent (eds), *Developments in the European Union* (London: Macmillan).

Hayes-Renshaw, F. and Wallace, H. (1997) *The Council of Ministers* (London: Macmillan).

Heath, E. (1998) *The Course of My Life: My Autobiography* (London: Hodder & Stoughton).

Heffernan, R. (2002) 'Beyond Euro-scepticism: Explaining the Europeanisation of the Labour Party Since 1983', *Political Quarterly*, 72 (2): 180–9.

Hirst, P. and Thompson, G. (1996) *Globalization in Question: The International Economy and the Possibilities of Governance* (Cambridge: Polity Press).

Hix, S., Noury, A. and Roland, G. (2009) 'Voting Patterns and Alliance Formation in the European Parliament', *Philosophical Transactions of the Royal Society B: Biological Sciences*, 364 (518): 821–31.

HM Government (1984) 'Europe: The Future', *Journal of Common Market Studies*, 23 (1): 74–81.

HM Treasury (2010) *Statement on the 2010 EU Budget and Measures to Counter Fraud and Mismanagement*, CM7978. London: Stationery Office.

HM Treasury (2011) *Treasury Analysis of Third Party Assessments of Cost–Benefit Analyses of EU Membership*, London: HM Treasury, http://www.hm-treasury.gov.uk/foi_costbenefit_eumembership.htm, accessed 30 May 2012.

Hobsbawm, E. and Ranger, T. (1983) *The Invention of Tradition* (Cambridge: Cambridge University Press).

Hoffmann, S. (1966) 'Obstinate or Obsolete: The Fate of the Nation State and the Case of Western Europe', *Daedalus*, 95: 892–908.

Holliday, I. (2000) 'Is the British State Hollowing Out?', *Political Quarterly*, 71 (2): 167–76.

Hood, C. (2006) 'Gaming in Targetworld: The Targets Approach to Managing British Public Services', *Public Administration* Review, 66 (4): 515–21.

Hooghe, L. (1997) 'Serving "Europe": Political Orientation of Senior Commission Officials', *European Integration On-line Papers*, http://eiop.or.at/eiop/texte/1997–008a.htm.

Hooghe, L. and Marks, G. (2007) 'Sources of Euroscepticism', *Acta Politica*, 42 (2–3): 1999–27.

Hooghe, L. and Marks, G. (2008) 'A Post-functional Theory of European Integration: From Permissive Consensus to Constraining Dissensus', *British Journal of Political Science*, 39(1): 1–23.

House of Commons (2012) *The UK and Europe: Time for a New Relationship?*, Standard Note SN/IA/6393, London: House of Commons.

House of Commons Foreign Affairs Committee (2011) *The Role of the FCO in UK Government*, Seventh Report of Session 2011–12. London: HMSO.

House of Commons Library (2010) *EU Legislation*, International Affairs and Defence Section Standard Note SN/IA5419. London: House of Commons.

House of Commons Treasury Select Committee (1998) *The UK and Preparations for Stage Three of Economic and Monetary Union*, HC503 1997–98. London: HMSO.

House of Lords (2008) *The Treaty of Lisbon: An Impact Assessment*, European Union Committee, 10th Report of Session 2007-8, London: The Stationery Office.

Howe, G. (1995) *Conflict of Loyalty* (London: Pan).

Howorth, J. (2000) *European Integration and Defence: The Ultimate Challenge* (Paris: Institute for Security Studies, West European Union).

Hughes, K. and Smith, E. (1998) 'New Labour, New Europe?', *International Affairs*, 74 (1): 93–103.

Inglehart, R. (1971) 'The Silent Revolution in Europe: Inter-generational Change in Post-industrial Societies', *American Political Science Review*, 65 (4): 991–1017.

James, S. (2011) *Managing Europe from Home: The Changing Face of European Policy-making under Blair and Ahern* (Manchester: Manchester University Press).

Jeffrey, C. (2000) 'Sub-national Mobilization and European Integration: Does It Make Any Difference?', *Journal of Common Market Studies*, 38 (1): 1–23.

Jenkins, R. (1991) *A Life at the Centre* (London: Macmillan).

Jordan, A. (2000) *The Europeanisation of UK Environmental Policy 1970–2000: A Departmental Perspective*, School of Environmental Science Working Paper No. 11/00, University of East Anglia.

Jordan, A. and Fairbrass, J. (2001) 'European Union Environmental Policy after the Nice Summit', *Environmental Politics*, 10 (4): 109–14.

Jordan, A. and Lenschow, A. (2010) 'Environmental Policy Integration: A State of the Art Review', *Environmental Policy and Governance*, 20 (3): 147–58.

Kaiser, W. (1996) *Using Europe, Abusing the Europeans: Britain and European Integration 1945–63* (New York: St Martin's Press).

Kassim, H. (2004) 'The United Kingdom and the Future of Europe: Winning the Battle, Losing the War, *Comparative European Politics*, 2 (2): 261–81.

Kassim, H. (2008) 'The Kinnock Reforms in Perspective: Why Reforming the Commission is an Heroic, but Thankless, Task', *Public Policy and Administration*, 19 (3): 25–41.

Keating, M. (2010) *The Government of Scotland. Public Policy-making after Devolution*, 2nd edn (Edinburgh: Edinburgh University Press).

Keating, M. (2011) *Scotland and Independence* (Montreal: Federal Idea).

King, A. (1977) *Britain Says Yes. The 1975 Referendum on the Common Market* (Washington, DC: American Enterprise Institute).

Knill, C. and Lenschow, A. (1998) 'Coping with Europe: The Impact of British and German Administrations on the Implementation of EU Environmental Policy', *Journal of European Public Policy*, 5 (4), 595–14.

Kwarteng, K., Skidmore, C., Raab, D., Truss, E. and Patel, P. (2011) *After the Coalition: A Conservative Agenda for Britain* (London: Biteback).

Laffan, B. (1992) *Integration and Co-operation in Europe* (London: Routledge).

Laffan, B. (1997) *The Finances of the European Union* (London: Macmillan).

Lambert, J. and Hoskyns, C. (2000) 'How Democratic is the European Parliament', in C. Hoskyns and M. Newman (eds), *Democratizing the European Union: Issues for the Twenty First Century* (Manchester: Manchester University Press).

Lamont, N. (1997) *In Office* (London: Warner Books).

Lenschow, A. (ed.) (2001) *Environmental Policy Integration: Greening Sectoral Policies in Europe* (London: Earthscan).

Levi, M. (1997) 'A Model, A Method and A Map: Rational Choice in Comparative and Historical Analysis', in M. Lichbach and A. Zuckerman (eds), *Comparative Politics: Rationality, Culture and Structure* (Cambridge: Cambridge University Press): 19–41.

Lindberg, L. and Scheingold, S. (19701) *Europe's Would-be Polity: Patterns of Change in the European Community* (Englewood Cliffs, NJ: Prentice Hall).

Lowe, P. and Ward, S. (eds) (1998) *British Environmental Policy and Europe* (London: Routledge).

Majone, G. (1996) *Regulating Europe* (London: Routledge).

Majone, G. (2002) 'The European Commission: The Limits of Centralization and the Perils of Parliamentarization'. *Governance*, 15 (3): 375–92.

Major, J. (1999) *John Major: The Autobiography* (London: HarperCollins).

Marks, G., Hooghe, L. and Blank, K. (1996) 'European Integration since the 1980s: State-centric versus Multi-level Governance', *Journal of Common Market Studies*, 34 (3): 341–78.

Marsh, D., Richards, D. and Smith, M. (2001) *Changing Patterns of Governance in the UK: Reinventing Whitehall?* (Basingstoke: Palgrave Macmillan).

Matthews, F. (2011) 'Constitutional Stretching, Coalition Governance and the Westminster Model', *Commonwealth and Comparative Politics*, 49 (4): 486–509.

Metcalfe, L. (2000) 'Reforming the Commission', *Journal of Common Market Studies,* 38 (5): 817–41.

Milward, A. (1992) *The European Rescue of the Nation State* (London: Routledge).

Mitchell, J. (2002) 'England and the Centre', *Regional Studies,* 36 (7): 757–65.

Moran, M. (2007) *The British Regulatory State: High Modernism and Hyper-innovation* (Oxford: Oxford University Press).

Moravcsik, A. (1994) *Why the European Union Strengthens the State: Domestic Politics and International Co-operation*, Harvard Centre for European Studies Working Paper series No. 52, http://www.ces.fas.harvard.edu/working_papers/Moravcsik52.pdf.

Moravcsik, A. (2002) 'In Defence of the "Democratic Deficit": Reassessing the Legitimacy of the European Union', *Journal of Common Market Studies*, 40 (4): 603–34.

Morgan, K. (1997) *Callaghan: A Life* (Oxford: Oxford University Press).

Murphy, M. (2011) 'Regional Representation in Brussels and Multi-level Governance: Evidence from Northern Ireland', *British Journal of Politics and International Relations*, 13 (4): 551–66.

National Audit Office (2011) *The Financial Stability Interventions*, Extract from the Certificate and Report of the Comptroller and Auditor General on HM Treasury Annual Report and Accounts 2010–11, HC 984 July 2011, London: HMSO.

Nicolaïdis, K. and Schmidt, S. (2007) 'Mutual Recognition "On Trial": The Long Road to Services Liberalisation', *Journal of European Public Policy*, 14 (5): 717–34.

Norris, P., Curtice, J., Sanders, D., Scammell, M. and Semetko, H. (1999) *On Message: Communicating the Campaign* (London: Sage).

Noury, A. and Roland, G. (2002) 'More Power to the European Parliament', *Economic Policy*, 17 (35): 279–319.

Oppermann, K. (2008) 'The Blair Government and Europe: The Policy of Containing the Salience of European Integration', *British Politics*, 3 (2): 156–82.

Page, E. (1998) 'The Impact of European Legislation on British Public Policy Making: A Research Note', *Public Administration*, 76 (4): 803–9.

Page, E. and Wright, V. (eds) (1999) *Bureaucratic Elites in Western European States: A Comparative Analysis of Top Officials* (Oxford: Oxford University Press).

Pierson, P. (1998) 'The Path of European Integration: A Historical Institutionalist Analysis', in W. Sandholtz and A. Stone Sweet (eds), *European Integration and Supranational Governance* (Oxford: Oxford University Press).

Pierson, P. (2000) 'Increasing Returns, Path Dependency and the Study of Politics', *American Political Science Review*, 94 (2): 251–67.

Pierson, P. (2004) *Politics in Time: History, Institutions and Social Analysis* (Princeton (NJ): Princeton University Press).

Ray, L. (2007) 'Mainstream Euroskepticism: Trend or Oxymoron?', *Acta Politica*, 42 (2–3): 153–72.

Quinn, T., Bara, J. and Bartle, J. (2011) 'The UK Coalition Agreement: Who Won?', *Journal of Public Opinion, Elections and Parties*, 21 (2): 295–312.

Rawnsley, A. (2001) *Servants of the People: The Inside Story of New Labour* (London: Penguin).

Rawnsley, A. (2010) *The End of the Party: The Rise and Fall of New Labour* (London: Penguin).

Reif, K. and Schmitt, H. (1980) 'Nine National Second Order Elections: A Systematic Framework for the Analysis of European Elections Results', *European Journal of Political Research*, 8 (1), 3–44.

Rhodes, R. (1997) *Understanding Governance: Policy Networks, Governance, Reflexivity and Accountability* (Buckingham: Open University Press).

Riddell, P. (1998) 'EMU and the Press', in A. Duff (ed.), *Understanding the Euro* (London: Federal Trust).

Risse, T. (2001) 'A European Identity? Europeanization and the Evolution of Nation-state Identities', in M. Green Cowles, J. Caporaso and T. Risse (eds), *Transforming Europe: Europeanization and Domestic Change* (Ithaca, NY: Cornell University Press).

Robins, L. (1979) *The Reluctant Party: Labour and the EC 1961–75* (Ormskirk: G.W. & A. Hesketh).

Rosamond, B. (1998) 'The Integration of Labour? British Trade Union Attitudes to European Integration', in D. Baker and D. Seawright (eds), *Britain For and Against Europe: British Politics and the Question of European Integration* (Oxford: Clarendon Press).

Rosamond, B. (2000) *Theories of European Integration* (London: Macmillan).

Rosamond, B. and Wincott, D. (2005) 'Constitutionalism, European Integration and British Political Economy, *British Journal of Politics and International Relations*, 8 (1): 1–14.

Russell, A. and Fieldhouse, E. (2005) *Neither Left Nor Right? The Liberal Democrats and the Electorate* (Manchester: Manchester University Press).

Seldon, A. (2005) *The Blair Effect 2001–5* (Cambridge: Cambridge University Press).

Smith, J. (2005) 'A Missed Opportunity: New Labour's European Policy', *International Affairs*, 81 (4): 703–21.

Smith, J. (2010) 'Sub-national Mobilization and the Scottish Government's Action Plan on European Engagement', *Public Policy and Administration*, 25 (2): 216–33.

Soames, C. (1972) 'Whitehall into Europe', *Public Administration*, 50 (2): 271–90.

Springford, J. (2012) *Britain Should Not Go Swiss*. London: Centre for European Reform.

Stephens, P. (1996) *Politics and the Pound: The Conservatives Struggle with Sterling* (London: Macmillan).

Stephens, P. (2001) 'Blair and Europe', *Political Quarterly*, 72 (1): 67–75.

Stern, N. (2007) *Stern Review on the Economics of Climate Change* (Cambridge: Cambridge University Press).

Stevens, A. (2002) *Europeanization and the Administration of the EU*, Queen's Papers on Europeanization, No. 4/2002.

Stevens, A. and Stevens, H. (2000) *Brussels Bureaucrats: The Administration of the European Union* (London: Macmillan).

Stone Sweet, A. and Sandholtz, W. (1998) 'Integration, Supranational Governance, and the Institutionalization of the European Polity', in W. Sandholtz and A. Stone Sweet (eds), *European Integration and Supranational Governance* (Oxford: Oxford University Press).

Story, J. (ed.) (1993) *The New Europe: Politics, Economy and Government since 1945* (Oxford: Basil Blackwell).

Streeck, W. (2001) 'International Competition, Supranational Integration, National Solidarity: the Emerging Construction of Social Europe', in M. Knoll and M. Novak (eds), *Will Europe Work: Integration, Employment and the Social Order* (London and New York: Routledge): 21–34.

Taggart, P. and Szczerbiak, A. (2004) 'Contemporary Euroscepticism in the Party Systems of the European Union Candidate States of Central and Eastern Europe', *European Journal of Political Research*, 43 (1): 1–27.

Temperton, P. (2001) *The UK and the Euro* (London: John Wiley).

Thatcher, M. (1993) *The Downing Street Years* (London: HarperCollins).

Turpin, C. and Tomkins, A. (2007) *British Government and the Constitution*, 6th edn (Cambridge: Cambridge University Press).

Urban, G. (1996) *Diplomacy and Disillusion at the Court of Margaret Thatcher: An Insider's View* (London: I.B. Tauris).

Usherwood, S. (2002) 'Opposition to the European Union in the UK: The Dilemma of Public Opinion and Party Management', *Government and Opposition*, 37 (2): 211–30.

Virilio, P. (2001) *Virilio Live: Selected Interviews with Paul Virilio* (edited by J. Armitage) (Cambridge: Polity).

Wall, S. (2002) 'Insider Interview', *Global Thinking*, Spring 2002 (London: Foreign Policy Centre).

Wallace, H. (1997) 'At Odds with Europe', *Political Studies*, 45 (4): 677–88.

Wallace, H. and Wallace, W. (1973) 'The Impact of Community Membership on the British Machinery of Government', *Journal of Common Market Studies*, 11 (4): 243–62.

Wallace, W. (1990) 'Introduction: The Dynamics of European Integration', in W. Wallace (ed.), *The Dynamics of European Integration* (London: Pinter/Royal Institute for International Affairs).

Wallace, W. (1991) 'Foreign Policy and National Identity in the United Kingdom', *International Affairs*, 67 (2): 65–80.

Walters, S. (2001) *Tory Wars: The Conservatives in Crisis* (London: Politicos).

Warleigh, A. (2003) *Democracy and the European Union: Theory, Practice and Reform* (London: Sage).

Watkins, A. (1991) *A Conservative Coup: The Fall of Margaret Thatcher* (London: Duckworth).

Weigall, D. and Stirk, P. (eds) (1992) *The Origins and Development of the European Community* (Leicester: Leicester University Press).

Westlake, M. (1999) *The Council of the European Union* (London: John Harper).

Westlake, M. (2001) *Kinnock: The Biography* (London: Little, Brown).

Wheare, K. (1963) *Federal Government* (Oxford: Oxford University Press).

Wickham Jones, M. (1997) 'How the Conservatives Lost the Economic Argument', in A. Geddes and J. Tonge (eds), *Labour's Landslide: The 1997 British General Election* (Manchester: Manchester University Press).

Wilks, S. (1996) 'Britain and Europe: An Awkward Partner or an Awkward State?', *Politics*, 16 (3): 159–67.

Williams, H. (1998) *Guilty Men: Conservative Decline and Fall 1992–1997* (London: Aurum Press).

Willis, V. (1982) *Britons in Brussels* (London: Policy Studies Institute).

Wright, A. (2005) *Who Governs Scotland?* (London: Routledge).

Wyn Jones, R. and Scully, R. (2012) *Wales Says Yes: Devolution and the 20112 Referendum* (Cardiff: University of Wales Press).

Young, H. (1989) *One of Us: A Biography of Mrs Thatcher* (London: Macmillan).

Young, H. (1999) *This Blessed Plot: Britain and Europe from Churchill to Blair* (London: Papermac).

Young, J. (1993) *Britain and European Unity* (London: Macmillan).

Index

275